Run for your life... the man is a cow.

by Cathy Guisewite

Selected Cartoons from
$14 IN THE BANK AND
A $200 FACE IN MY PURSE.
Volume 1

FAWCETT CREST • NEW YORK

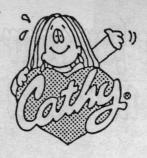

A Fawcett Crest Book
Published by Ballantine Books
 Published in the United States by Ballantine Books, a division of Random House, Inc., New York, and simultaneously in Canada by Random House of Canada Limited, Toronto.

This title is comprised of portions of $14 IN THE BANK AND A $200 FACE IN MY PURSE.

Library of Congress Catalog Card Number: 90-82673

ISBN 0-449-22036-2

This edition published by arrangement with Andrews and McMeel, a Universal Press Syndicate Company.

Printed in Canada

First Ballantine Books Edition: November 1991

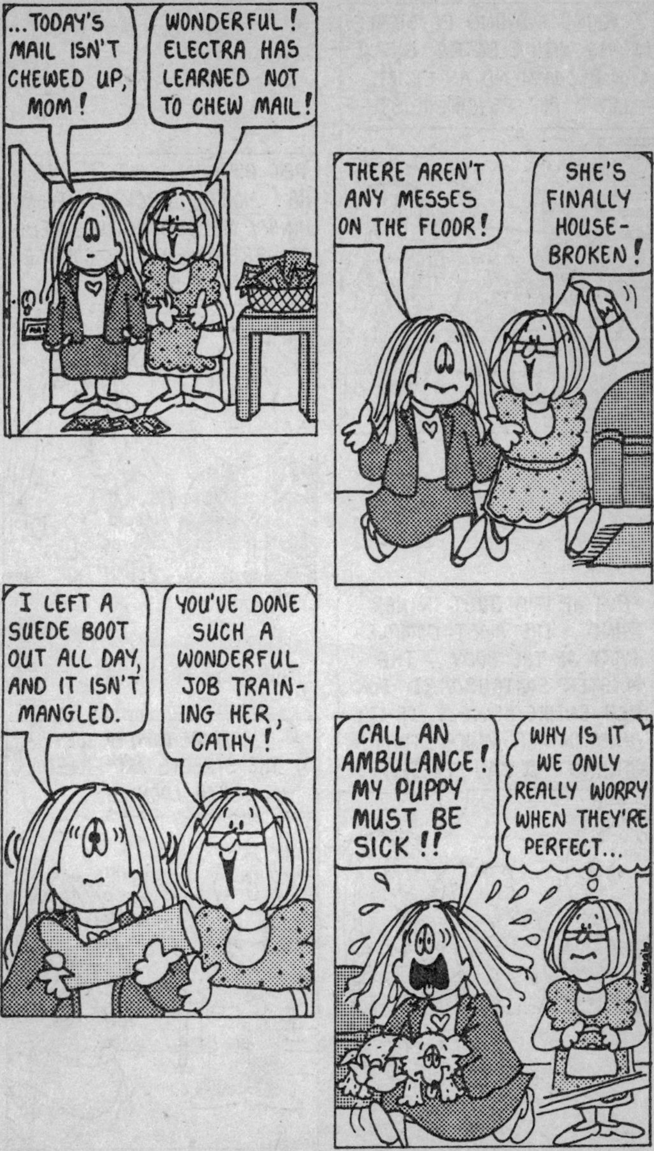
...TODAY'S MAIL ISN'T CHEWED UP, MOM!
WONDERFUL! ELECTRA HAS LEARNED NOT TO CHEW MAIL!
THERE AREN'T ANY MESSES ON THE FLOOR!
SHE'S FINALLY HOUSE-BROKEN!
I LEFT A SUEDE BOOT OUT ALL DAY, AND IT ISN'T MANGLED.
YOU'VE DONE SUCH A WONDERFUL JOB TRAINING HER, CATHY!
CALL AN AMBULANCE! MY PUPPY MUST BE SICK!!
WHY IS IT WE ONLY REALLY WORRY WHEN THEY'RE PERFECT...

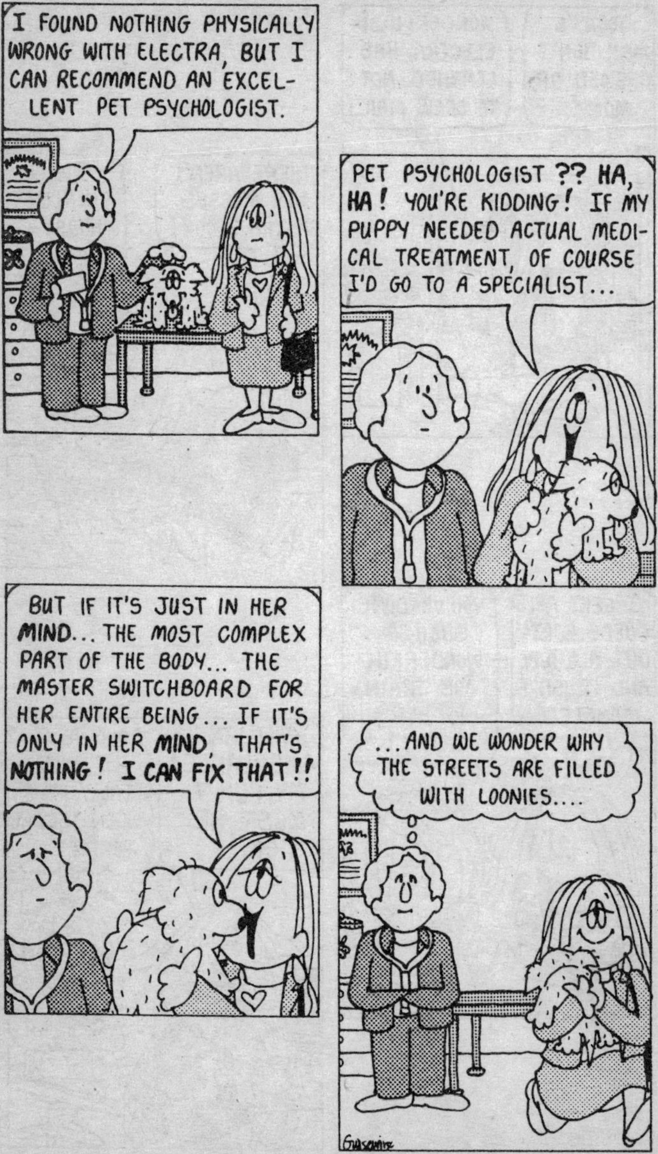
I FOUND NOTHING PHYSICALLY WRONG WITH ELECTRA, BUT I CAN RECOMMEND AN EXCELLENT PET PSYCHOLOGIST.
PET PSYCHOLOGIST ?? HA, HA! YOU'RE KIDDING! IF MY PUPPY NEEDED ACTUAL MEDICAL TREATMENT, OF COURSE I'D GO TO A SPECIALIST...
BUT IF IT'S JUST IN HER MIND... THE MOST COMPLEX PART OF THE BODY... THE MASTER SWITCHBOARD FOR HER ENTIRE BEING... IF IT'S ONLY IN HER MIND, THAT'S NOTHING! I CAN FIX THAT!!
...AND WE WONDER WHY THE STREETS ARE FILLED WITH LOONIES....
Guisewite

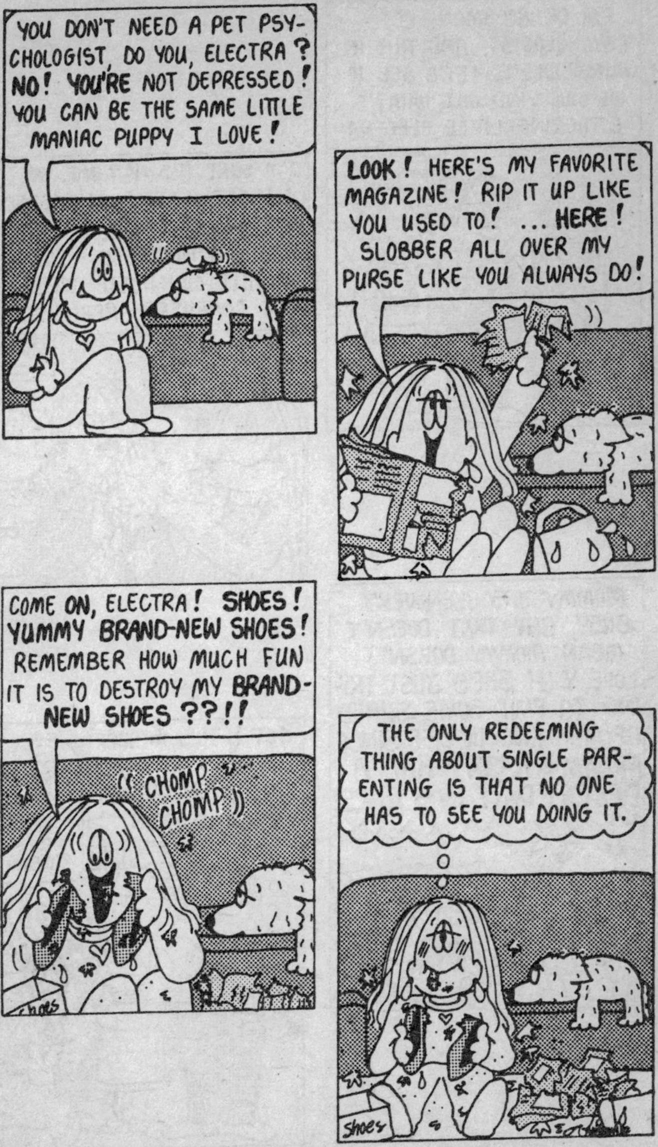
YOU DON'T NEED A PET PSY-CHOLOGIST, DO YOU, ELECTRA? NO! YOU'RE NOT DEPRESSED! YOU CAN BE THE SAME LITTLE MANIAC PUPPY I LOVE!
LOOK! HERE'S MY FAVORITE MAGAZINE! RIP IT UP LIKE YOU USED TO! ... HERE! SLOBBER ALL OVER MY PURSE LIKE YOU ALWAYS DO!
COME ON, ELECTRA! SHOES! YUMMY BRAND-NEW SHOES! REMEMBER HOW MUCH FUN IT IS TO DESTROY MY BRAND-NEW SHOES??!!
CHOMP CHOMP
THE ONLY REDEEMING THING ABOUT SINGLE PAR-ENTING IS THAT NO ONE HAS TO SEE YOU DOING IT.
SHOES

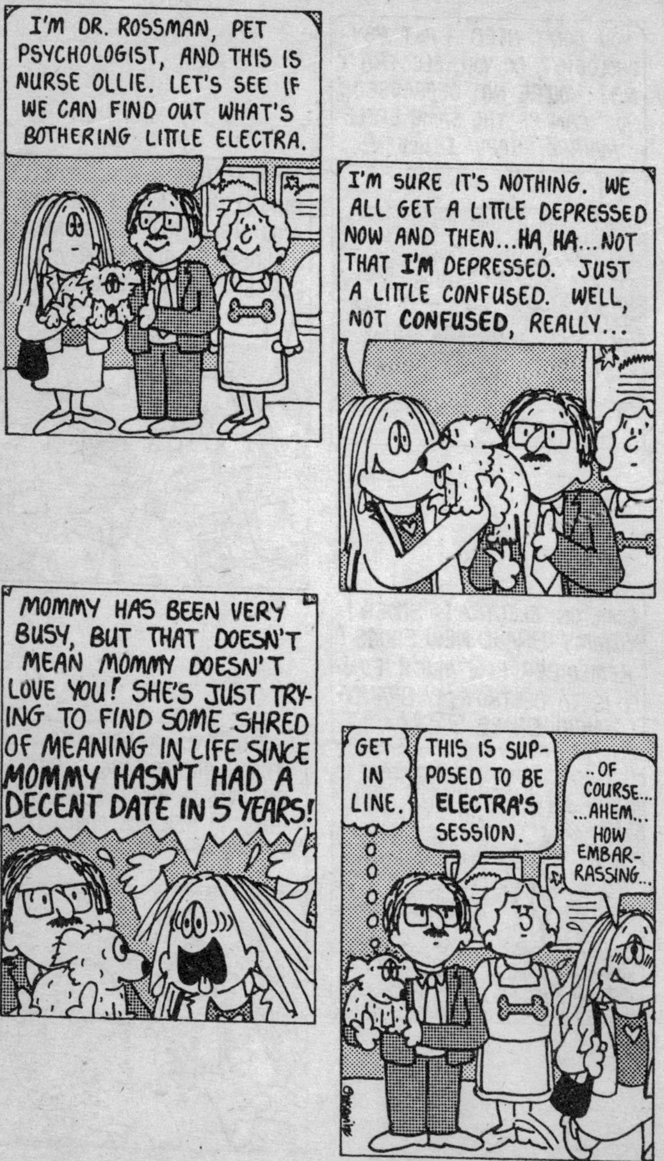
I'M DR. ROSSMAN, PET PSYCHOLOGIST, AND THIS IS NURSE OLLIE. LET'S SEE IF WE CAN FIND OUT WHAT'S BOTHERING LITTLE ELECTRA.
I'M SURE IT'S NOTHING. WE ALL GET A LITTLE DEPRESSED NOW AND THEN...HA, HA...NOT THAT I'M DEPRESSED. JUST A LITTLE CONFUSED. WELL, NOT CONFUSED, REALLY...
MOMMY HAS BEEN VERY BUSY, BUT THAT DOESN'T MEAN MOMMY DOESN'T LOVE YOU! SHE'S JUST TRYING TO FIND SOME SHRED OF MEANING IN LIFE SINCE MOMMY HASN'T HAD A DECENT DATE IN 5 YEARS!
GET IN LINE.
THIS IS SUPPOSED TO BE ELECTRA'S SESSION.
..OF COURSE... ...AHEM... HOW EMBARRASSING...

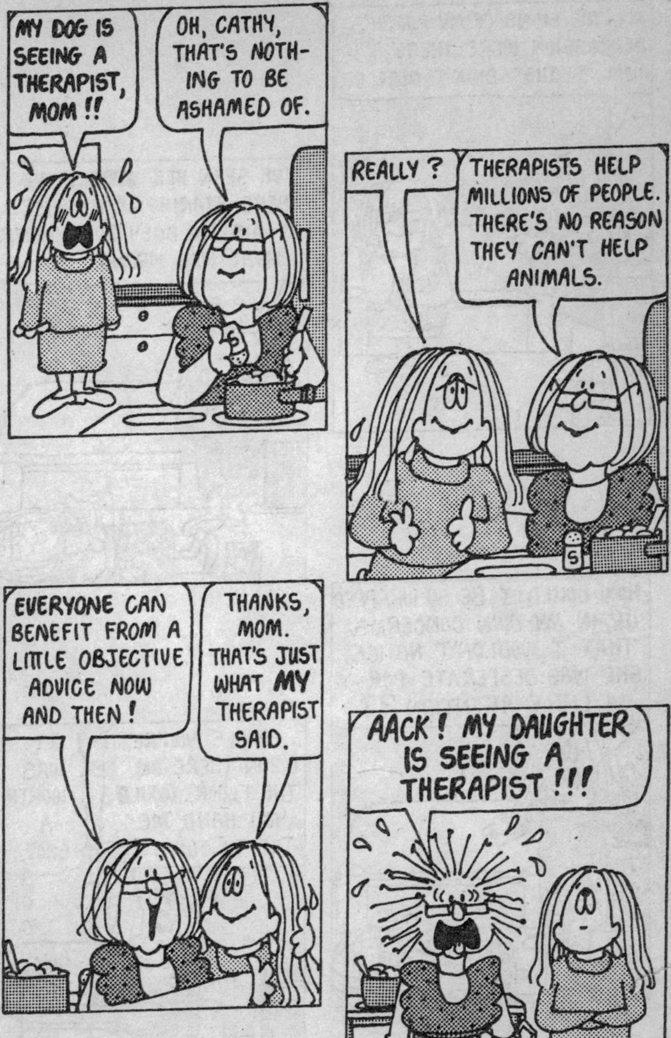
MY DOG IS SEEING A THERAPIST, MOM !!
OH, CATHY, THAT'S NOTHING TO BE ASHAMED OF.
REALLY ?
THERAPISTS HELP MILLIONS OF PEOPLE. THERE'S NO REASON THEY CAN'T HELP ANIMALS.
EVERYONE CAN BENEFIT FROM A LITTLE OBJECTIVE ADVICE NOW AND THEN !
THANKS, MOM. THAT'S JUST WHAT MY THERAPIST SAID.
AACK ! MY DAUGHTER IS SEEING A THERAPIST !!!

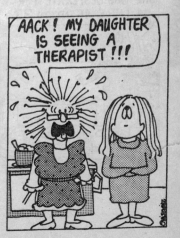

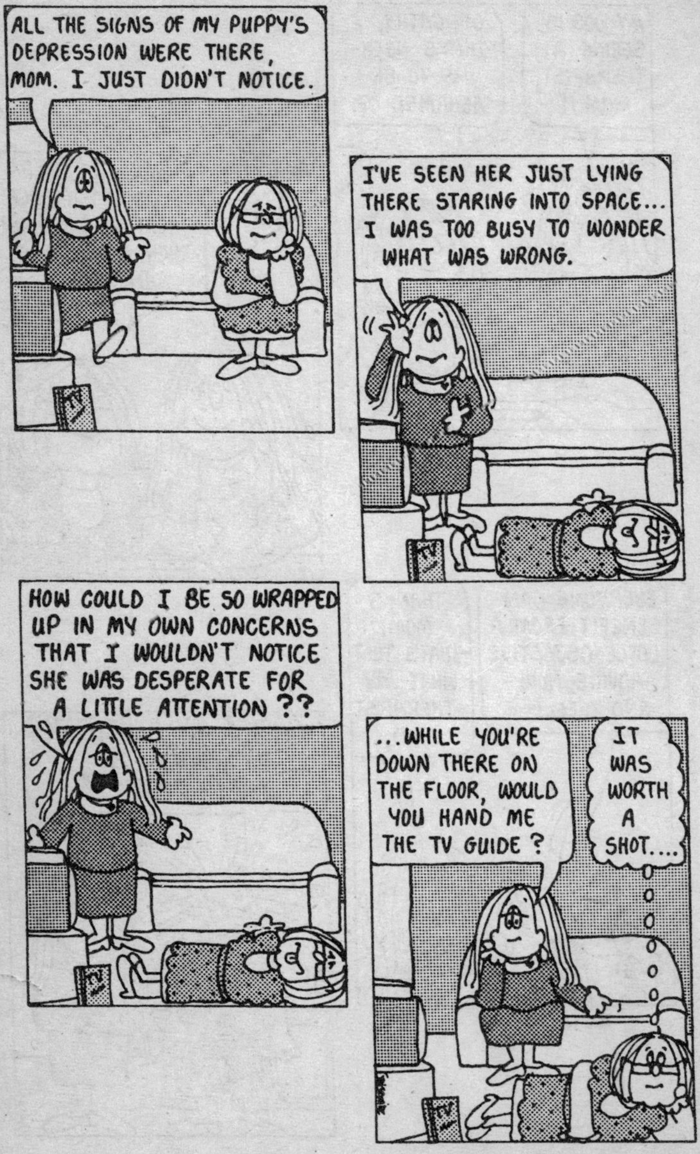
ALL THE SIGNS OF MY PUPPY'S DEPRESSION WERE THERE, MOM. I JUST DIDN'T NOTICE.
I'VE SEEN HER JUST LYING THERE STARING INTO SPACE... I WAS TOO BUSY TO WONDER WHAT WAS WRONG.
HOW COULD I BE SO WRAPPED UP IN MY OWN CONCERNS THAT I WOULDN'T NOTICE SHE WAS DESPERATE FOR A LITTLE ATTENTION??
...WHILE YOU'RE DOWN THERE ON THE FLOOR, WOULD YOU HAND ME THE TV GUIDE?
IT WAS WORTH A SHOT....
TV

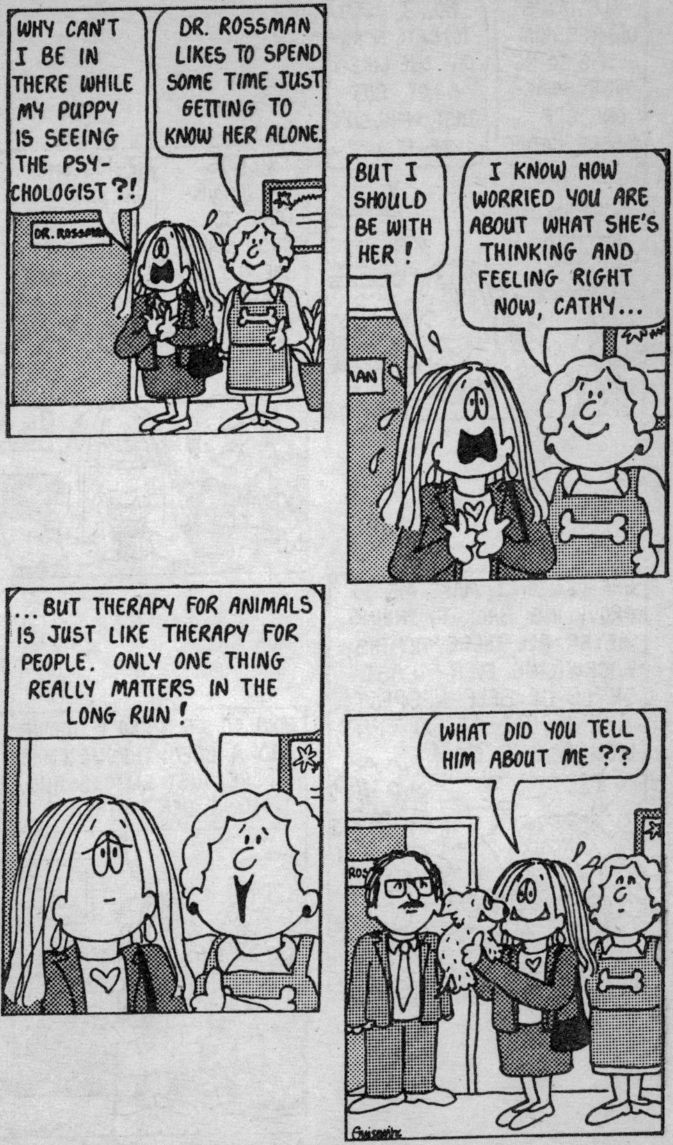

WHY CAN'T I BE IN THERE WHILE MY PUPPY IS SEEING THE PSYCHOLOGIST?!
DR. ROSSMAN LIKES TO SPEND SOME TIME JUST GETTING TO KNOW HER ALONE.
DR. ROSSMAN
BUT I SHOULD BE WITH HER!
I KNOW HOW WORRIED YOU ARE ABOUT WHAT SHE'S THINKING AND FEELING RIGHT NOW, CATHY...
...BUT THERAPY FOR ANIMALS IS JUST LIKE THERAPY FOR PEOPLE. ONLY ONE THING REALLY MATTERS IN THE LONG RUN!
WHAT DID YOU TELL HIM ABOUT ME??
Guisewite

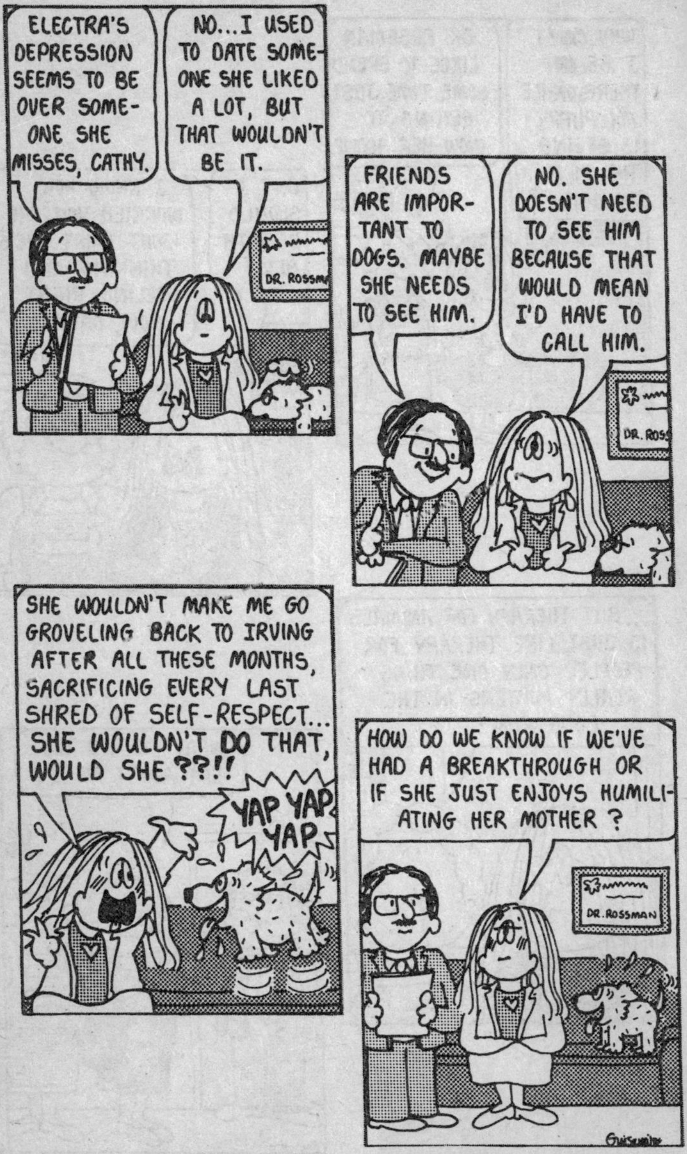
ELECTRA'S DEPRESSION SEEMS TO BE OVER SOMEONE SHE MISSES, CATHY.
NO...I USED TO DATE SOMEONE SHE LIKED A LOT, BUT THAT WOULDN'T BE IT.
DR. ROSSMAN
FRIENDS ARE IMPORTANT TO DOGS. MAYBE SHE NEEDS TO SEE HIM.
NO. SHE DOESN'T NEED TO SEE HIM BECAUSE THAT WOULD MEAN I'D HAVE TO CALL HIM.
SHE WOULDN'T MAKE ME GO GROVELING BACK TO IRVING AFTER ALL THESE MONTHS, SACRIFICING EVERY LAST SHRED OF SELF-RESPECT... SHE WOULDN'T DO THAT, WOULD SHE ??!!
YAP YAP YAP
HOW DO WE KNOW IF WE'VE HAD A BREAKTHROUGH OR IF SHE JUST ENJOYS HUMILIATING HER MOTHER ?
DR. ROSSMAN

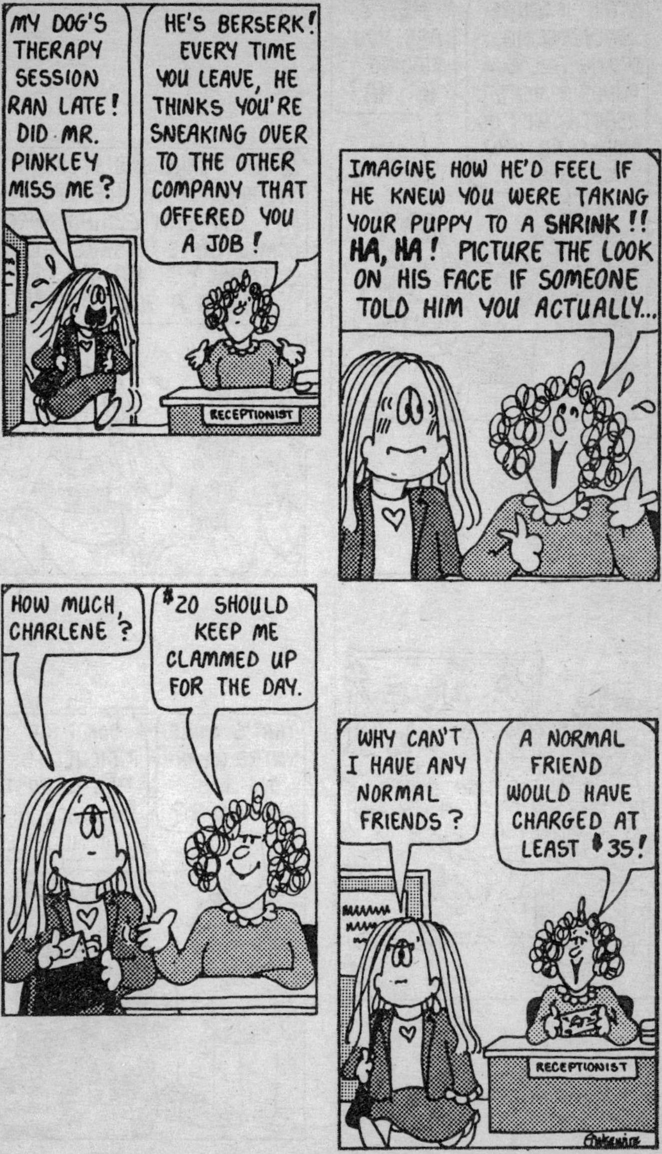
MY DOG'S THERAPY SESSION RAN LATE! DID MR. PINKLEY MISS ME?
HE'S BERSERK! EVERY TIME YOU LEAVE, HE THINKS YOU'RE SNEAKING OVER TO THE OTHER COMPANY THAT OFFERED YOU A JOB!
RECEPTIONIST
IMAGINE HOW HE'D FEEL IF HE KNEW YOU WERE TAKING YOUR PUPPY TO A SHRINK!! HA, HA! PICTURE THE LOOK ON HIS FACE IF SOMEONE TOLD HIM YOU ACTUALLY...
HOW MUCH, CHARLENE?
$20 SHOULD KEEP ME CLAMMED UP FOR THE DAY.
WHY CAN'T I HAVE ANY NORMAL FRIENDS?
A NORMAL FRIEND WOULD HAVE CHARGED AT LEAST $35!
RECEPTIONIST

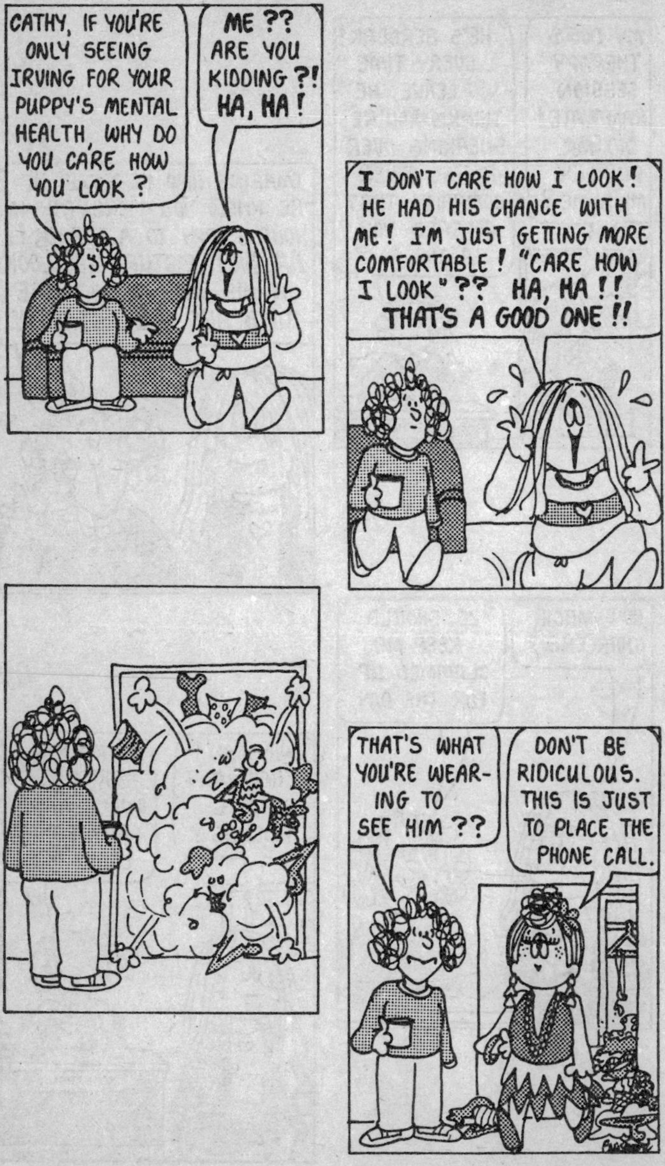
CATHY, IF YOU'RE ONLY SEEING IRVING FOR YOUR PUPPY'S MENTAL HEALTH, WHY DO YOU CARE HOW YOU LOOK?
ME?? ARE YOU KIDDING?! HA, HA!
I DON'T CARE HOW I LOOK! HE HAD HIS CHANCE WITH ME! I'M JUST GETTING MORE COMFORTABLE! "CARE HOW I LOOK"?? HA, HA!! THAT'S A GOOD ONE!!
THAT'S WHAT YOU'RE WEAR-ING TO SEE HIM??
DON'T BE RIDICULOUS. THIS IS JUST TO PLACE THE PHONE CALL.

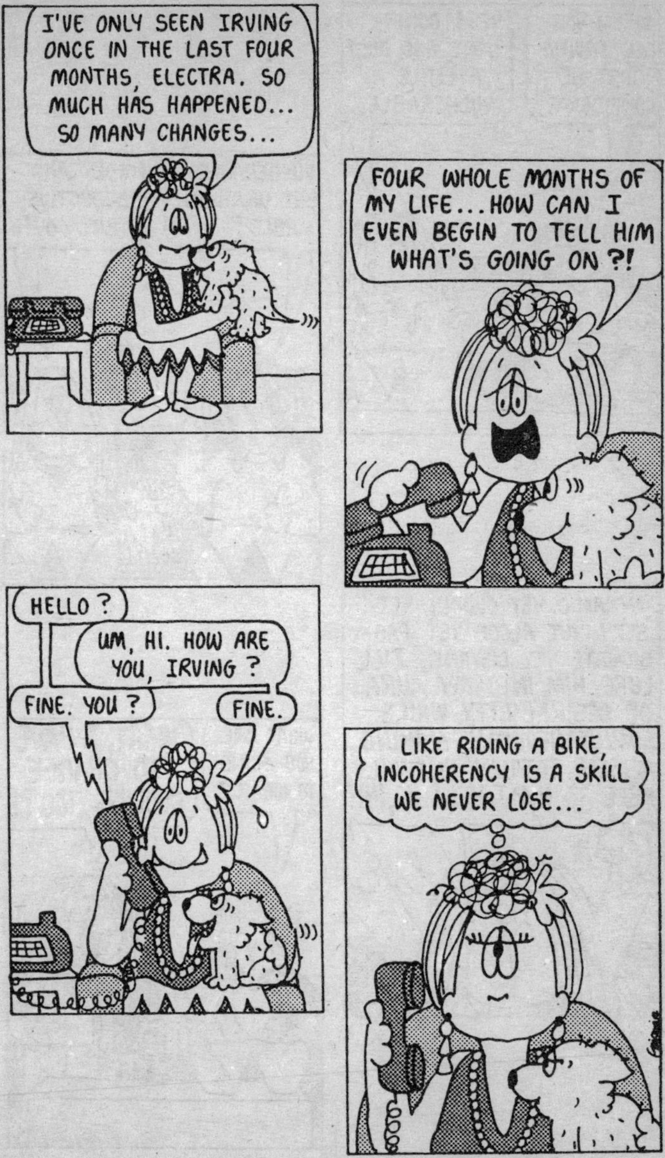
I'VE ONLY SEEN IRVING ONCE IN THE LAST FOUR MONTHS, ELECTRA. SO MUCH HAS HAPPENED... SO MANY CHANGES...
FOUR WHOLE MONTHS OF MY LIFE...HOW CAN I EVEN BEGIN TO TELL HIM WHAT'S GOING ON?!
HELLO?
UM, HI. HOW ARE YOU, IRVING?
FINE. YOU?
FINE.
LIKE RIDING A BIKE, INCOHERENCY IS A SKILL WE NEVER LOSE...

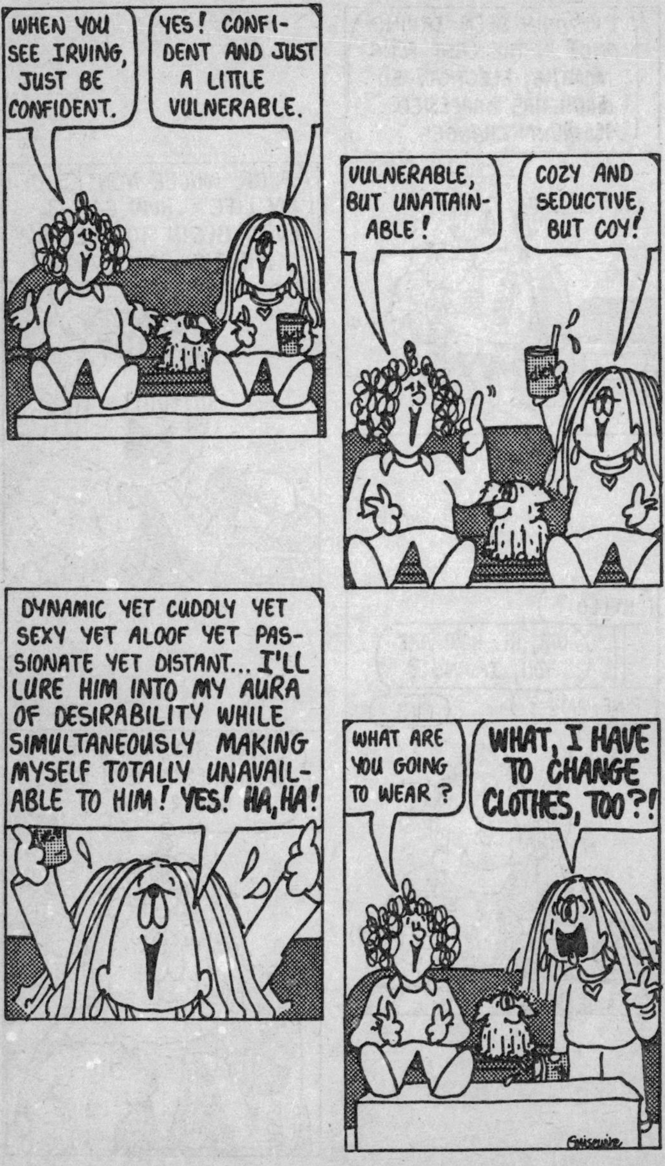

WHEN YOU SEE IRVING, JUST BE CONFIDENT.
YES! CONFI- DENT AND JUST A LITTLE VULNERABLE.
VULNERABLE, BUT UNATTAIN- ABLE!
COZY AND SEDUCTIVE, BUT COY!
DYNAMIC YET CUDDLY YET SEXY YET ALOOF YET PAS- SIONATE YET DISTANT... I'LL LURE HIM INTO MY AURA OF DESIRABILITY WHILE SIMULTANEOUSLY MAKING MYSELF TOTALLY UNAVAIL- ABLE TO HIM! YES! HA, HA!
WHAT ARE YOU GOING TO WEAR?
WHAT, I HAVE TO CHANGE CLOTHES, TOO?!
Guisewite

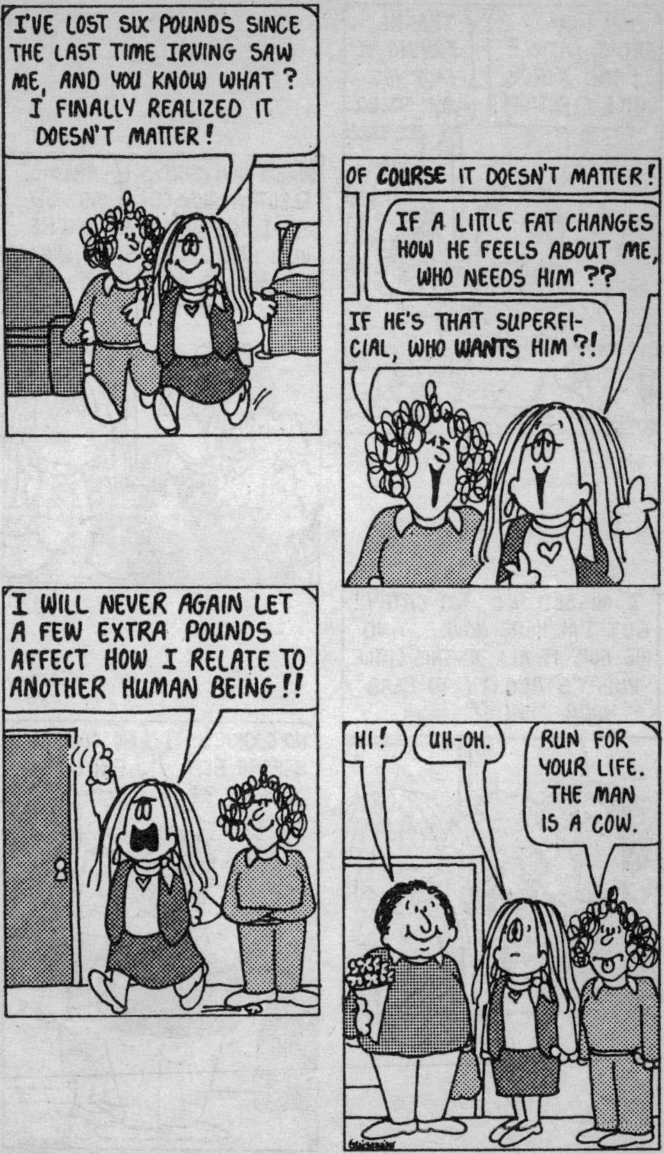
I'VE LOST SIX POUNDS SINCE THE LAST TIME IRVING SAW ME, AND YOU KNOW WHAT? I FINALLY REALIZED IT DOESN'T MATTER!
OF COURSE IT DOESN'T MATTER!
IF A LITTLE FAT CHANGES HOW HE FEELS ABOUT ME, WHO NEEDS HIM??
IF HE'S THAT SUPERFICIAL, WHO WANTS HIM?!
I WILL NEVER AGAIN LET A FEW EXTRA POUNDS AFFECT HOW I RELATE TO ANOTHER HUMAN BEING!!
HI!
UH-OH.
RUN FOR YOUR LIFE. THE MAN IS A COW.

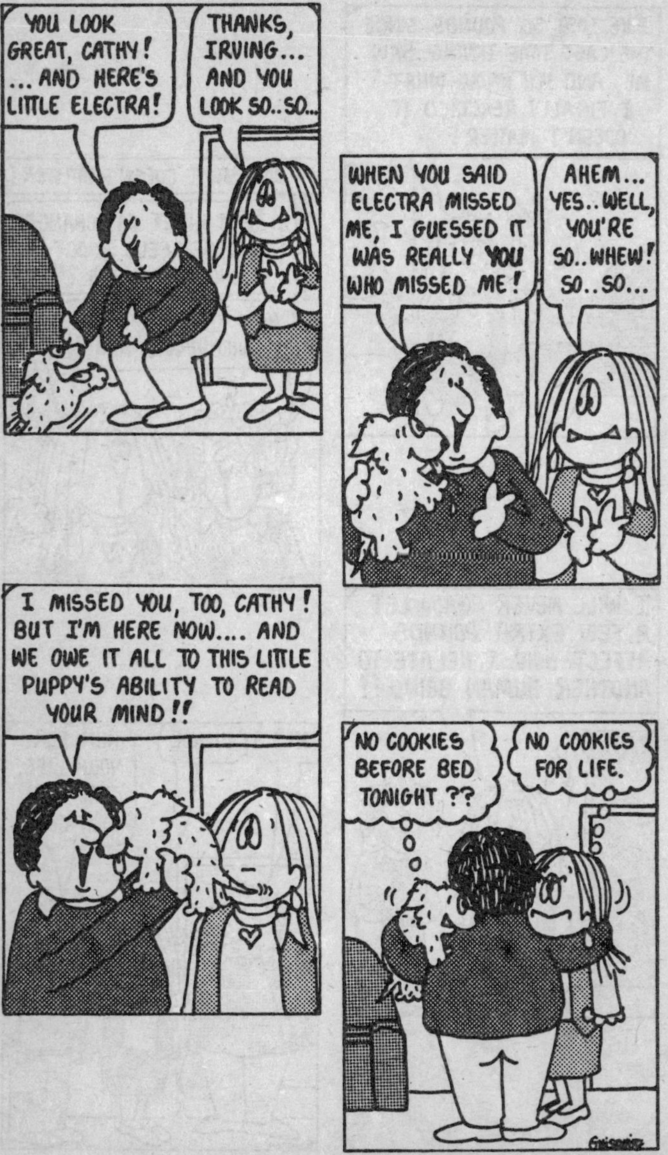

YOU LOOK GREAT, CATHY! ... AND HERE'S LITTLE ELECTRA!
THANKS, IRVING... AND YOU LOOK SO..SO...
WHEN YOU SAID ELECTRA MISSED ME, I GUESSED IT WAS REALLY YOU WHO MISSED ME!
AHEM... YES..WELL, YOU'RE SO..WHEW! SO..SO...
I MISSED YOU, TOO, CATHY! BUT I'M HERE NOW.... AND WE OWE IT ALL TO THIS LITTLE PUPPY'S ABILITY TO READ YOUR MIND!!
NO COOKIES BEFORE BED TONIGHT??
NO COOKIES FOR LIFE.

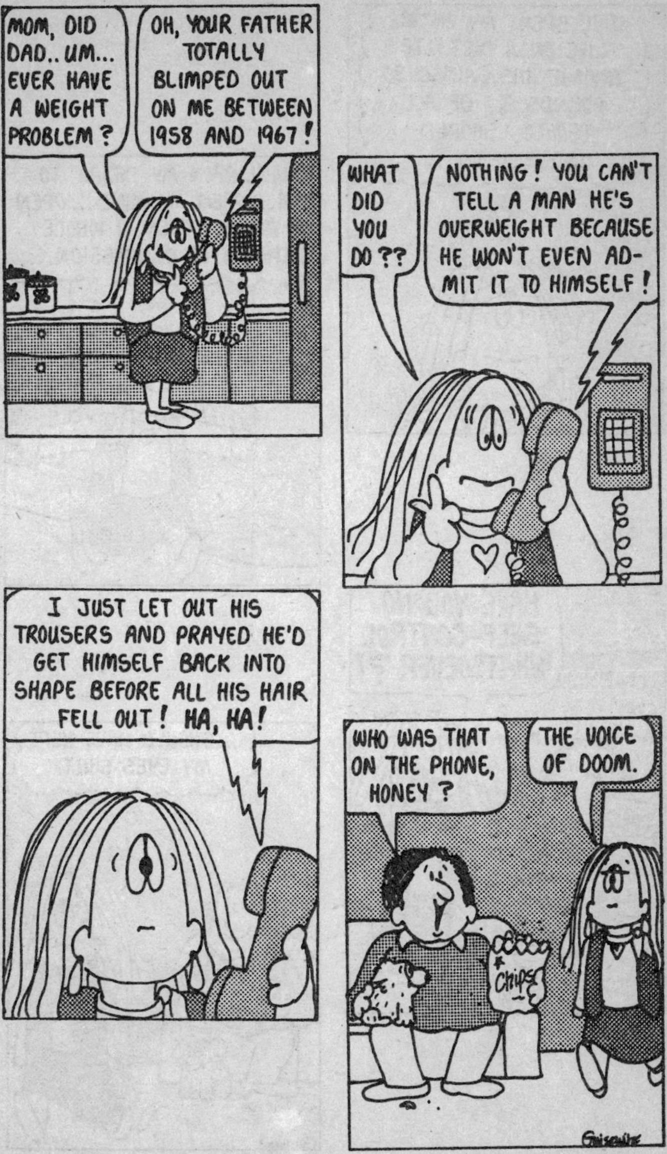
MOM, DID DAD.. UM... EVER HAVE A WEIGHT PROBLEM?
OH, YOUR FATHER TOTALLY BLIMPED OUT ON ME BETWEEN 1958 AND 1967!
WHAT DID YOU DO??
NOTHING! YOU CAN'T TELL A MAN HE'S OVERWEIGHT BECAUSE HE WON'T EVEN ADMIT IT TO HIMSELF!
I JUST LET OUT HIS TROUSERS AND PRAYED HE'D GET HIMSELF BACK INTO SHAPE BEFORE ALL HIS HAIR FELL OUT! HA, HA!
WHO WAS THAT ON THE PHONE, HONEY?
THE VOICE OF DOOM.
CHIPS
Guisewite

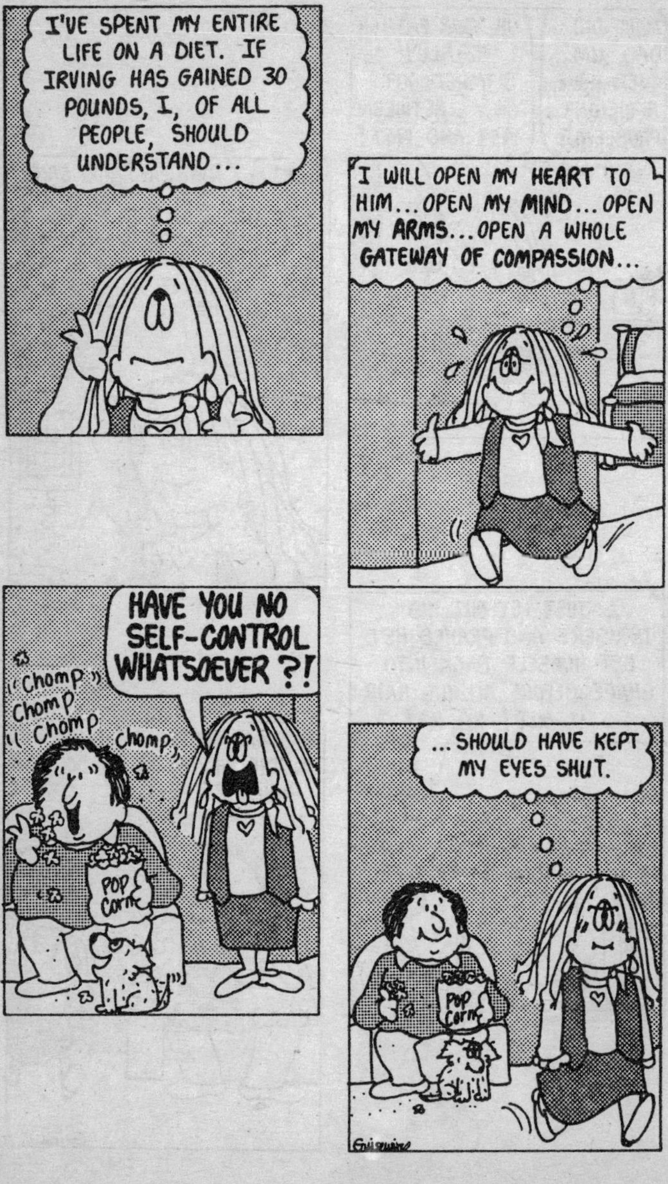
I'VE SPENT MY ENTIRE LIFE ON A DIET. IF IRVING HAS GAINED 30 POUNDS, I, OF ALL PEOPLE, SHOULD UNDERSTAND...
I WILL OPEN MY HEART TO HIM...OPEN MY MIND...OPEN MY ARMS...OPEN A WHOLE GATEWAY OF COMPASSION...
"Chomp" Chomp "Chomp Chomp"
HAVE YOU NO SELF-CONTROL WHATSOEVER?!
POP Corn
...SHOULD HAVE KEPT MY EYES SHUT.
POP Corn

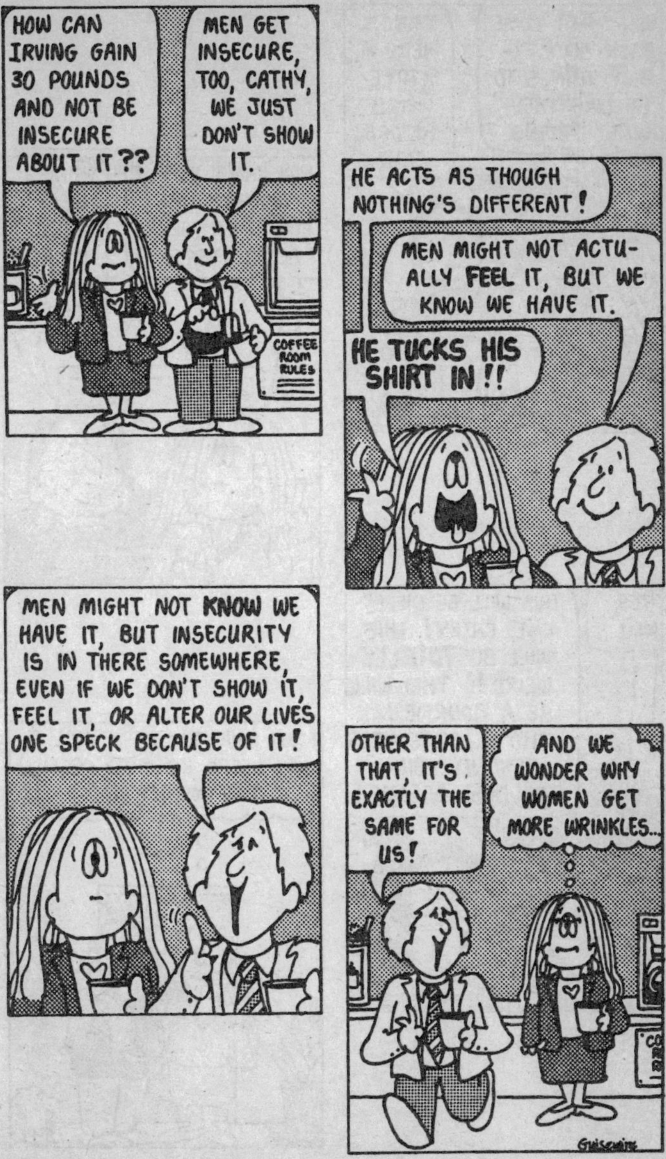
HOW CAN IRVING GAIN 30 POUNDS AND NOT BE INSECURE ABOUT IT??
MEN GET INSECURE, TOO, CATHY, WE JUST DON'T SHOW IT.
COFFEE ROOM RULES
HE ACTS AS THOUGH NOTHING'S DIFFERENT!
MEN MIGHT NOT ACTUALLY FEEL IT, BUT WE KNOW WE HAVE IT.
HE TUCKS HIS SHIRT IN!!
MEN MIGHT NOT KNOW WE HAVE IT, BUT INSECURITY IS IN THERE SOMEWHERE, EVEN IF WE DON'T SHOW IT, FEEL IT, OR ALTER OUR LIVES ONE SPECK BECAUSE OF IT!
OTHER THAN THAT, IT'S EXACTLY THE SAME FOR US!
AND WE WONDER WHY WOMEN GET MORE WRINKLES...
Guisewite

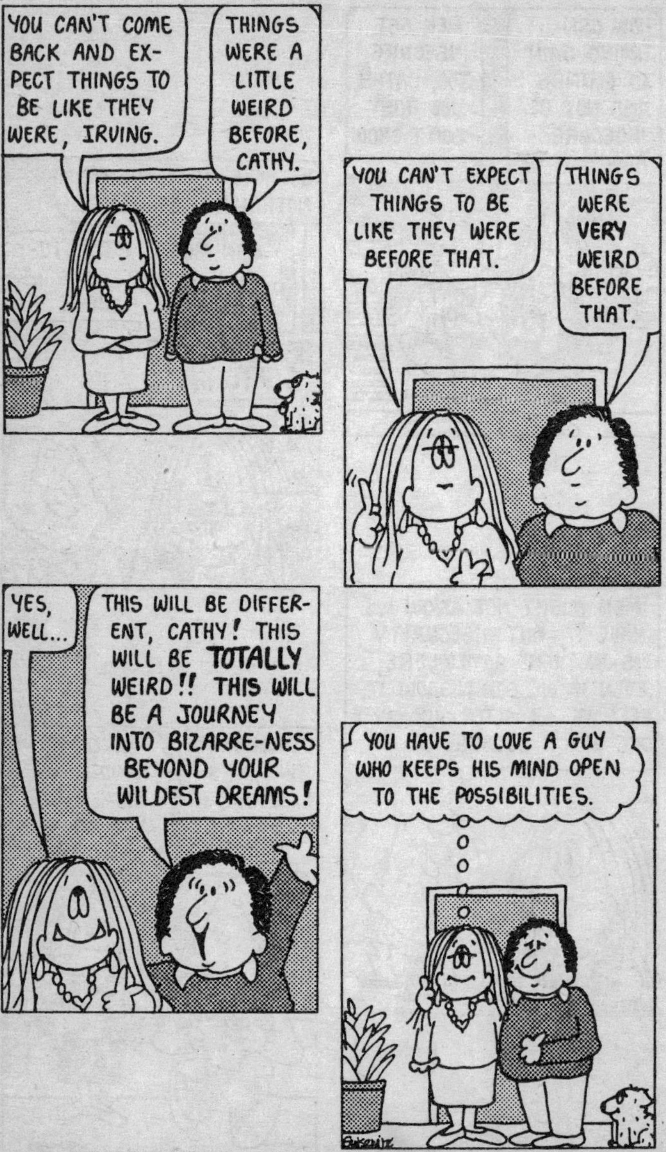
YOU CAN'T COME BACK AND EX-PECT THINGS TO BE LIKE THEY WERE, IRVING.
THINGS WERE A LITTLE WEIRD BEFORE, CATHY.
YOU CAN'T EXPECT THINGS TO BE LIKE THEY WERE BEFORE THAT.
THINGS WERE VERY WEIRD BEFORE THAT.
YES, WELL...
THIS WILL BE DIFFER-ENT, CATHY! THIS WILL BE TOTALLY WEIRD!! THIS WILL BE A JOURNEY INTO BIZARRE-NESS BEYOND YOUR WILDEST DREAMS!
YOU HAVE TO LOVE A GUY WHO KEEPS HIS MIND OPEN TO THE POSSIBILITIES.

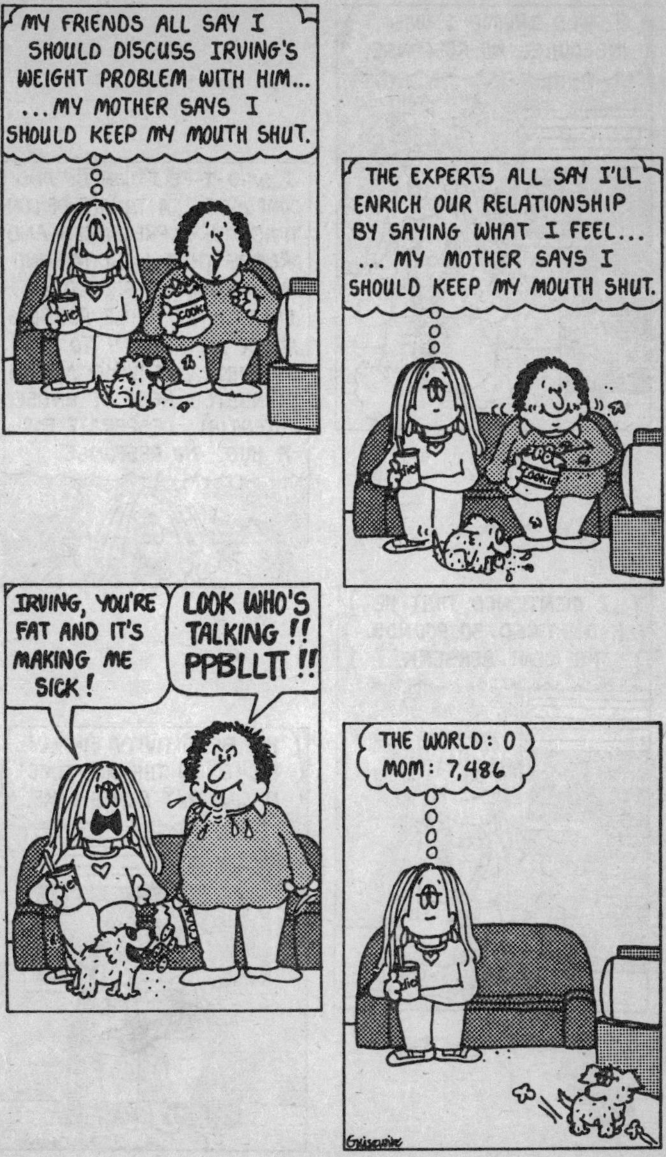
MY FRIENDS ALL SAY I SHOULD DISCUSS IRVING'S WEIGHT PROBLEM WITH HIM... ...MY MOTHER SAYS I SHOULD KEEP MY MOUTH SHUT.
THE EXPERTS ALL SAY I'LL ENRICH OUR RELATIONSHIP BY SAYING WHAT I FEEL... ...MY MOTHER SAYS I SHOULD KEEP MY MOUTH SHUT.
IRVING, YOU'RE FAT AND IT'S MAKING ME SICK!
LOOK WHO'S TALKING!! PPBLLTT!!
THE WORLD: 0
MOM: 7,486

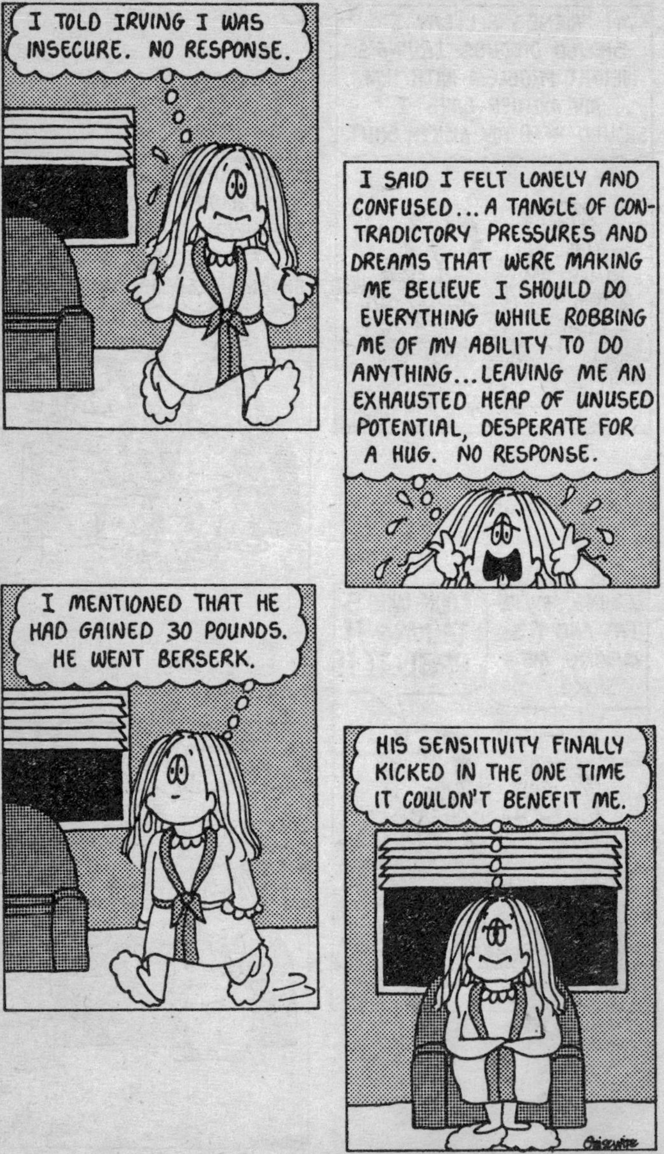
I TOLD IRVING I WAS INSECURE. NO RESPONSE.
I SAID I FELT LONELY AND CONFUSED... A TANGLE OF CONTRADICTORY PRESSURES AND DREAMS THAT WERE MAKING ME BELIEVE I SHOULD DO EVERYTHING WHILE ROBBING ME OF MY ABILITY TO DO ANYTHING... LEAVING ME AN EXHAUSTED HEAP OF UNUSED POTENTIAL, DESPERATE FOR A HUG. NO RESPONSE.
I MENTIONED THAT HE HAD GAINED 30 POUNDS. HE WENT BERSERK.
HIS SENSITIVITY FINALLY KICKED IN THE ONE TIME IT COULDN'T BENEFIT ME.

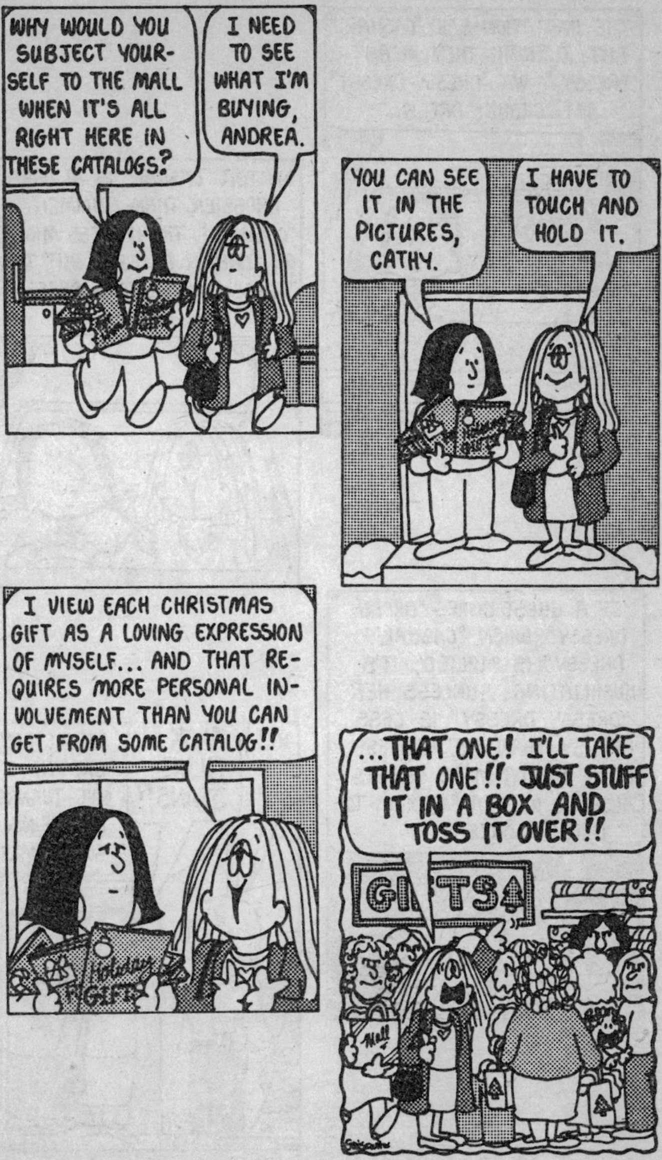
WHY WOULD YOU SUBJECT YOURSELF TO THE MALL WHEN IT'S ALL RIGHT HERE IN THESE CATALOGS?
I NEED TO SEE WHAT I'M BUYING, ANDREA.
YOU CAN SEE IT IN THE PICTURES, CATHY.
I HAVE TO TOUCH AND HOLD IT.
I VIEW EACH CHRISTMAS GIFT AS A LOVING EXPRESSION OF MYSELF... AND THAT REQUIRES MORE PERSONAL INVOLVEMENT THAN YOU CAN GET FROM SOME CATALOG!!
...THAT ONE! I'LL TAKE THAT ONE!! JUST STUFF IT IN A BOX AND TOSS IT OVER!!

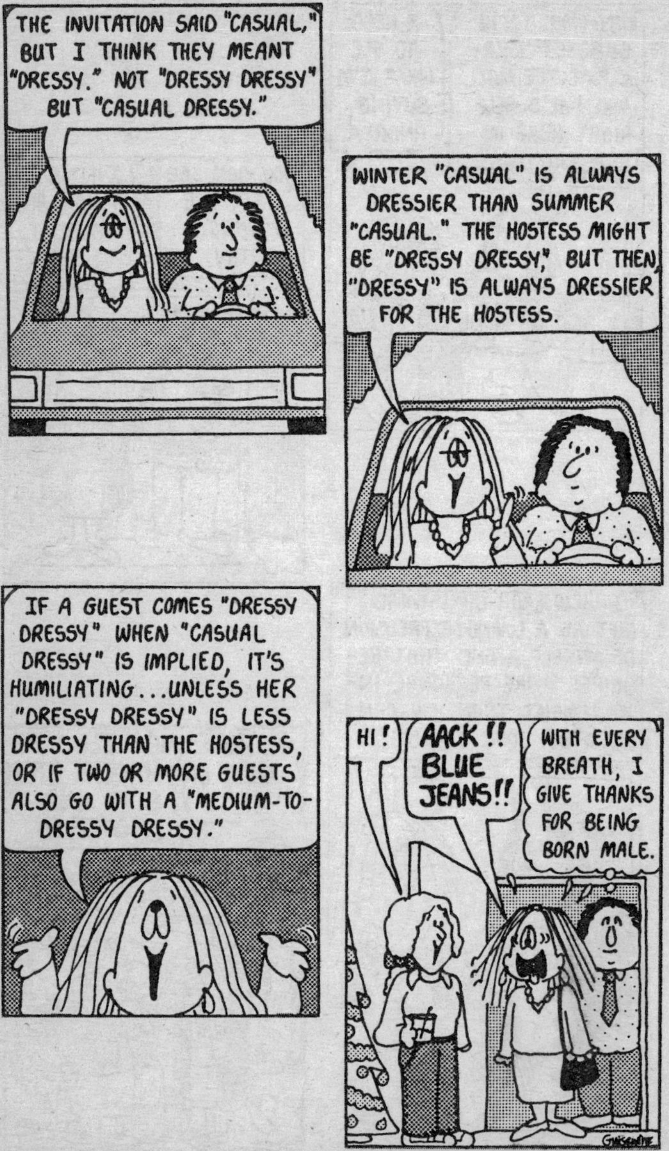
THE INVITATION SAID "CASUAL," BUT I THINK THEY MEANT "DRESSY." NOT "DRESSY DRESSY" BUT "CASUAL DRESSY."
WINTER "CASUAL" IS ALWAYS DRESSIER THAN SUMMER "CASUAL." THE HOSTESS MIGHT BE "DRESSY DRESSY," BUT THEN, "DRESSY" IS ALWAYS DRESSIER FOR THE HOSTESS.
IF A GUEST COMES "DRESSY DRESSY" WHEN "CASUAL DRESSY" IS IMPLIED, IT'S HUMILIATING...UNLESS HER "DRESSY DRESSY" IS LESS DRESSY THAN THE HOSTESS, OR IF TWO OR MORE GUESTS ALSO GO WITH A "MEDIUM-TO-DRESSY DRESSY."
HI!
AACK!! BLUE JEANS!!
WITH EVERY BREATH, I GIVE THANKS FOR BEING BORN MALE.

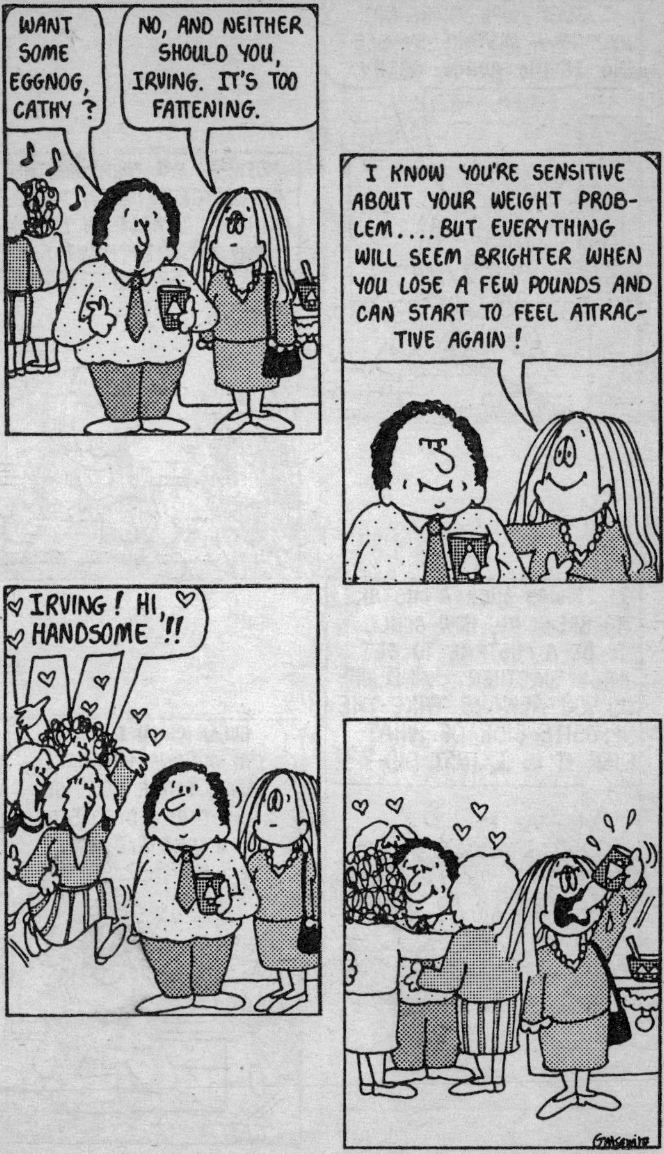
WANT SOME EGGNOG, CATHY ?
NO, AND NEITHER SHOULD YOU, IRVING. IT'S TOO FATTENING.
I KNOW YOU'RE SENSITIVE ABOUT YOUR WEIGHT PROBLEM.... BUT EVERYTHING WILL SEEM BRIGHTER WHEN YOU LOSE A FEW POUNDS AND CAN START TO FEEL ATTRACTIVE AGAIN !
IRVING ! HI, HANDSOME !!

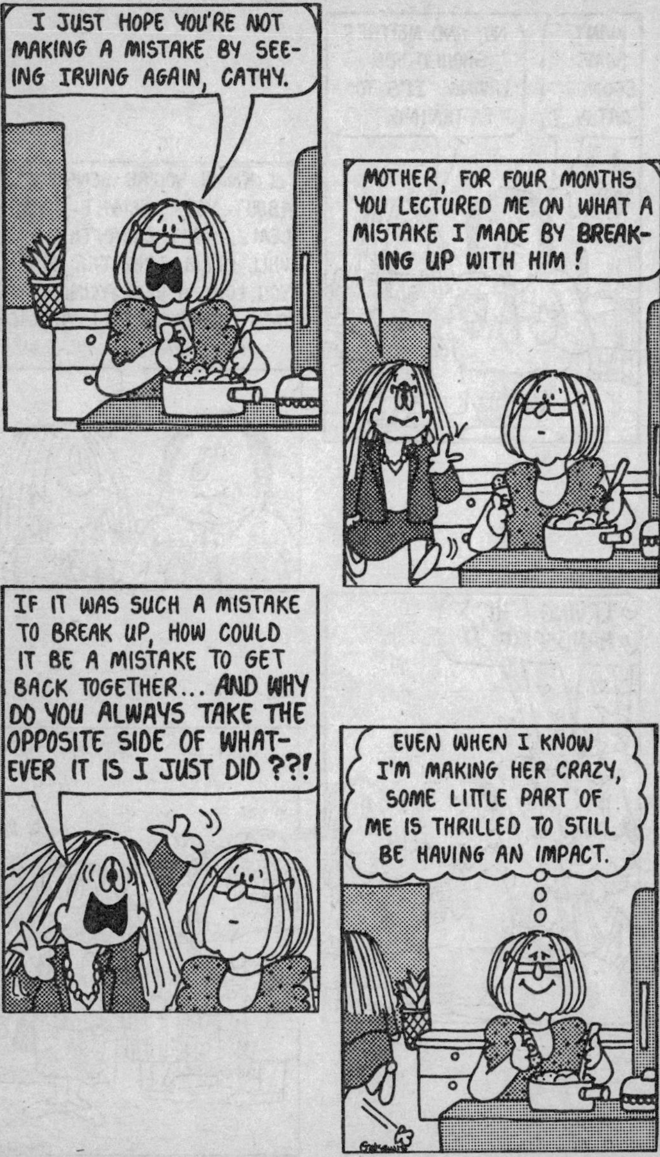
I JUST HOPE YOU'RE NOT MAKING A MISTAKE BY SEEING IRVING AGAIN, CATHY.
MOTHER, FOR FOUR MONTHS YOU LECTURED ME ON WHAT A MISTAKE I MADE BY BREAKING UP WITH HIM!
IF IT WAS SUCH A MISTAKE TO BREAK UP, HOW COULD IT BE A MISTAKE TO GET BACK TOGETHER... AND WHY DO YOU ALWAYS TAKE THE OPPOSITE SIDE OF WHATEVER IT IS I JUST DID??!
EVEN WHEN I KNOW I'M MAKING HER CRAZY, SOME LITTLE PART OF ME IS THRILLED TO STILL BE HAVING AN IMPACT.

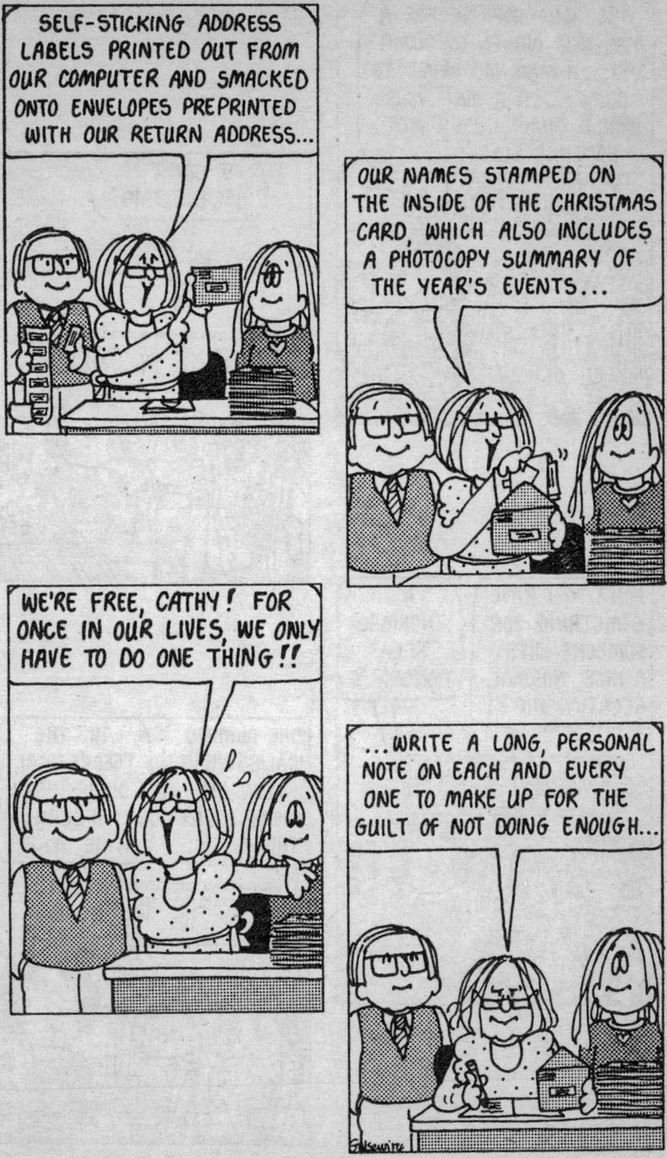
SELF-STICKING ADDRESS LABELS PRINTED OUT FROM OUR COMPUTER AND SMACKED ONTO ENVELOPES PREPRINTED WITH OUR RETURN ADDRESS...
OUR NAMES STAMPED ON THE INSIDE OF THE CHRISTMAS CARD, WHICH ALSO INCLUDES A PHOTOCOPY SUMMARY OF THE YEAR'S EVENTS...
WE'RE FREE, CATHY! FOR ONCE IN OUR LIVES, WE ONLY HAVE TO DO ONE THING!!
...WRITE A LONG, PERSONAL NOTE ON EACH AND EVERY ONE TO MAKE UP FOR THE GUILT OF NOT DOING ENOUGH...

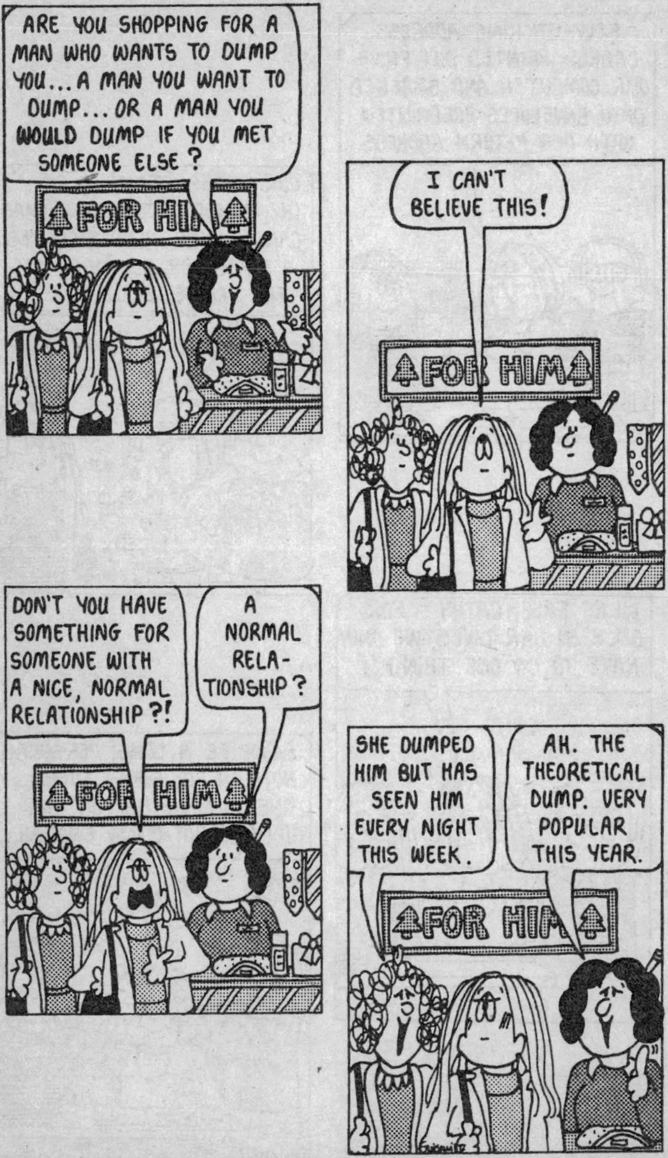

ARE YOU SHOPPING FOR A MAN WHO WANTS TO DUMP YOU... A MAN YOU WANT TO DUMP... OR A MAN YOU WOULD DUMP IF YOU MET SOMEONE ELSE?
FOR HIM
I CAN'T BELIEVE THIS!
FOR HIM
DON'T YOU HAVE SOMETHING FOR SOMEONE WITH A NICE, NORMAL RELATIONSHIP?!
A NORMAL RELA-TIONSHIP?
FOR HIM
SHE DUMPED HIM BUT HAS SEEN HIM EVERY NIGHT THIS WEEK.
AH. THE THEORETICAL DUMP. VERY POPULAR THIS YEAR.

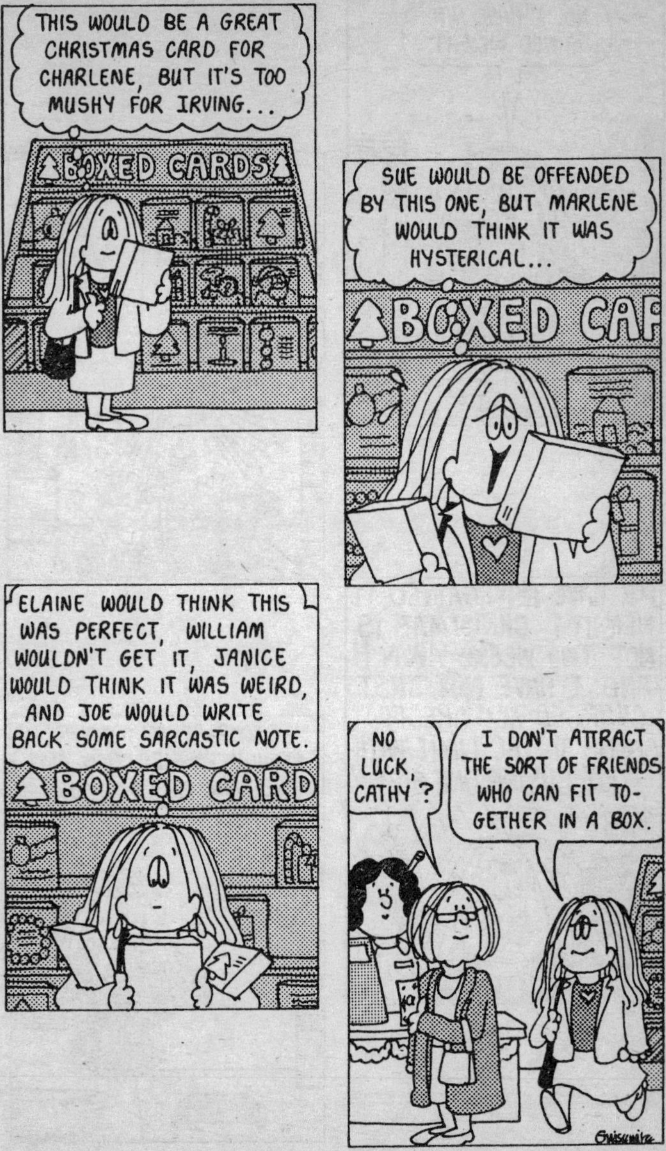
THIS WOULD BE A GREAT CHRISTMAS CARD FOR CHARLENE, BUT IT'S TOO MUSHY FOR IRVING...
BOXED CARDS
SUE WOULD BE OFFENDED BY THIS ONE, BUT MARLENE WOULD THINK IT WAS HYSTERICAL...
ELAINE WOULD THINK THIS WAS PERFECT, WILLIAM WOULDN'T GET IT, JANICE WOULD THINK IT WAS WEIRD, AND JOE WOULD WRITE BACK SOME SARCASTIC NOTE.
NO LUCK, CATHY?
I DON'T ATTRACT THE SORT OF FRIENDS WHO CAN FIT TOGETHER IN A BOX.
Guisewite

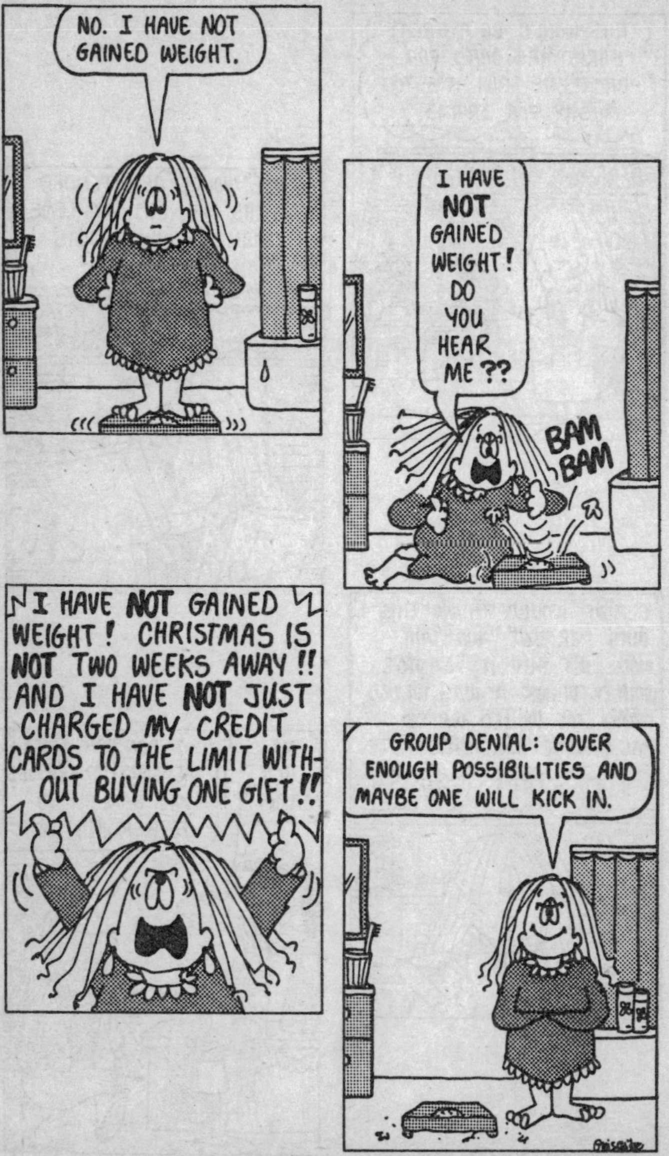
NO. I HAVE NOT GAINED WEIGHT.
I HAVE NOT GAINED WEIGHT! DO YOU HEAR ME??
BAM BAM
I HAVE NOT GAINED WEIGHT! CHRISTMAS IS NOT TWO WEEKS AWAY!! AND I HAVE NOT JUST CHARGED MY CREDIT CARDS TO THE LIMIT WITH-OUT BUYING ONE GIFT!!
GROUP DENIAL: COVER ENOUGH POSSIBILITIES AND MAYBE ONE WILL KICK IN.

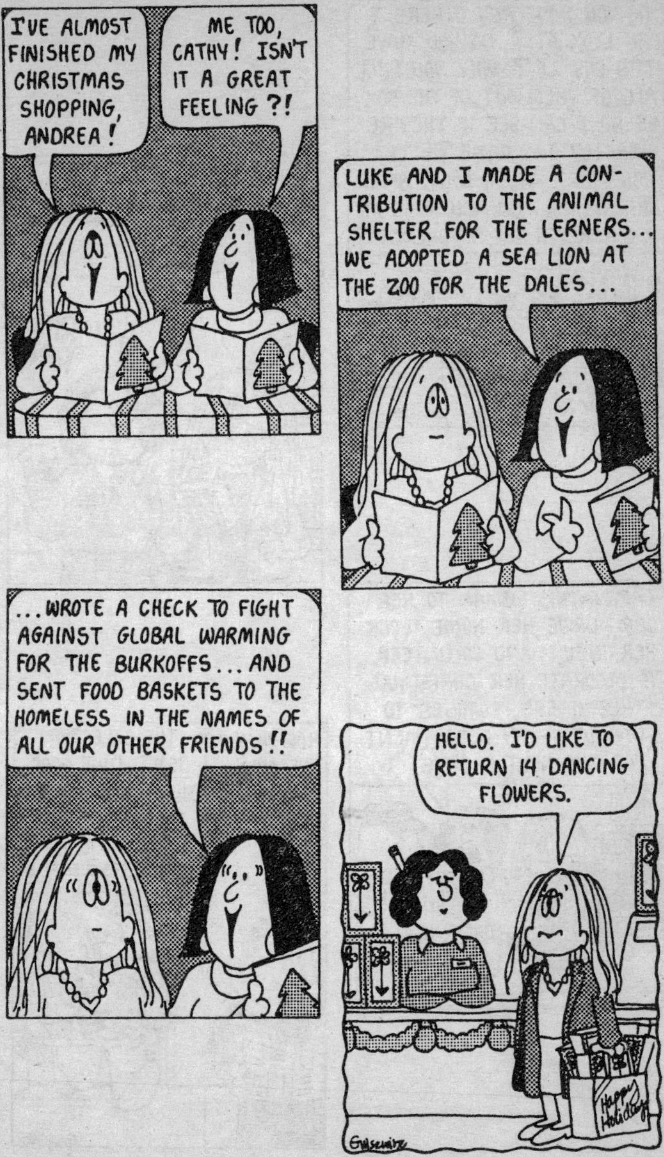
I'VE ALMOST FINISHED MY CHRISTMAS SHOPPING, ANDREA!
ME TOO, CATHY! ISN'T IT A GREAT FEELING?!
LUKE AND I MADE A CONTRIBUTION TO THE ANIMAL SHELTER FOR THE LERNERS... WE ADOPTED A SEA LION AT THE ZOO FOR THE DALES...
...WROTE A CHECK TO FIGHT AGAINST GLOBAL WARMING FOR THE BURKOFFS... AND SENT FOOD BASKETS TO THE HOMELESS IN THE NAMES OF ALL OUR OTHER FRIENDS!!
HELLO. I'D LIKE TO RETURN 14 DANCING FLOWERS.

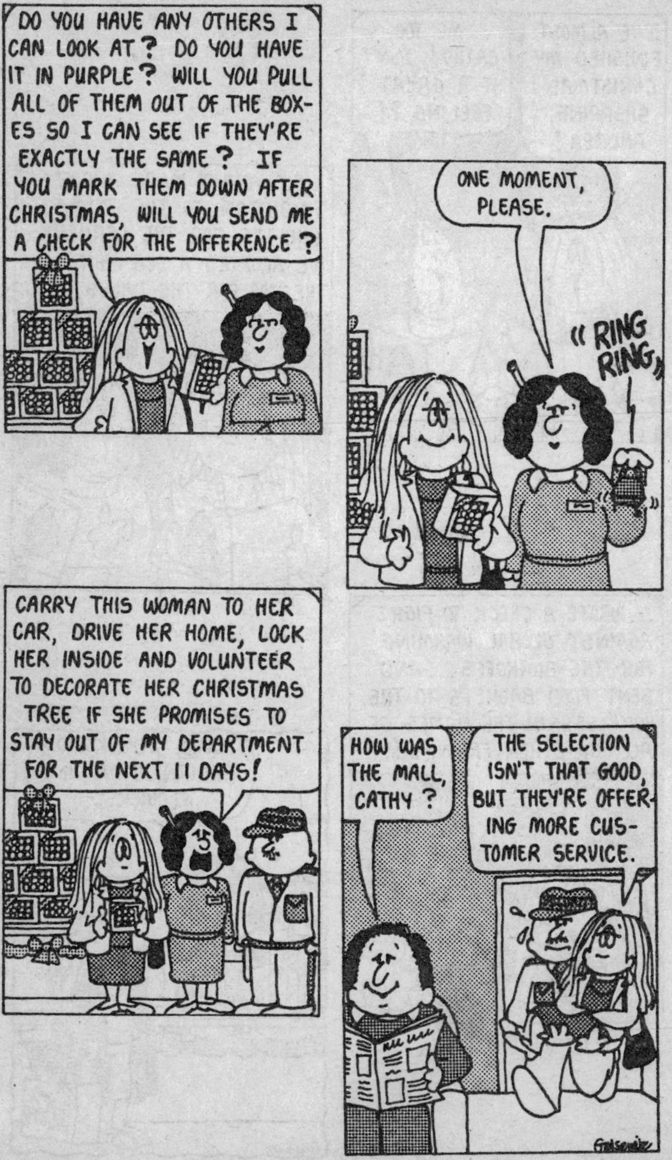
DO YOU HAVE ANY OTHERS I CAN LOOK AT? DO YOU HAVE IT IN PURPLE? WILL YOU PULL ALL OF THEM OUT OF THE BOX-ES SO I CAN SEE IF THEY'RE EXACTLY THE SAME? IF YOU MARK THEM DOWN AFTER CHRISTMAS, WILL YOU SEND ME A CHECK FOR THE DIFFERENCE?
ONE MOMENT, PLEASE.
« RING RING »
CARRY THIS WOMAN TO HER CAR, DRIVE HER HOME, LOCK HER INSIDE AND VOLUNTEER TO DECORATE HER CHRISTMAS TREE IF SHE PROMISES TO STAY OUT OF MY DEPARTMENT FOR THE NEXT 11 DAYS!
HOW WAS THE MALL, CATHY?
THE SELECTION ISN'T THAT GOOD, BUT THEY'RE OFFER-ING MORE CUS-TOMER SERVICE.

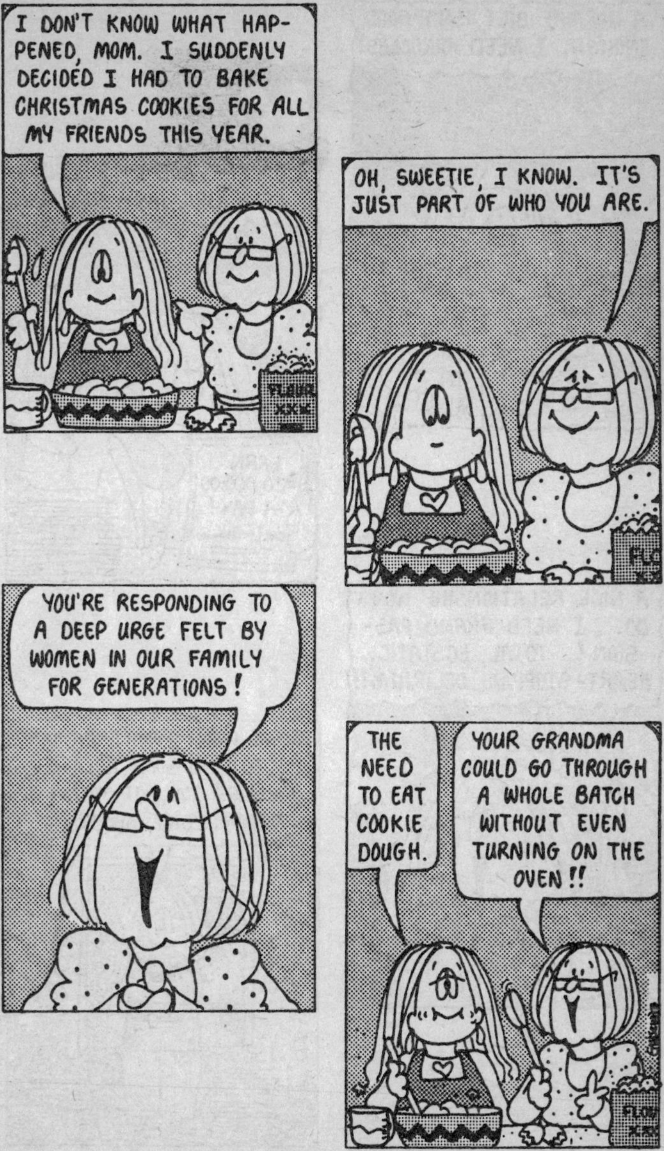
I DON'T KNOW WHAT HAPPENED, MOM. I SUDDENLY DECIDED I HAD TO BAKE CHRISTMAS COOKIES FOR ALL MY FRIENDS THIS YEAR.
FLOUR XXX
OH, SWEETIE, I KNOW. IT'S JUST PART OF WHO YOU ARE.
YOU'RE RESPONDING TO A DEEP URGE FELT BY WOMEN IN OUR FAMILY FOR GENERATIONS!
THE NEED TO EAT COOKIE DOUGH.
YOUR GRANDMA COULD GO THROUGH A WHOLE BATCH WITHOUT EVEN TURNING ON THE OVEN!!

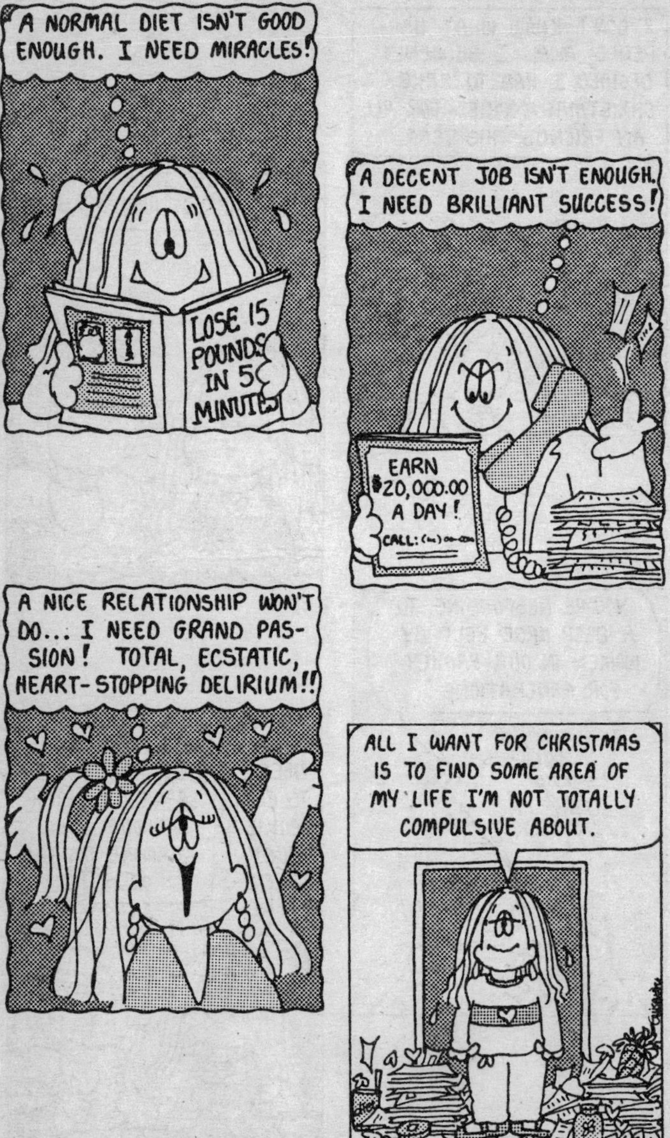
A NORMAL DIET ISN'T GOOD ENOUGH. I NEED MIRACLES!
LOSE 15 POUNDS IN 5 MINUTES
A DECENT JOB ISN'T ENOUGH. I NEED BRILLIANT SUCCESS!
EARN $20,000.00 A DAY!
CALL:
A NICE RELATIONSHIP WON'T DO... I NEED GRAND PASSION! TOTAL, ECSTATIC, HEART-STOPPING DELIRIUM!!
ALL I WANT FOR CHRISTMAS IS TO FIND SOME AREA OF MY LIFE I'M NOT TOTALLY COMPULSIVE ABOUT.

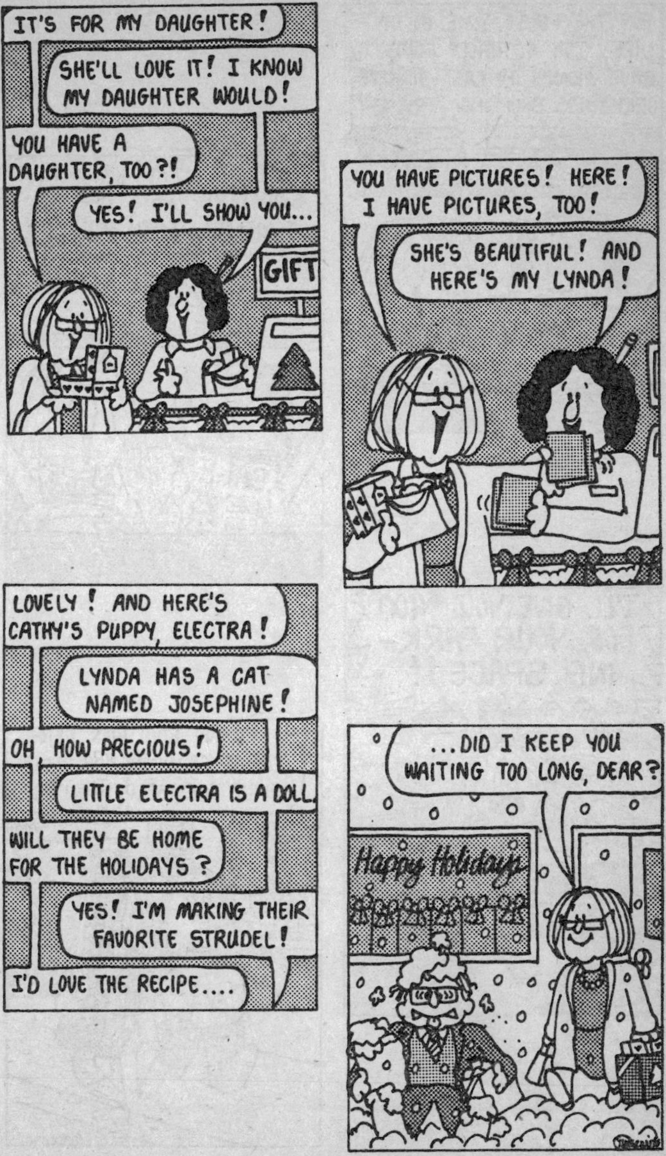
IT'S FOR MY DAUGHTER!
SHE'LL LOVE IT! I KNOW MY DAUGHTER WOULD!
YOU HAVE A DAUGHTER, TOO?!
YES! I'LL SHOW YOU...
GIFT
YOU HAVE PICTURES! HERE! I HAVE PICTURES, TOO!
SHE'S BEAUTIFUL! AND HERE'S MY LYNDA!
LOVELY! AND HERE'S CATHY'S PUPPY, ELECTRA!
LYNDA HAS A CAT NAMED JOSEPHINE!
OH, HOW PRECIOUS!
LITTLE ELECTRA IS A DOLL.
WILL THEY BE HOME FOR THE HOLIDAYS?
YES! I'M MAKING THEIR FAVORITE STRUDEL!
I'D LOVE THE RECIPE....
...DID I KEEP YOU WAITING TOO LONG, DEAR?
Happy Holidays

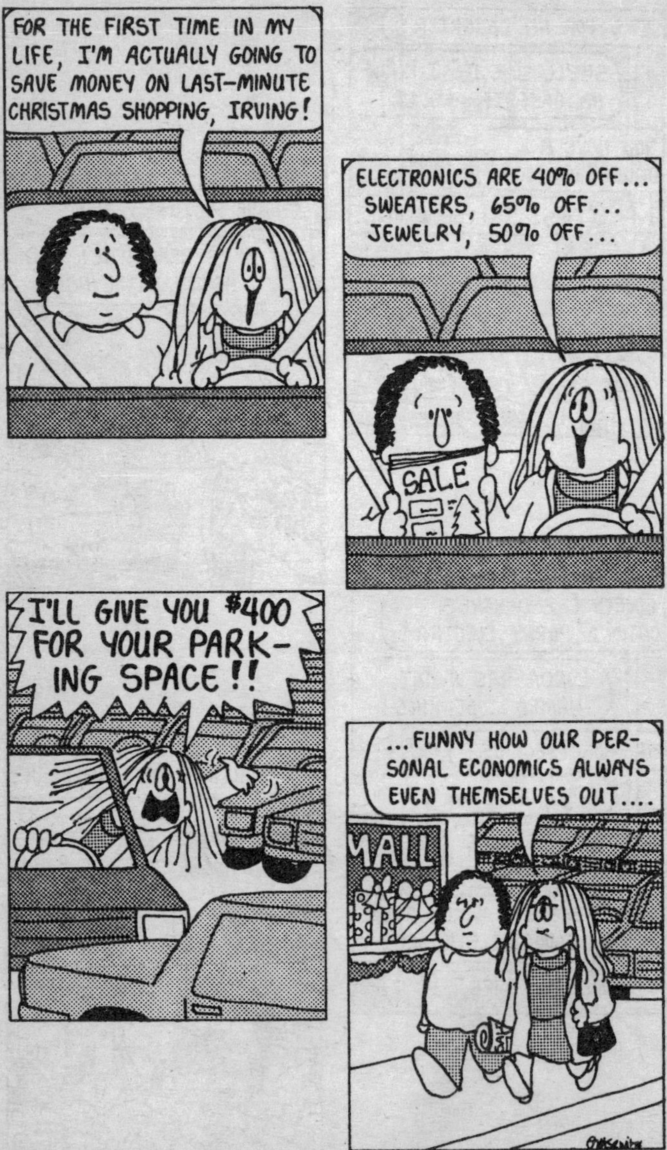
FOR THE FIRST TIME IN MY LIFE, I'M ACTUALLY GOING TO SAVE MONEY ON LAST-MINUTE CHRISTMAS SHOPPING, IRVING!
ELECTRONICS ARE 40% OFF... SWEATERS, 65% OFF... JEWELRY, 50% OFF...
SALE
I'LL GIVE YOU $400 FOR YOUR PARK-ING SPACE!!
...FUNNY HOW OUR PER-SONAL ECONOMICS ALWAYS EVEN THEMSELVES OUT....
MALL

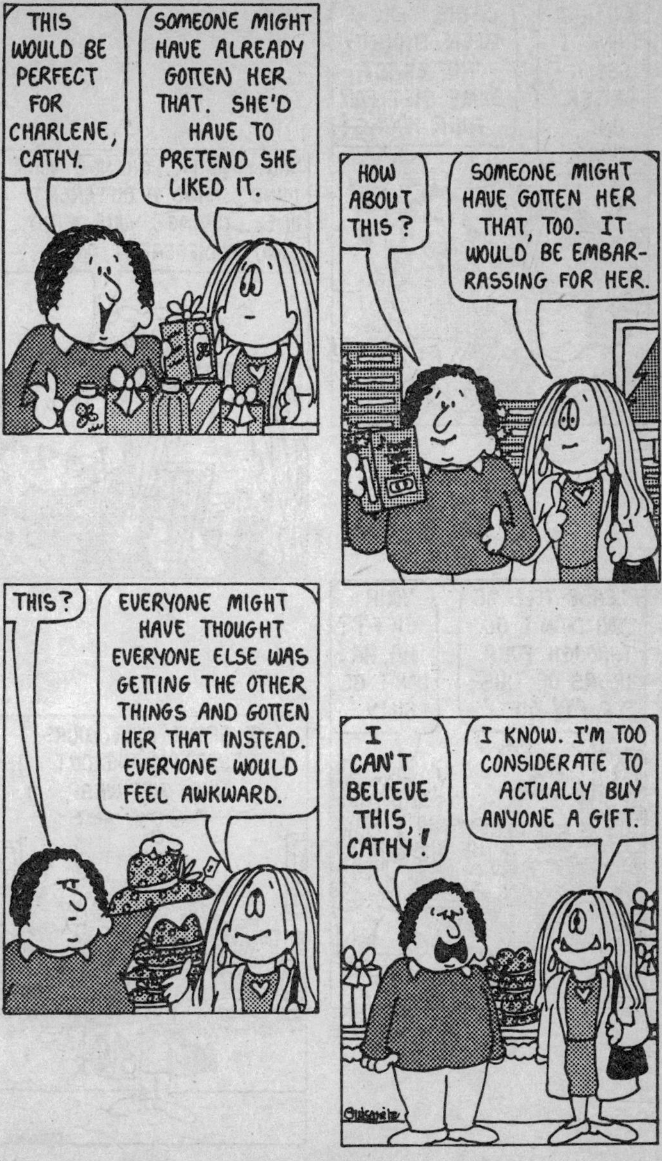
THIS WOULD BE PERFECT FOR CHARLENE, CATHY.
SOMEONE MIGHT HAVE ALREADY GOTTEN HER THAT. SHE'D HAVE TO PRETEND SHE LIKED IT.
HOW ABOUT THIS?
SOMEONE MIGHT HAVE GOTTEN HER THAT, TOO. IT WOULD BE EMBARRASSING FOR HER.
THIS?
EVERYONE MIGHT HAVE THOUGHT EVERYONE ELSE WAS GETTING THE OTHER THINGS AND GOTTEN HER THAT INSTEAD. EVERYONE WOULD FEEL AWKWARD.
I CAN'T BELIEVE THIS, CATHY!
I KNOW. I'M TOO CONSIDERATE TO ACTUALLY BUY ANYONE A GIFT.

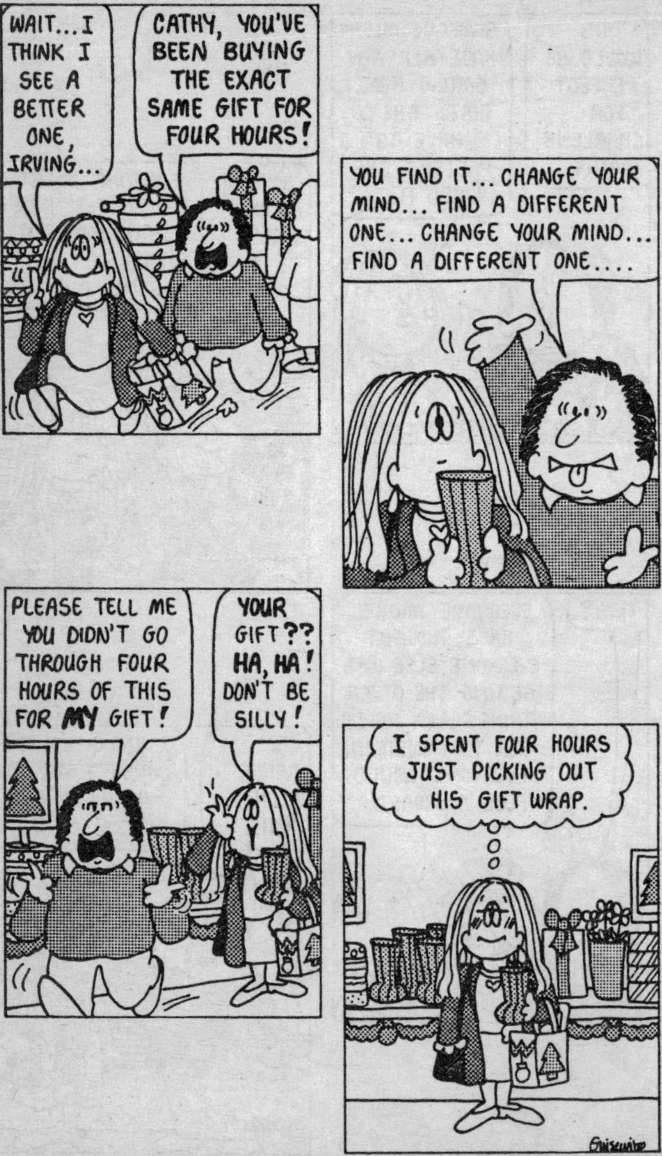
WAIT... I THINK I SEE A BETTER ONE, IRVING...
CATHY, YOU'VE BEEN BUYING THE EXACT SAME GIFT FOR FOUR HOURS!
YOU FIND IT... CHANGE YOUR MIND... FIND A DIFFERENT ONE... CHANGE YOUR MIND... FIND A DIFFERENT ONE....
PLEASE TELL ME YOU DIDN'T GO THROUGH FOUR HOURS OF THIS FOR MY GIFT!
YOUR GIFT?? HA, HA! DON'T BE SILLY!
I SPENT FOUR HOURS JUST PICKING OUT HIS GIFT WRAP.

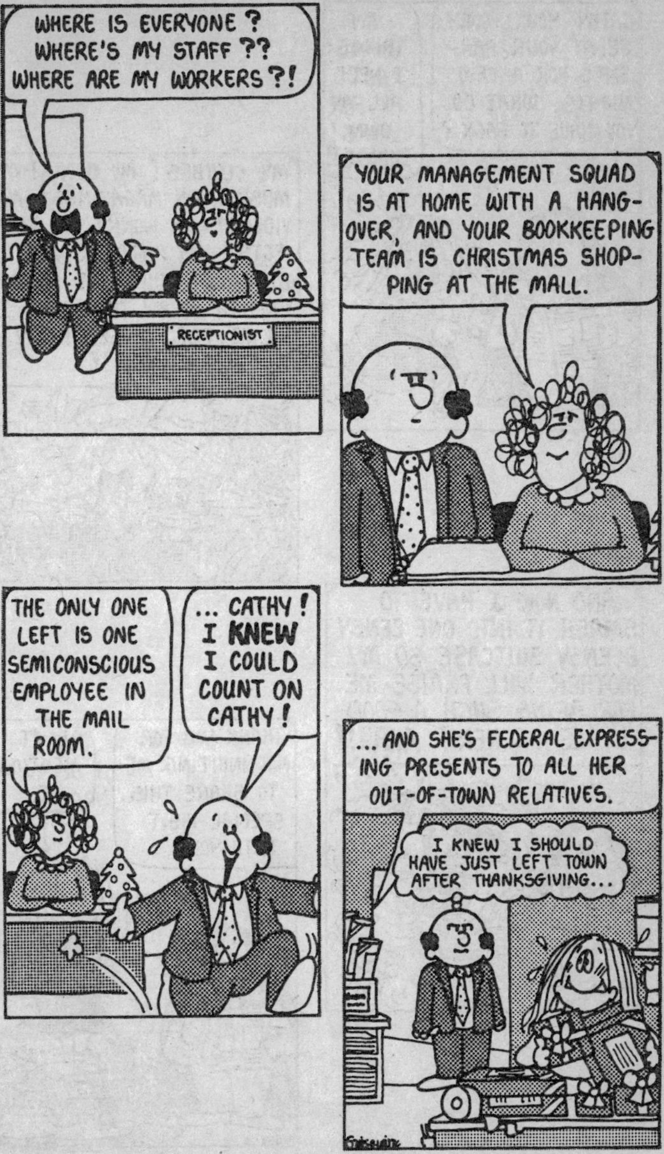
WHERE IS EVERYONE? WHERE'S MY STAFF?? WHERE ARE MY WORKERS?!
RECEPTIONIST
YOUR MANAGEMENT SQUAD IS AT HOME WITH A HANG-OVER, AND YOUR BOOKKEEPING TEAM IS CHRISTMAS SHOP-PING AT THE MALL.
THE ONLY ONE LEFT IS ONE SEMICONSCIOUS EMPLOYEE IN THE MAIL ROOM.
... CATHY! I KNEW I COULD COUNT ON CATHY!
... AND SHE'S FEDERAL EXPRESS-ING PRESENTS TO ALL HER OUT-OF-TOWN RELATIVES.
I KNEW I SHOULD HAVE JUST LEFT TOWN AFTER THANKSGIVING...

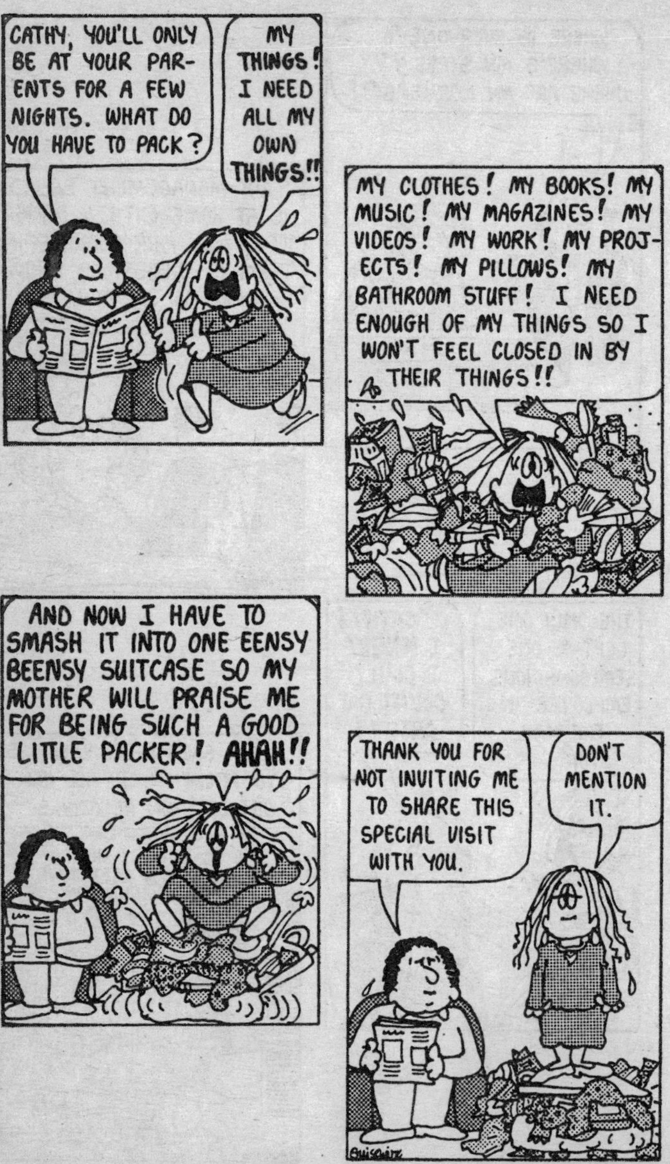
CATHY, YOU'LL ONLY BE AT YOUR PARENTS FOR A FEW NIGHTS. WHAT DO YOU HAVE TO PACK?
MY THINGS! I NEED ALL MY OWN THINGS!!
MY CLOTHES! MY BOOKS! MY MUSIC! MY MAGAZINES! MY VIDEOS! MY WORK! MY PROJECTS! MY PILLOWS! MY BATHROOM STUFF! I NEED ENOUGH OF MY THINGS SO I WON'T FEEL CLOSED IN BY THEIR THINGS!!
AND NOW I HAVE TO SMASH IT INTO ONE EENSY BEENSY SUITCASE SO MY MOTHER WILL PRAISE ME FOR BEING SUCH A GOOD LITTLE PACKER! AHAH!!
THANK YOU FOR NOT INVITING ME TO SHARE THIS SPECIAL VISIT WITH YOU.
DON'T MENTION IT.

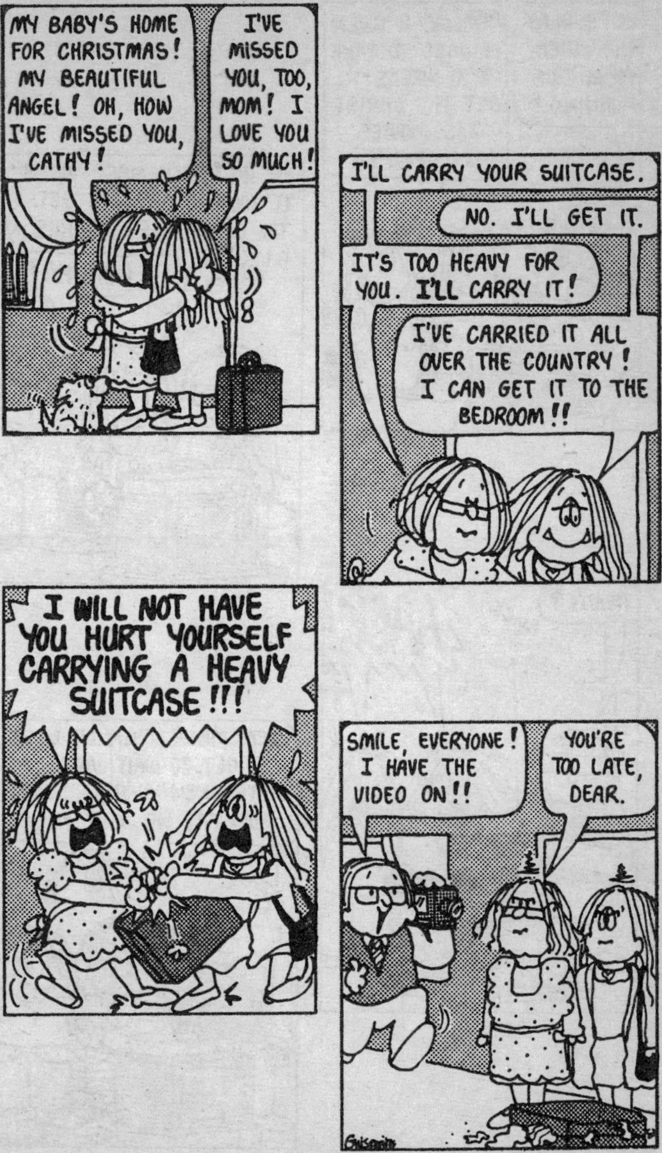
MY BABY'S HOME FOR CHRISTMAS! MY BEAUTIFUL ANGEL! OH, HOW I'VE MISSED YOU, CATHY!
I'VE MISSED YOU, TOO, MOM! I LOVE YOU SO MUCH!
I'LL CARRY YOUR SUITCASE.
NO. I'LL GET IT.
IT'S TOO HEAVY FOR YOU. I'LL CARRY IT!
I'VE CARRIED IT ALL OVER THE COUNTRY! I CAN GET IT TO THE BEDROOM!!
I WILL NOT HAVE YOU HURT YOURSELF CARRYING A HEAVY SUITCASE!!!
SMILE, EVERYONE! I HAVE THE VIDEO ON!!
YOU'RE TOO LATE, DEAR.

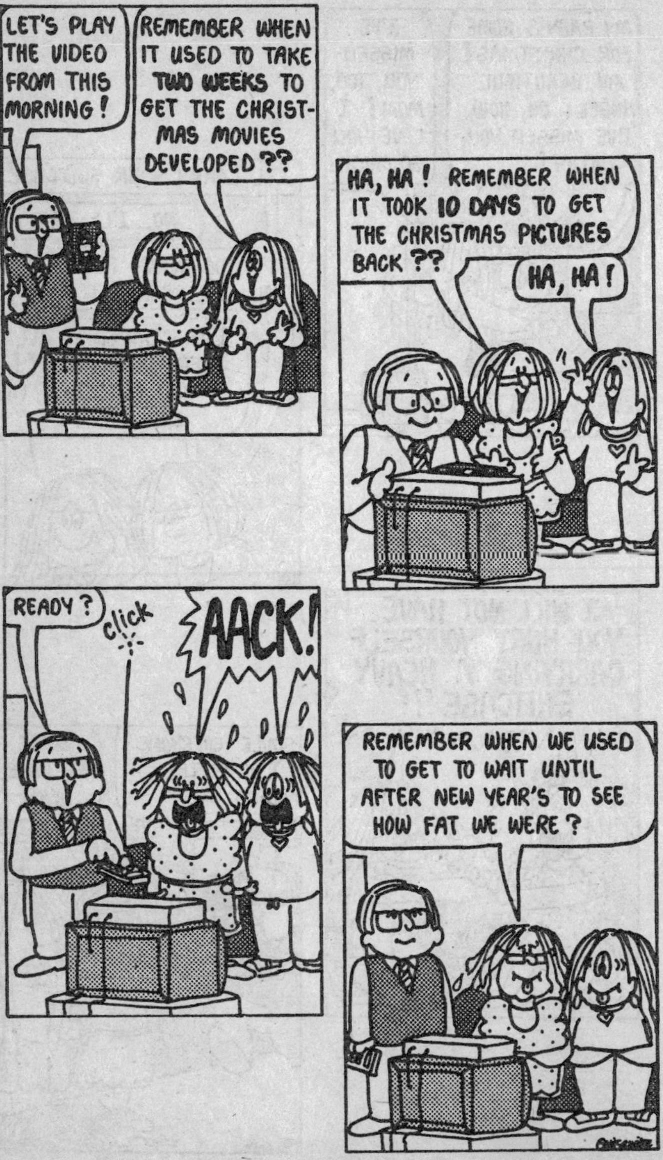
LET'S PLAY THE VIDEO FROM THIS MORNING!
REMEMBER WHEN IT USED TO TAKE TWO WEEKS TO GET THE CHRIST-MAS MOVIES DEVELOPED??
HA, HA! REMEMBER WHEN IT TOOK 10 DAYS TO GET THE CHRISTMAS PICTURES BACK??
HA, HA!
READY?
click
AACK!
REMEMBER WHEN WE USED TO GET TO WAIT UNTIL AFTER NEW YEAR'S TO SEE HOW FAT WE WERE?

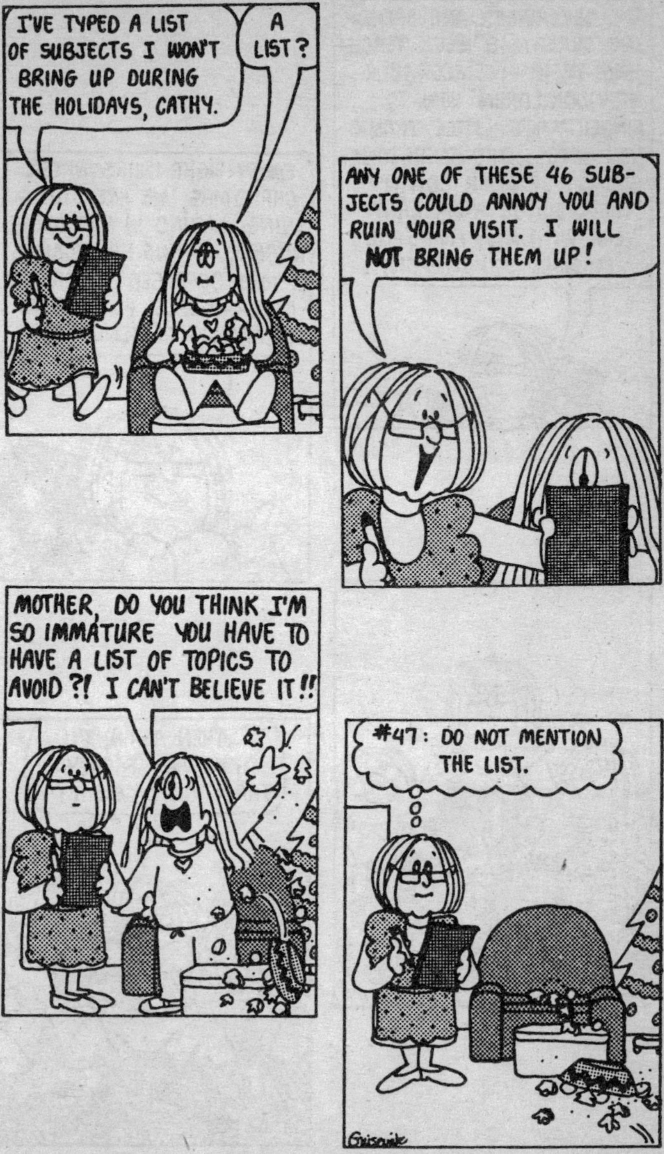
I'VE TYPED A LIST OF SUBJECTS I WON'T BRING UP DURING THE HOLIDAYS, CATHY.
A LIST?
ANY ONE OF THESE 46 SUBJECTS COULD ANNOY YOU AND RUIN YOUR VISIT. I WILL NOT BRING THEM UP!
MOTHER, DO YOU THINK I'M SO IMMATURE YOU HAVE TO HAVE A LIST OF TOPICS TO AVOID?! I CAN'T BELIEVE IT!!
#47: DO NOT MENTION THE LIST.
Guisewite

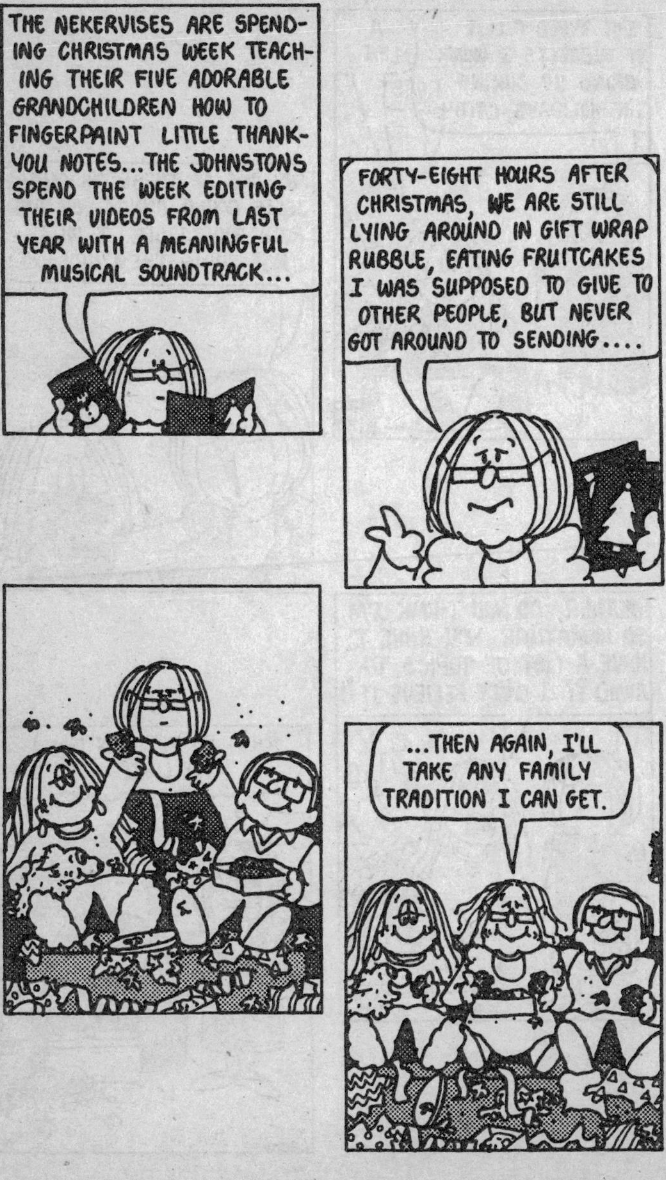
THE NEKERVISES ARE SPENDING CHRISTMAS WEEK TEACHING THEIR FIVE ADORABLE GRANDCHILDREN HOW TO FINGERPAINT LITTLE THANK-YOU NOTES...THE JOHNSTONS SPEND THE WEEK EDITING THEIR VIDEOS FROM LAST YEAR WITH A MEANINGFUL MUSICAL SOUNDTRACK...
FORTY-EIGHT HOURS AFTER CHRISTMAS, WE ARE STILL LYING AROUND IN GIFT WRAP RUBBLE, EATING FRUITCAKES I WAS SUPPOSED TO GIVE TO OTHER PEOPLE, BUT NEVER GOT AROUND TO SENDING....
...THEN AGAIN, I'LL TAKE ANY FAMILY TRADITION I CAN GET.

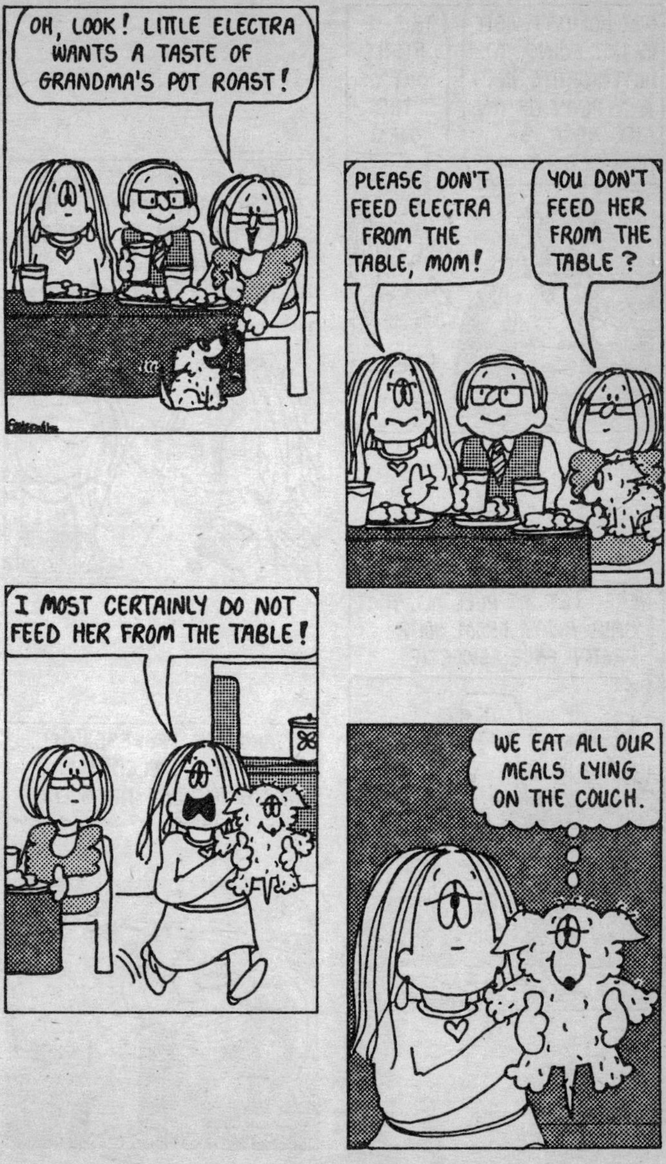
OH, LOOK! LITTLE ELECTRA WANTS A TASTE OF GRANDMA'S POT ROAST!
PLEASE DON'T FEED ELECTRA FROM THE TABLE, MOM!
YOU DON'T FEED HER FROM THE TABLE?
I MOST CERTAINLY DO NOT FEED HER FROM THE TABLE!
WE EAT ALL OUR MEALS LYING ON THE COUCH.

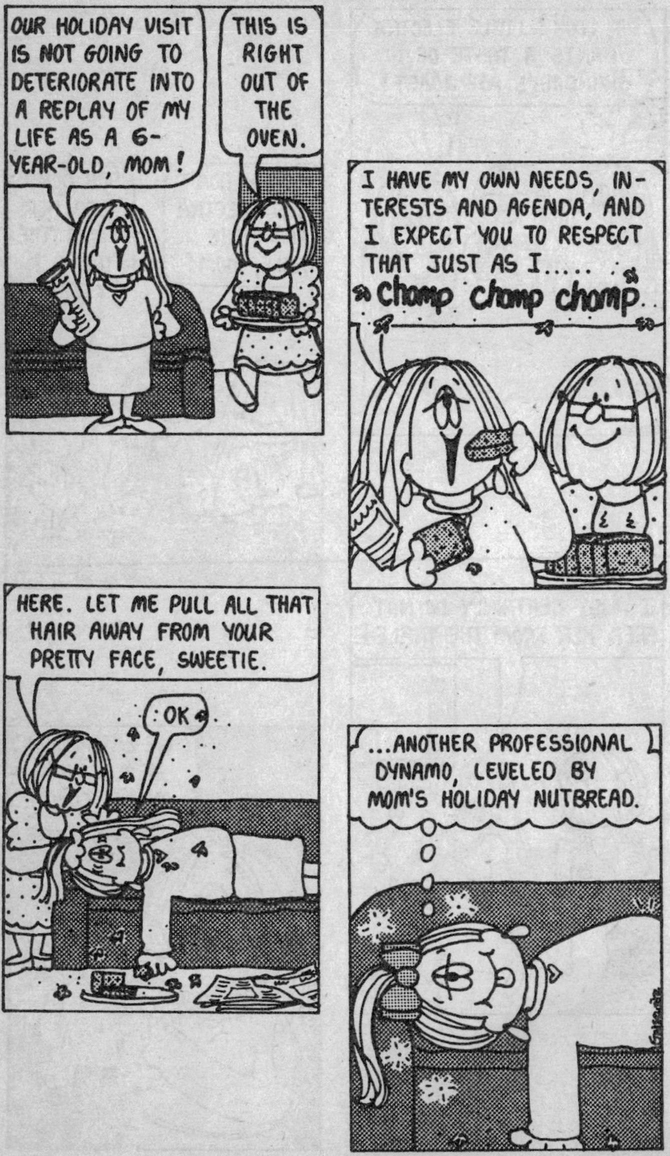
OUR HOLIDAY VISIT IS NOT GOING TO DETERIORATE INTO A REPLAY OF MY LIFE AS A 6-YEAR-OLD, MOM!
THIS IS RIGHT OUT OF THE OVEN.
I HAVE MY OWN NEEDS, INTERESTS AND AGENDA, AND I EXPECT YOU TO RESPECT THAT JUST AS I.....
chomp chomp chomp
HERE. LET ME PULL ALL THAT HAIR AWAY FROM YOUR PRETTY FACE, SWEETIE.
OK
...ANOTHER PROFESSIONAL DYNAMO, LEVELED BY MOM'S HOLIDAY NUTBREAD.

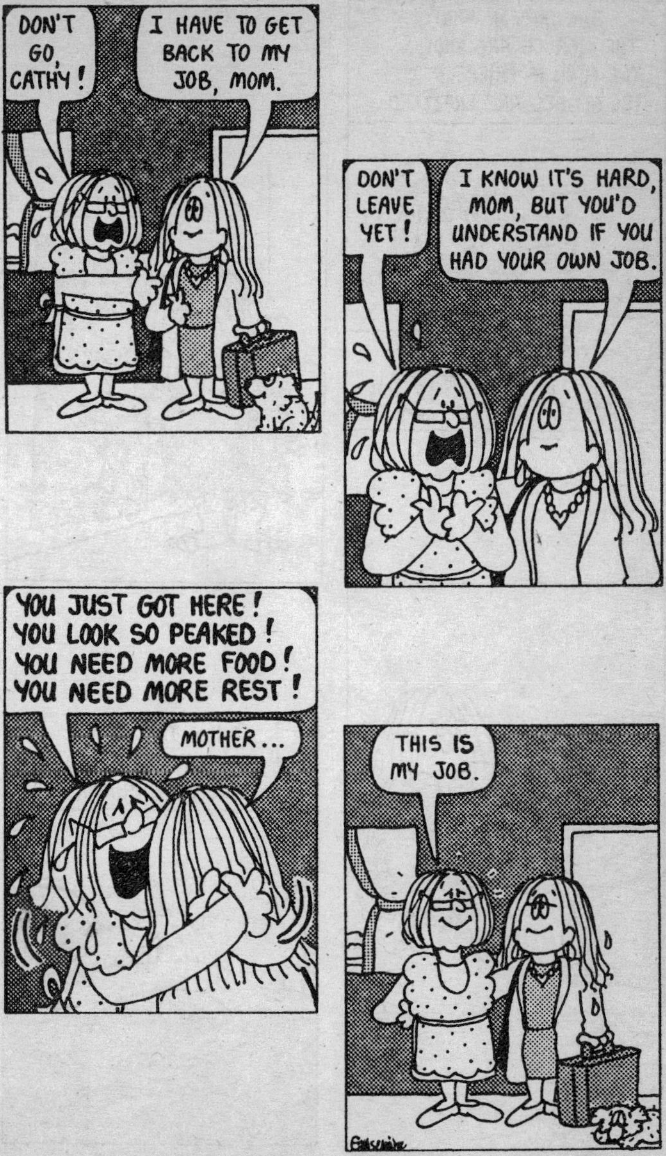
DON'T GO, CATHY!
I HAVE TO GET BACK TO MY JOB, MOM.
DON'T LEAVE YET!
I KNOW IT'S HARD, MOM, BUT YOU'D UNDERSTAND IF YOU HAD YOUR OWN JOB.
YOU JUST GOT HERE! YOU LOOK SO PEAKED! YOU NEED MORE FOOD! YOU NEED MORE REST!
MOTHER...
THIS IS MY JOB.

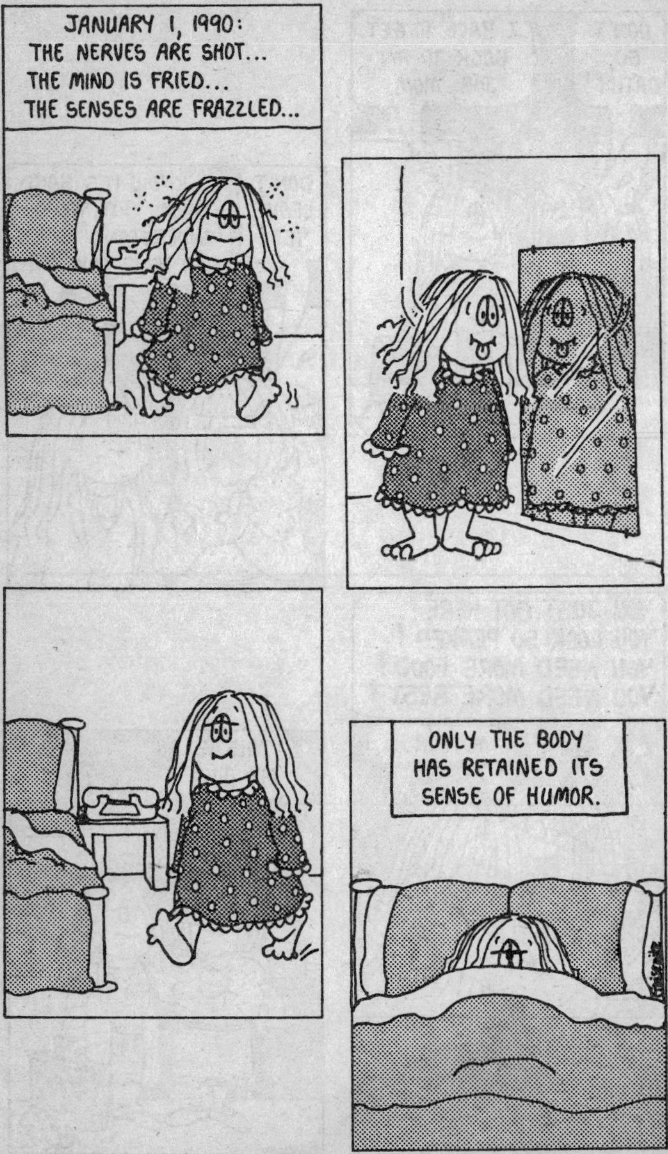
JANUARY 1, 1990:
THE NERVES ARE SHOT...
THE MIND IS FRIED...
THE SENSES ARE FRAZZLED...
ONLY THE BODY
HAS RETAINED ITS
SENSE OF HUMOR.

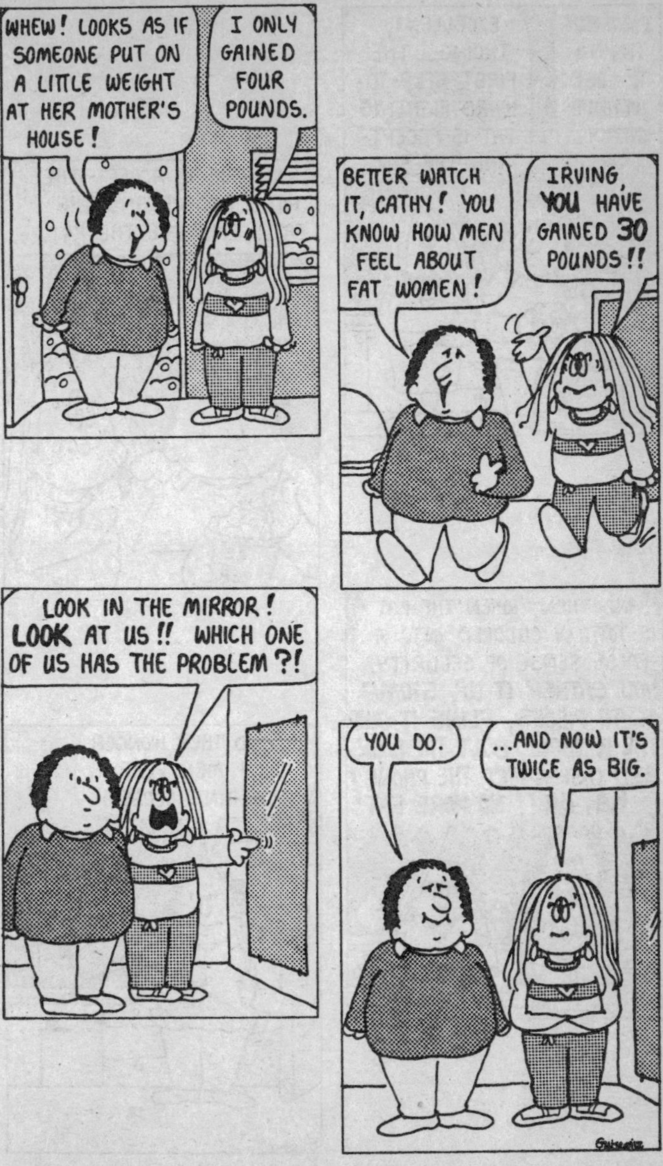
WHEW! LOOKS AS IF SOMEONE PUT ON A LITTLE WEIGHT AT HER MOTHER'S HOUSE!
I ONLY GAINED FOUR POUNDS.
BETTER WATCH IT, CATHY! YOU KNOW HOW MEN FEEL ABOUT FAT WOMEN!
IRVING, YOU HAVE GAINED 30 POUNDS!!
LOOK IN THE MIRROR! LOOK AT US!! WHICH ONE OF US HAS THE PROBLEM?!
YOU DO.
...AND NOW IT'S TWICE AS BIG.

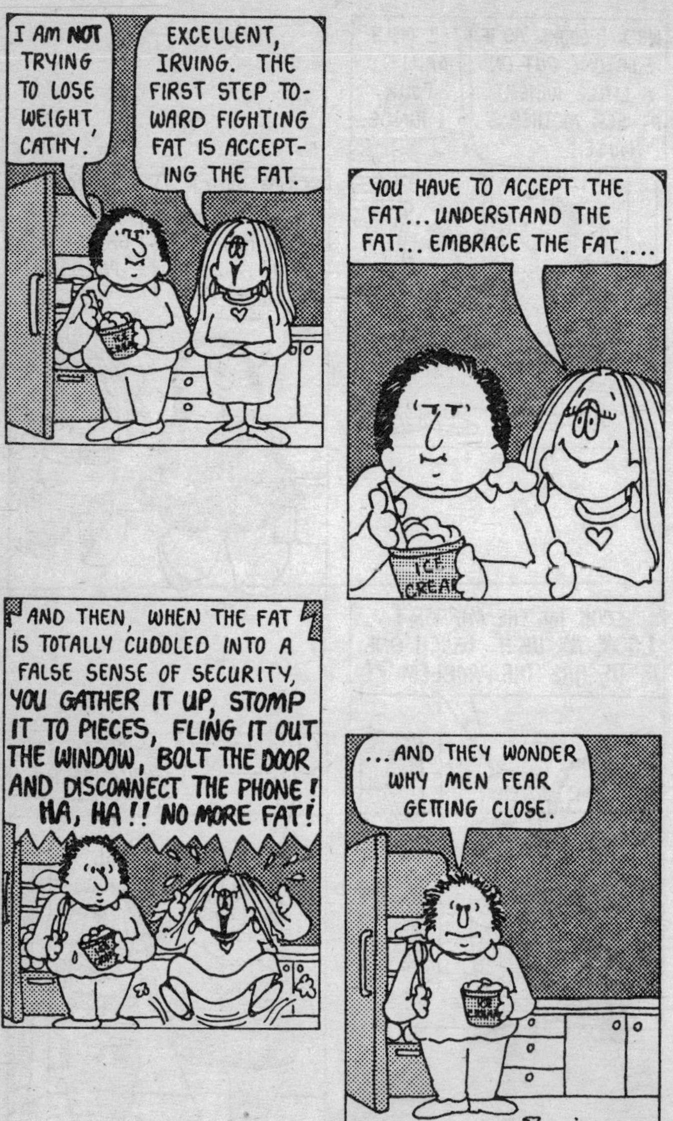
I AM NOT TRYING TO LOSE WEIGHT, CATHY.
EXCELLENT, IRVING. THE FIRST STEP TOWARD FIGHTING FAT IS ACCEPTING THE FAT.
YOU HAVE TO ACCEPT THE FAT... UNDERSTAND THE FAT... EMBRACE THE FAT....
ICE CREAM
AND THEN, WHEN THE FAT IS TOTALLY CUDDLED INTO A FALSE SENSE OF SECURITY, YOU GATHER IT UP, STOMP IT TO PIECES, FLING IT OUT THE WINDOW, BOLT THE DOOR AND DISCONNECT THE PHONE! HA, HA!! NO MORE FAT!
...AND THEY WONDER WHY MEN FEAR GETTING CLOSE.

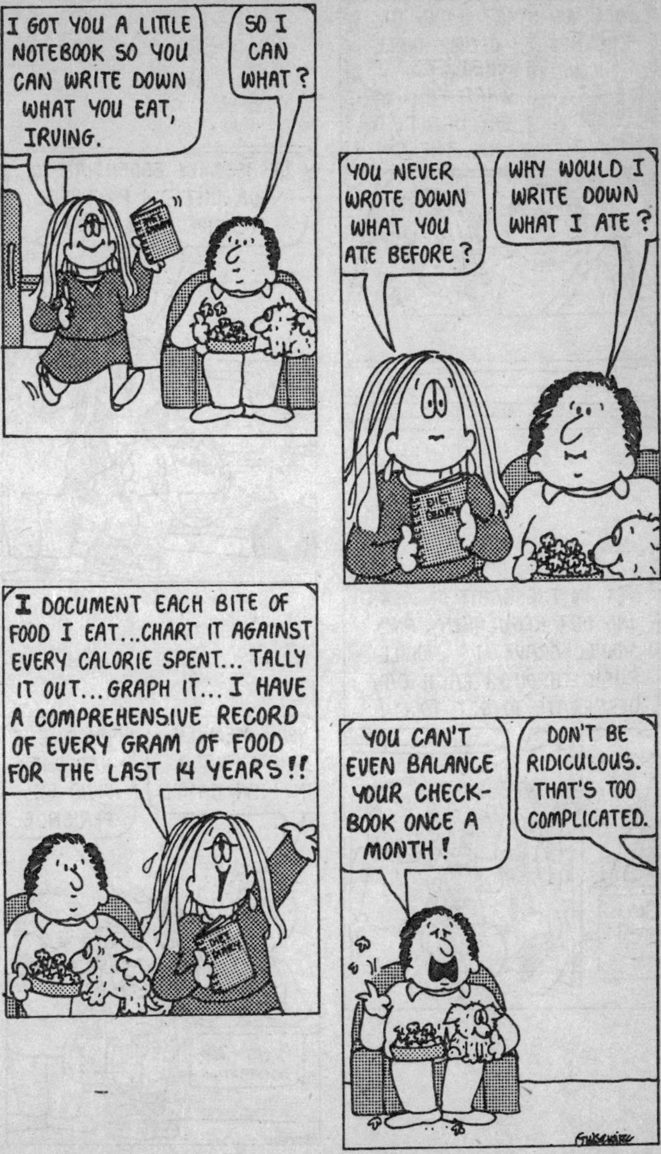

I GOT YOU A LITTLE NOTEBOOK SO YOU CAN WRITE DOWN WHAT YOU EAT, IRVING.
SO I CAN WHAT?
YOU NEVER WROTE DOWN WHAT YOU ATE BEFORE?
WHY WOULD I WRITE DOWN WHAT I ATE?
I DOCUMENT EACH BITE OF FOOD I EAT...CHART IT AGAINST EVERY CALORIE SPENT... TALLY IT OUT...GRAPH IT... I HAVE A COMPREHENSIVE RECORD OF EVERY GRAM OF FOOD FOR THE LAST 14 YEARS!!
YOU CAN'T EVEN BALANCE YOUR CHECK-BOOK ONCE A MONTH!
DON'T BE RIDICULOUS. THAT'S TOO COMPLICATED.

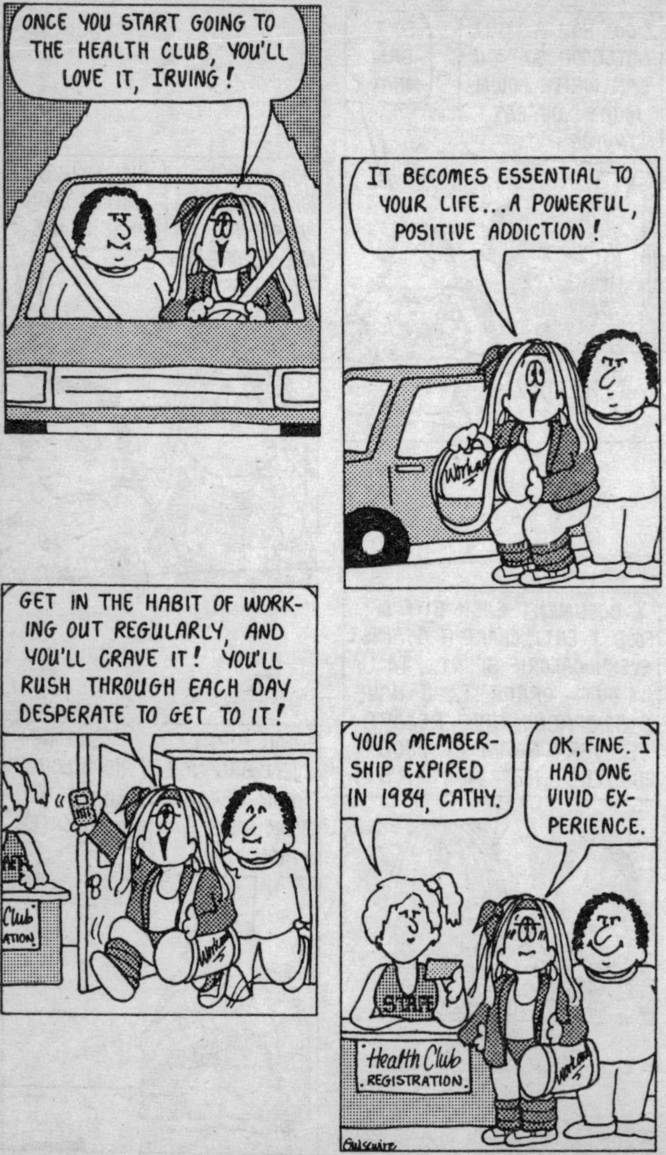
ONCE YOU START GOING TO THE HEALTH CLUB, YOU'LL LOVE IT, IRVING!
IT BECOMES ESSENTIAL TO YOUR LIFE... A POWERFUL, POSITIVE ADDICTION!
GET IN THE HABIT OF WORKING OUT REGULARLY, AND YOU'LL CRAVE IT! YOU'LL RUSH THROUGH EACH DAY DESPERATE TO GET TO IT!
YOUR MEMBERSHIP EXPIRED IN 1984, CATHY.
OK, FINE. I HAD ONE VIVID EXPERIENCE.
STAFF
Health Club
REGISTRATION

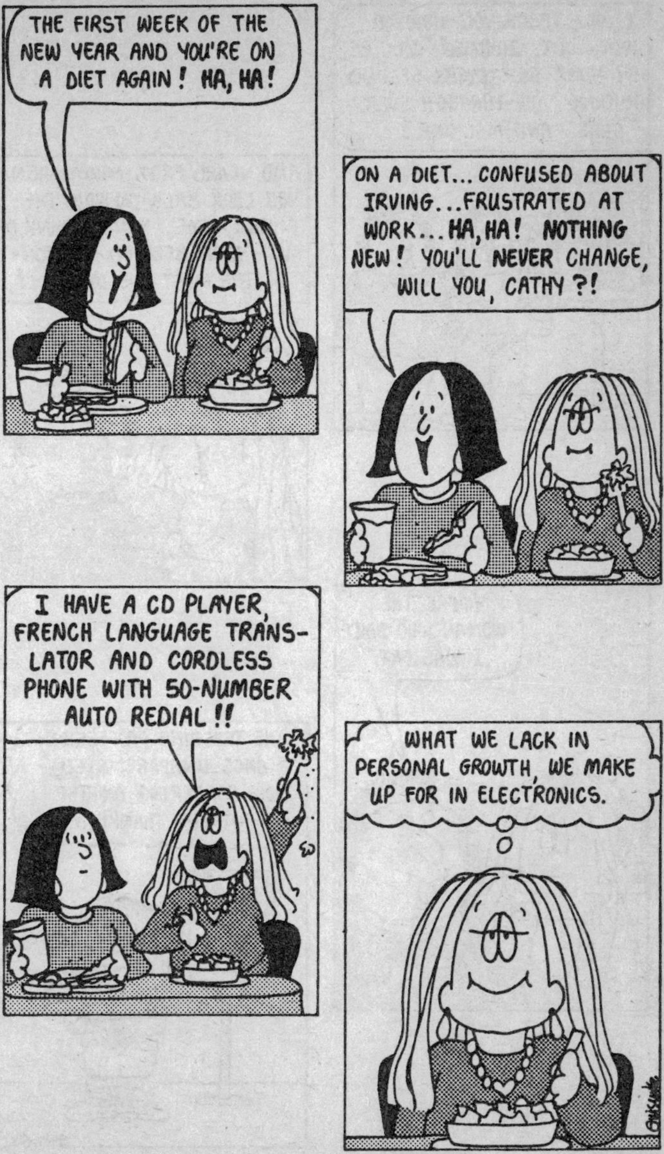
THE FIRST WEEK OF THE NEW YEAR AND YOU'RE ON A DIET AGAIN! HA, HA!
ON A DIET... CONFUSED ABOUT IRVING...FRUSTRATED AT WORK... HA, HA! NOTHING NEW! YOU'LL NEVER CHANGE, WILL YOU, CATHY ?!
I HAVE A CD PLAYER, FRENCH LANGUAGE TRANSLATOR AND CORDLESS PHONE WITH 50-NUMBER AUTO REDIAL !!
WHAT WE LACK IN PERSONAL GROWTH, WE MAKE UP FOR IN ELECTRONICS.

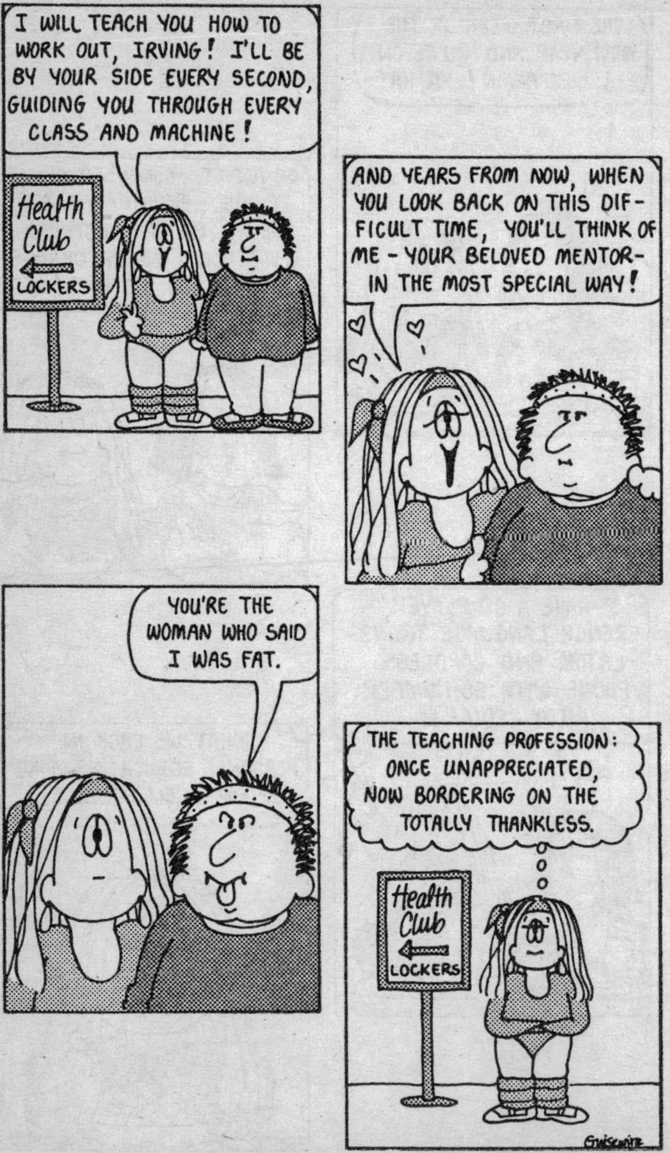
I WILL TEACH YOU HOW TO WORK OUT, IRVING! I'LL BE BY YOUR SIDE EVERY SECOND, GUIDING YOU THROUGH EVERY CLASS AND MACHINE!
Health Club
LOCKERS
AND YEARS FROM NOW, WHEN YOU LOOK BACK ON THIS DIFFICULT TIME, YOU'LL THINK OF ME - YOUR BELOVED MENTOR- IN THE MOST SPECIAL WAY!
YOU'RE THE WOMAN WHO SAID I WAS FAT.
THE TEACHING PROFESSION: ONCE UNAPPRECIATED, NOW BORDERING ON THE TOTALLY THANKLESS.
Health Club
LOCKERS
Guisewite

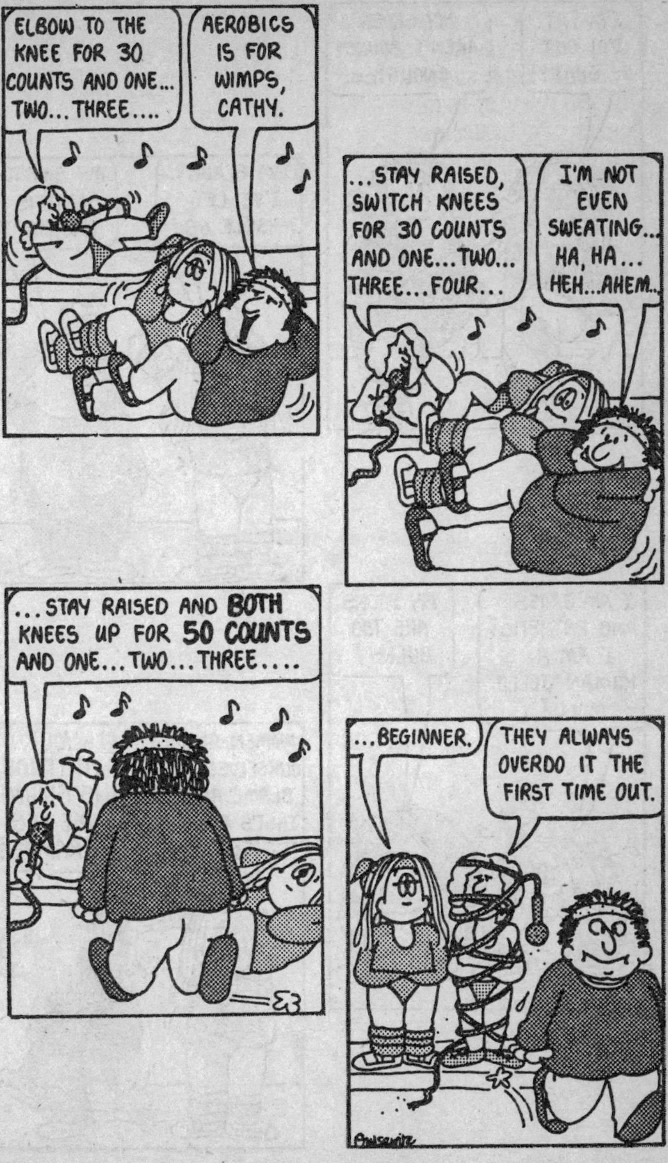
ELBOW TO THE KNEE FOR 30 COUNTS AND ONE... TWO... THREE....
AEROBICS IS FOR WIMPS, CATHY.
...STAY RAISED, SWITCH KNEES FOR 30 COUNTS AND ONE... TWO... THREE... FOUR...
I'M NOT EVEN SWEATING... HA, HA... HEH...AHEM...
...STAY RAISED AND BOTH KNEES UP FOR 50 COUNTS AND ONE... TWO... THREE....
...BEGINNER.
THEY ALWAYS OVERDO IT THE FIRST TIME OUT.
Guisewite

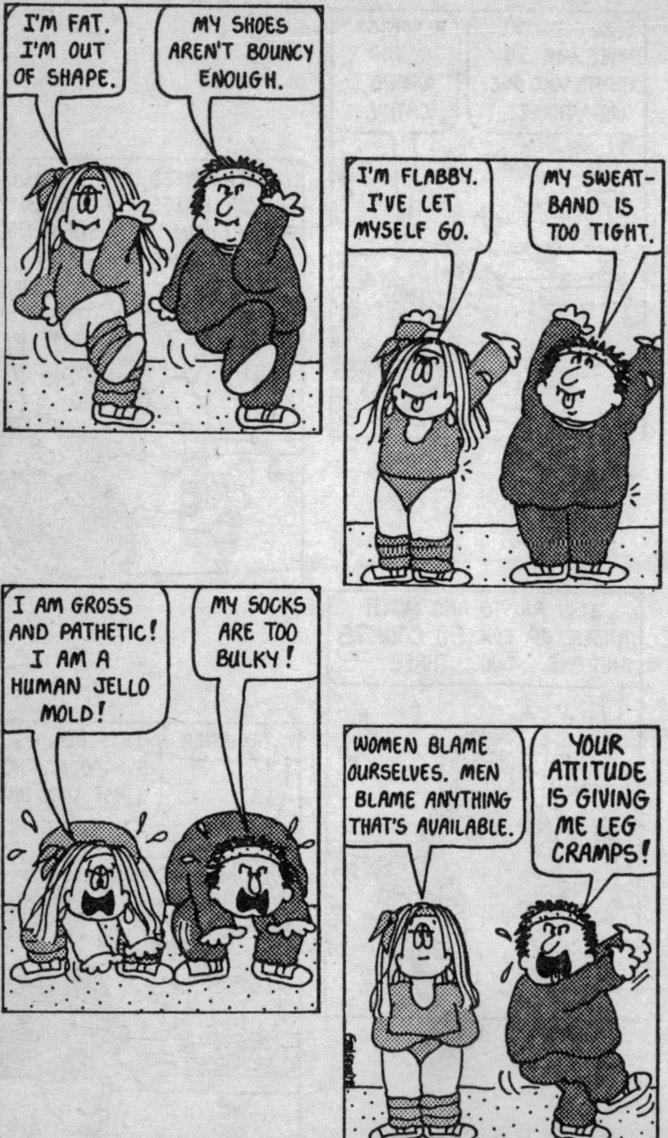
I'M FAT. I'M OUT OF SHAPE.
MY SHOES AREN'T BOUNCY ENOUGH.
I'M FLABBY. I'VE LET MYSELF GO.
MY SWEAT-BAND IS TOO TIGHT.
I AM GROSS AND PATHETIC! I AM A HUMAN JELLO MOLD!
MY SOCKS ARE TOO BULKY!
WOMEN BLAME OURSELVES. MEN BLAME ANYTHING THAT'S AVAILABLE.
YOUR ATTITUDE IS GIVING ME LEG CRAMPS!

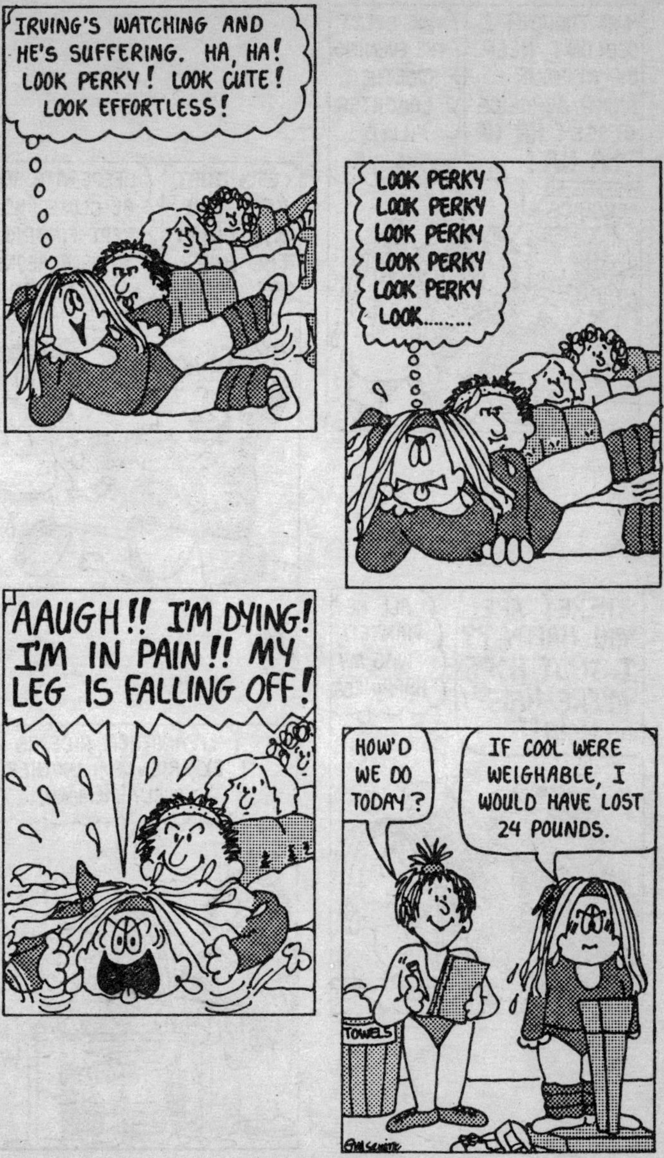
IRVING'S WATCHING AND HE'S SUFFERING. HA, HA! LOOK PERKY! LOOK CUTE! LOOK EFFORTLESS!
LOOK PERKY LOOK PERKY LOOK PERKY LOOK PERKY LOOK PERKY LOOK.........
AAUGH!! I'M DYING! I'M IN PAIN!! MY LEG IS FALLING OFF!
HOW'D WE DO TODAY?
IF COOL WERE WEIGHABLE, I WOULD HAVE LOST 24 POUNDS.
TOWELS

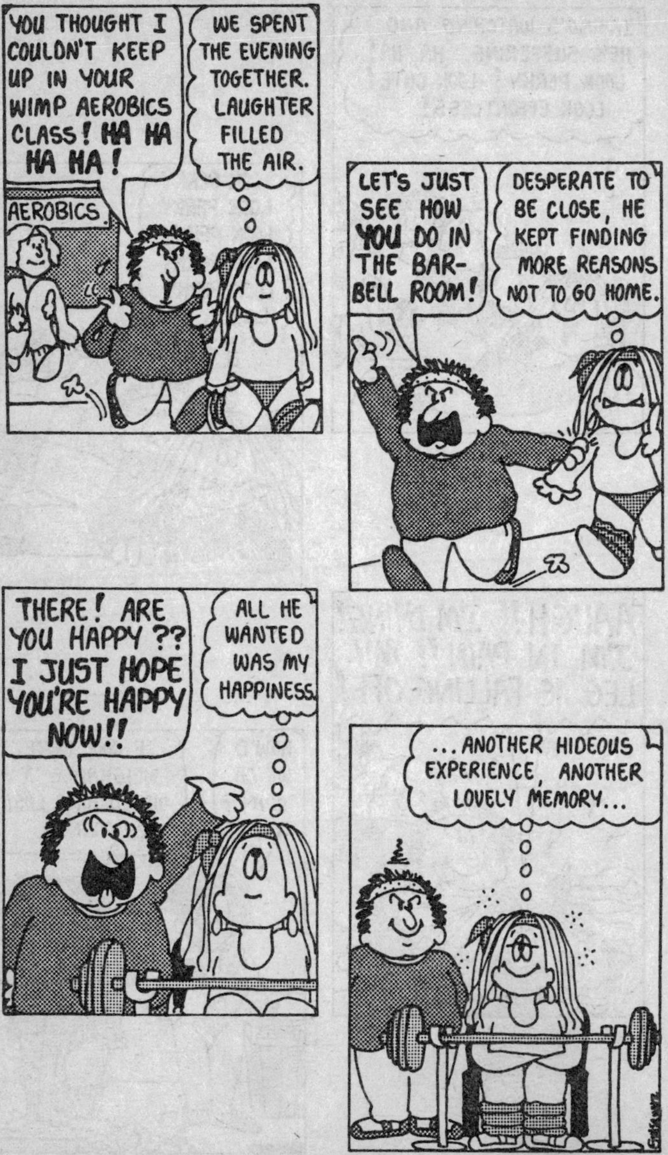
YOU THOUGHT I COULDN'T KEEP UP IN YOUR WIMP AEROBICS CLASS! HA HA HA HA!
WE SPENT THE EVENING TOGETHER. LAUGHTER FILLED THE AIR.
AEROBICS
LET'S JUST SEE HOW YOU DO IN THE BAR-BELL ROOM!
DESPERATE TO BE CLOSE, HE KEPT FINDING MORE REASONS NOT TO GO HOME.
THERE! ARE YOU HAPPY?? I JUST HOPE YOU'RE HAPPY NOW!!
ALL HE WANTED WAS MY HAPPINESS.
...ANOTHER HIDEOUS EXPERIENCE, ANOTHER LOVELY MEMORY...

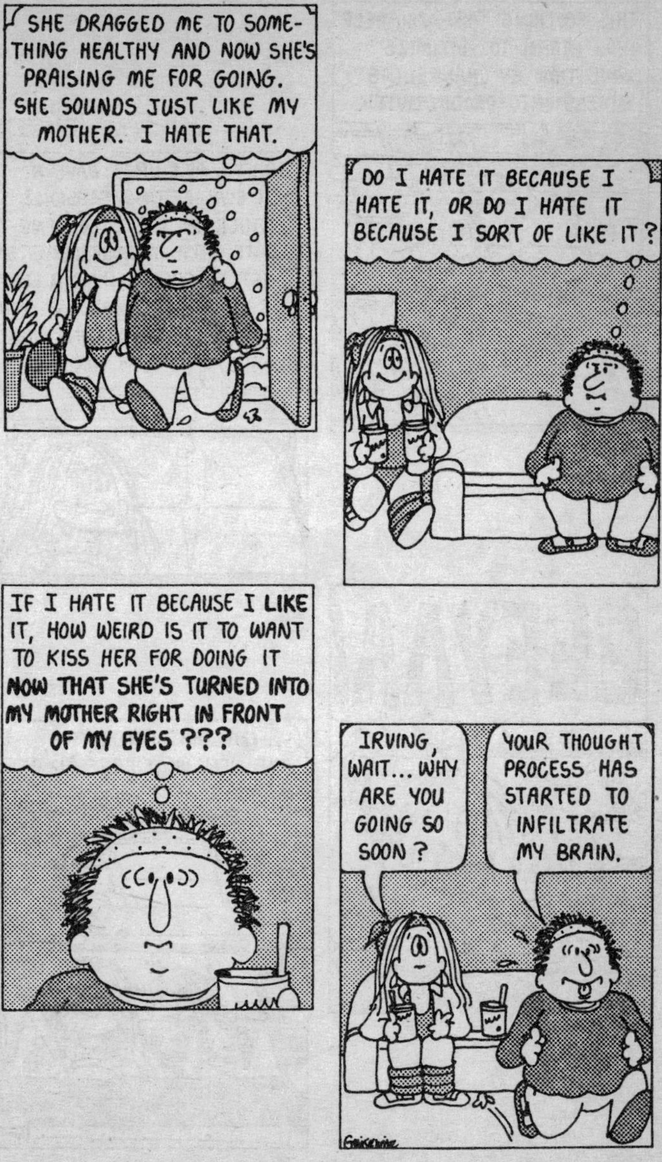
SHE DRAGGED ME TO SOMETHING HEALTHY AND NOW SHE'S PRAISING ME FOR GOING. SHE SOUNDS JUST LIKE MY MOTHER. I HATE THAT.
DO I HATE IT BECAUSE I HATE IT, OR DO I HATE IT BECAUSE I SORT OF LIKE IT?
IF I HATE IT BECAUSE I LIKE IT, HOW WEIRD IS IT TO WANT TO KISS HER FOR DOING IT NOW THAT SHE'S TURNED INTO MY MOTHER RIGHT IN FRONT OF MY EYES???
IRVING, WAIT... WHY ARE YOU GOING SO SOON?
YOUR THOUGHT PROCESS HAS STARTED TO INFILTRATE MY BRAIN.

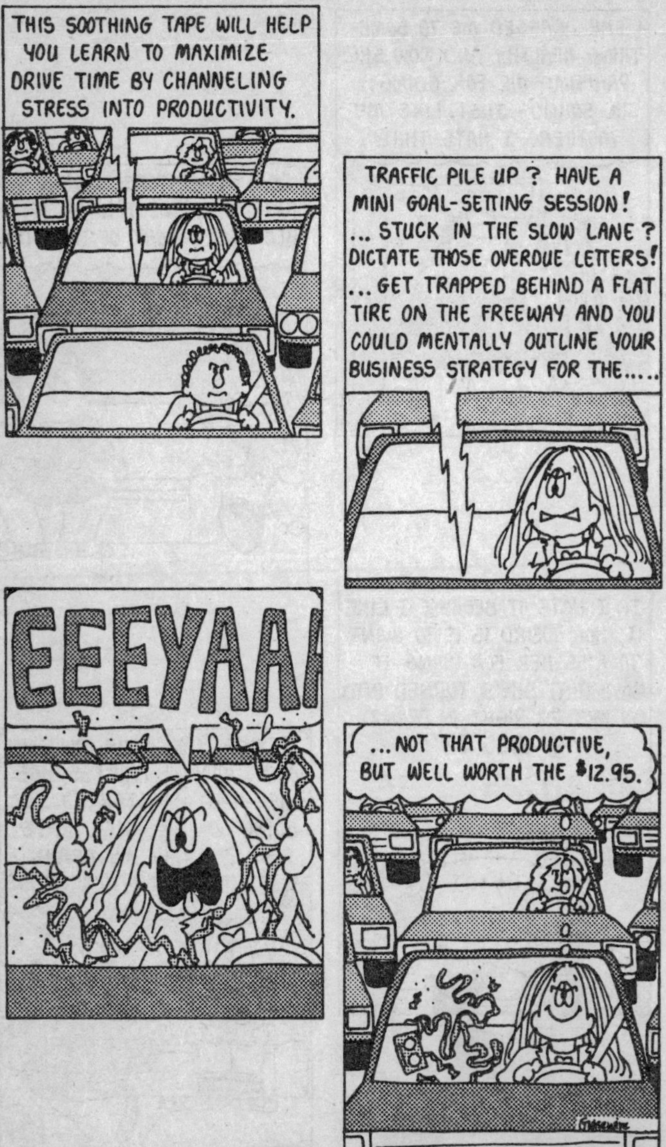
THIS SOOTHING TAPE WILL HELP YOU LEARN TO MAXIMIZE DRIVE TIME BY CHANNELING STRESS INTO PRODUCTIVITY.
TRAFFIC PILE UP ? HAVE A MINI GOAL-SETTING SESSION! ... STUCK IN THE SLOW LANE ? DICTATE THOSE OVERDUE LETTERS! ... GET TRAPPED BEHIND A FLAT TIRE ON THE FREEWAY AND YOU COULD MENTALLY OUTLINE YOUR BUSINESS STRATEGY FOR THE.....
EEEYAA
... NOT THAT PRODUCTIVE, BUT WELL WORTH THE $12.95.

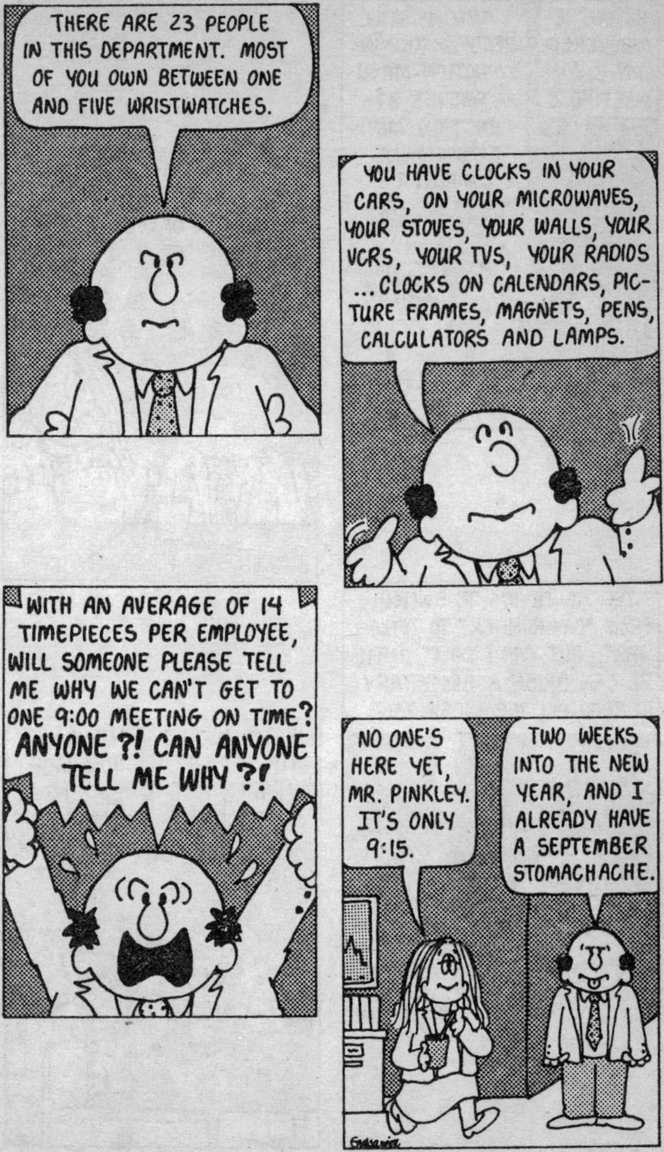
THERE ARE 23 PEOPLE IN THIS DEPARTMENT. MOST OF YOU OWN BETWEEN ONE AND FIVE WRISTWATCHES.
YOU HAVE CLOCKS IN YOUR CARS, ON YOUR MICROWAVES, YOUR STOVES, YOUR WALLS, YOUR VCRS, YOUR TVS, YOUR RADIOS ...CLOCKS ON CALENDARS, PICTURE FRAMES, MAGNETS, PENS, CALCULATORS AND LAMPS.
WITH AN AVERAGE OF 14 TIMEPIECES PER EMPLOYEE, WILL SOMEONE PLEASE TELL ME WHY WE CAN'T GET TO ONE 9:00 MEETING ON TIME? ANYONE ?! CAN ANYONE TELL ME WHY ?!
NO ONE'S HERE YET, MR. PINKLEY. IT'S ONLY 9:15.
TWO WEEKS INTO THE NEW YEAR, AND I ALREADY HAVE A SEPTEMBER STOMACHACHE.

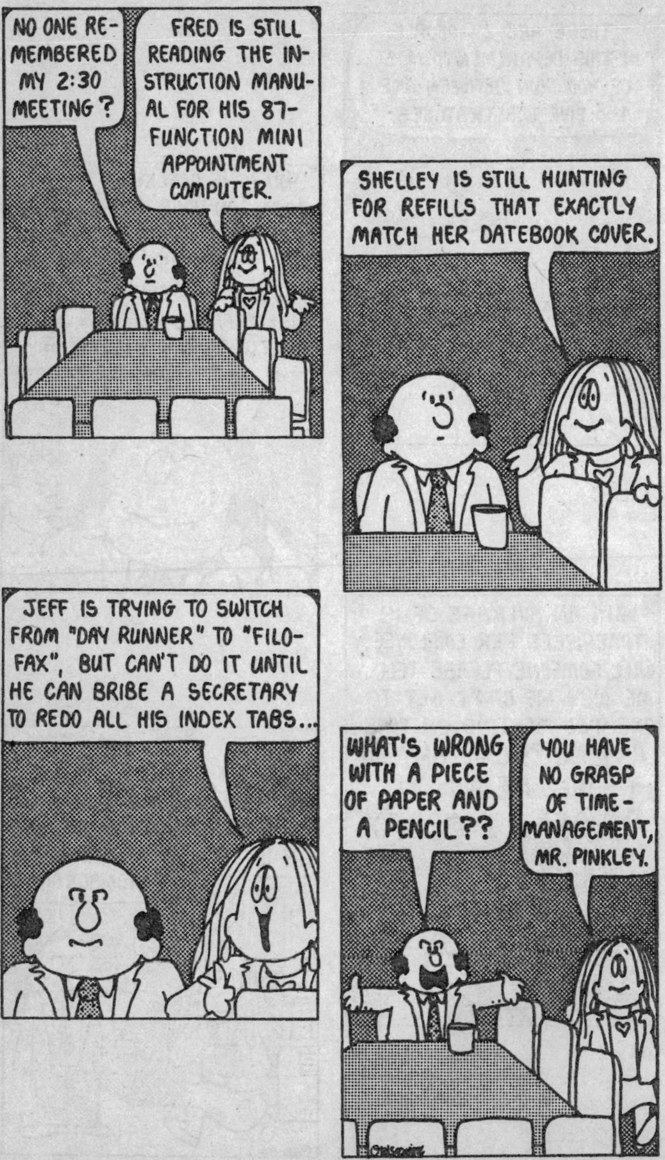
NO ONE REMEMBERED MY 2:30 MEETING?
FRED IS STILL READING THE INSTRUCTION MANUAL FOR HIS 87-FUNCTION MINI APPOINTMENT COMPUTER.
SHELLEY IS STILL HUNTING FOR REFILLS THAT EXACTLY MATCH HER DATEBOOK COVER.
JEFF IS TRYING TO SWITCH FROM "DAY RUNNER" TO "FILO-FAX", BUT CAN'T DO IT UNTIL HE CAN BRIBE A SECRETARY TO REDO ALL HIS INDEX TABS...
WHAT'S WRONG WITH A PIECE OF PAPER AND A PENCIL??
YOU HAVE NO GRASP OF TIME-MANAGEMENT, MR. PINKLEY.

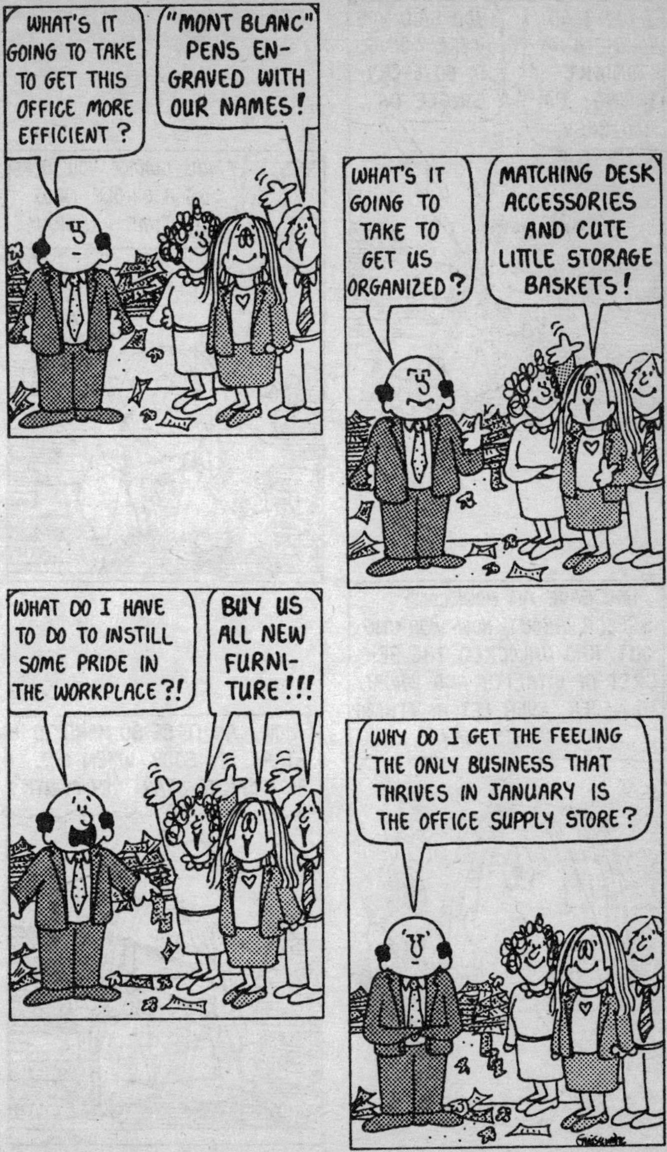
WHAT'S IT GOING TO TAKE TO GET THIS OFFICE MORE EFFICIENT ?
"MONT BLANC" PENS EN- GRAVED WITH OUR NAMES!
WHAT'S IT GOING TO TAKE TO GET US ORGANIZED?
MATCHING DESK ACCESSORIES AND CUTE LITTLE STORAGE BASKETS!
WHAT DO I HAVE TO DO TO INSTILL SOME PRIDE IN THE WORKPLACE?!
BUY US ALL NEW FURNI- TURE!!!
WHY DO I GET THE FEELING THE ONLY BUSINESS THAT THRIVES IN JANUARY IS THE OFFICE SUPPLY STORE?

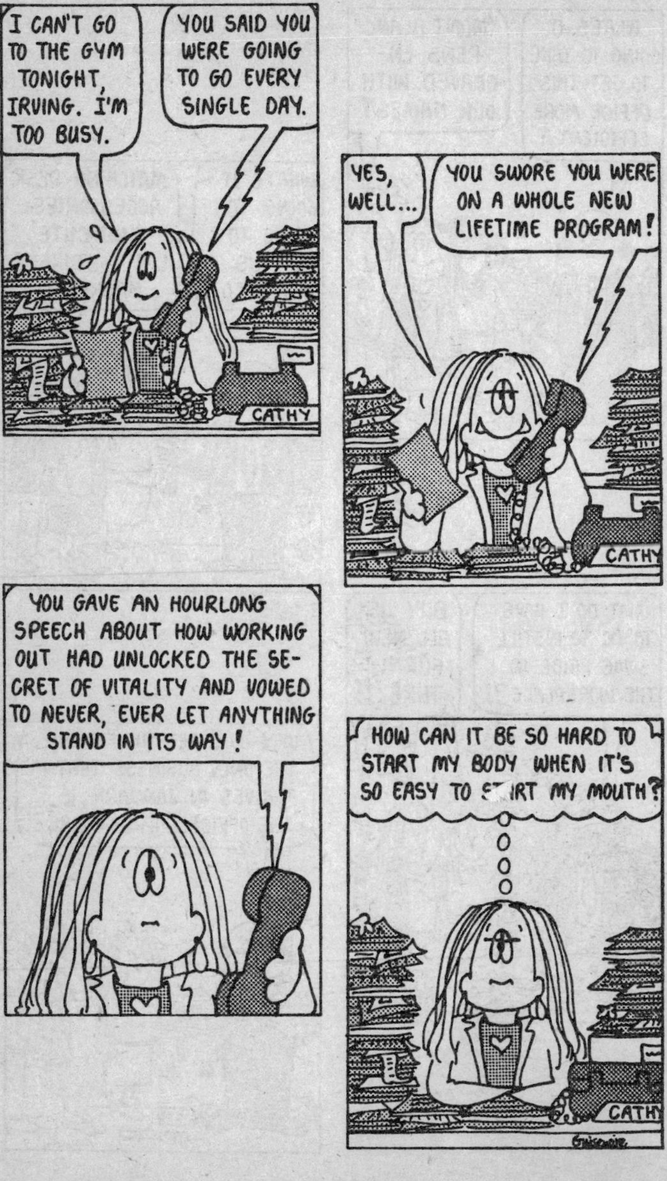
I CAN'T GO TO THE GYM TONIGHT, IRVING. I'M TOO BUSY.
YOU SAID YOU WERE GOING TO GO EVERY SINGLE DAY.
CATHY
YES, WELL...
YOU SWORE YOU WERE ON A WHOLE NEW LIFETIME PROGRAM!
CATHY
YOU GAVE AN HOURLONG SPEECH ABOUT HOW WORKING OUT HAD UNLOCKED THE SECRET OF VITALITY AND VOWED TO NEVER, EVER LET ANYTHING STAND IN ITS WAY!
HOW CAN IT BE SO HARD TO START MY BODY WHEN IT'S SO EASY TO START MY MOUTH?
CATHY

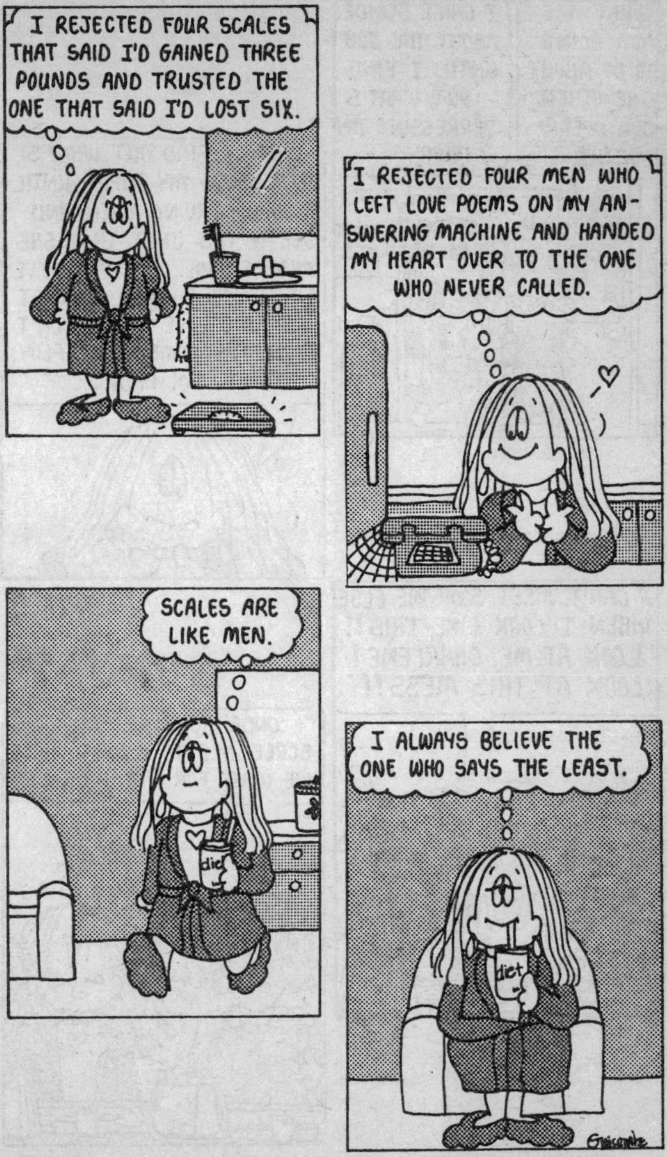
I REJECTED FOUR SCALES THAT SAID I'D GAINED THREE POUNDS AND TRUSTED THE ONE THAT SAID I'D LOST SIX.
I REJECTED FOUR MEN WHO LEFT LOVE POEMS ON MY ANSWERING MACHINE AND HANDED MY HEART OVER TO THE ONE WHO NEVER CALLED.
SCALES ARE LIKE MEN.
I ALWAYS BELIEVE THE ONE WHO SAYS THE LEAST.
diet
diet
Guisewite

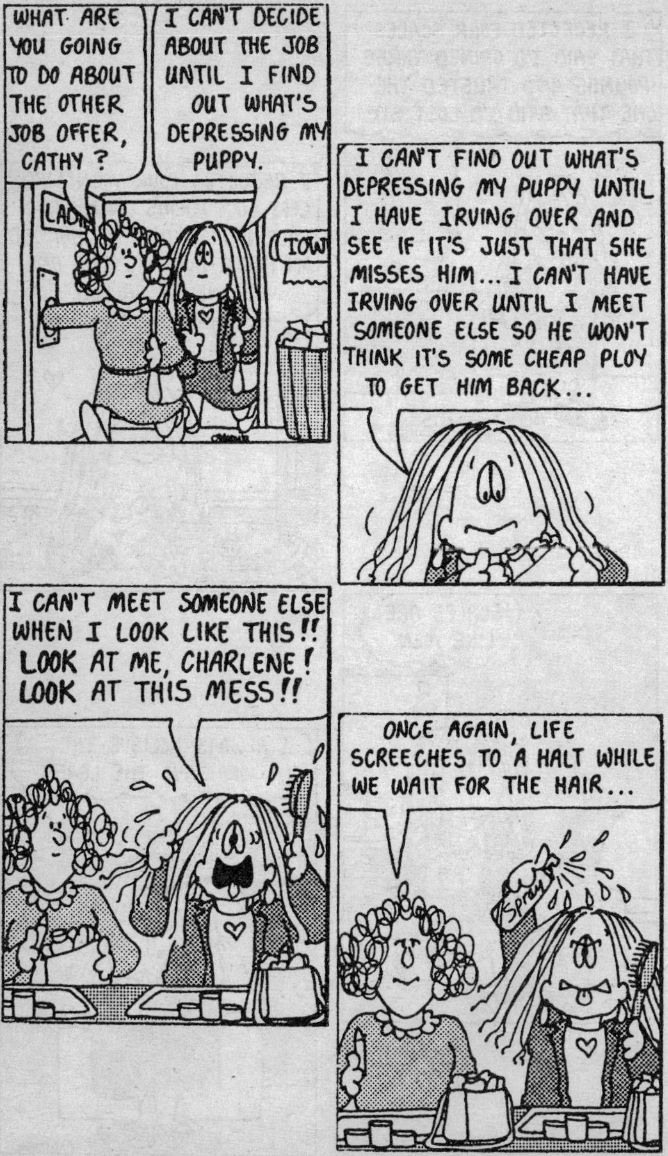
WHAT ARE YOU GOING TO DO ABOUT THE OTHER JOB OFFER, CATHY ?
I CAN'T DECIDE ABOUT THE JOB UNTIL I FIND OUT WHAT'S DEPRESSING MY PUPPY.
I CAN'T FIND OUT WHAT'S DEPRESSING MY PUPPY UNTIL I HAVE IRVING OVER AND SEE IF IT'S JUST THAT SHE MISSES HIM... I CAN'T HAVE IRVING OVER UNTIL I MEET SOMEONE ELSE SO HE WON'T THINK IT'S SOME CHEAP PLOY TO GET HIM BACK...
I CAN'T MEET SOMEONE ELSE WHEN I LOOK LIKE THIS!! LOOK AT ME, CHARLENE! LOOK AT THIS MESS!!
ONCE AGAIN, LIFE SCREECHES TO A HALT WHILE WE WAIT FOR THE HAIR...
Spray

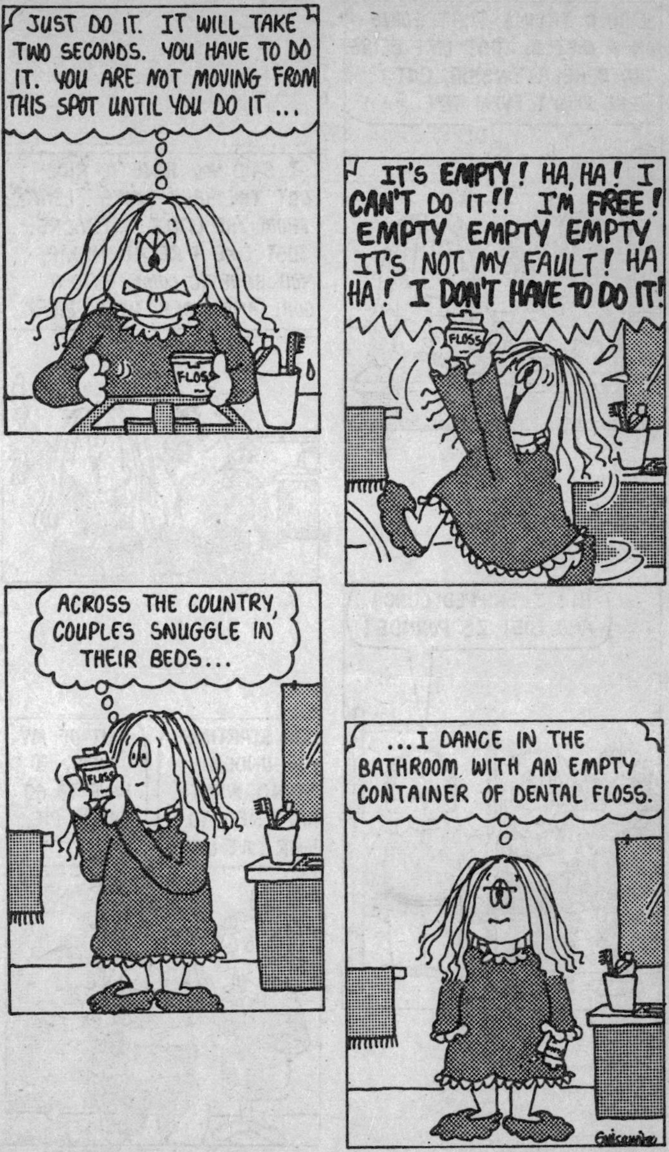
JUST DO IT. IT WILL TAKE TWO SECONDS. YOU HAVE TO DO IT. YOU ARE NOT MOVING FROM THIS SPOT UNTIL YOU DO IT ...
FLOSS
IT'S EMPTY! HA, HA! I CAN'T DO IT!! I'M FREE! EMPTY EMPTY EMPTY IT'S NOT MY FAULT! HA HA! I DON'T HAVE TO DO IT!
FLOSS
ACROSS THE COUNTRY, COUPLES SNUGGLE IN THEIR BEDS...
FLOSS
...I DANCE IN THE BATHROOM WITH AN EMPTY CONTAINER OF DENTAL FLOSS.

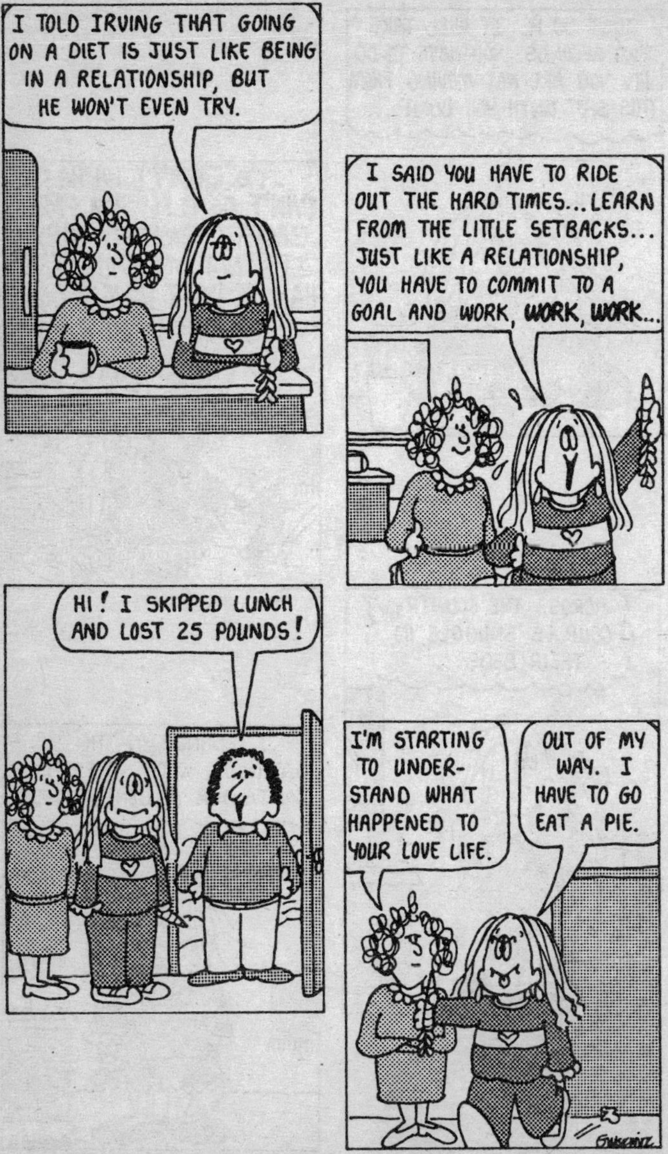
I TOLD IRVING THAT GOING ON A DIET IS JUST LIKE BEING IN A RELATIONSHIP, BUT HE WON'T EVEN TRY.
I SAID YOU HAVE TO RIDE OUT THE HARD TIMES... LEARN FROM THE LITTLE SETBACKS... JUST LIKE A RELATIONSHIP, YOU HAVE TO COMMIT TO A GOAL AND WORK, WORK, WORK...
HI! I SKIPPED LUNCH AND LOST 25 POUNDS!
I'M STARTING TO UNDER-STAND WHAT HAPPENED TO YOUR LOVE LIFE.
OUT OF MY WAY. I HAVE TO GO EAT A PIE.

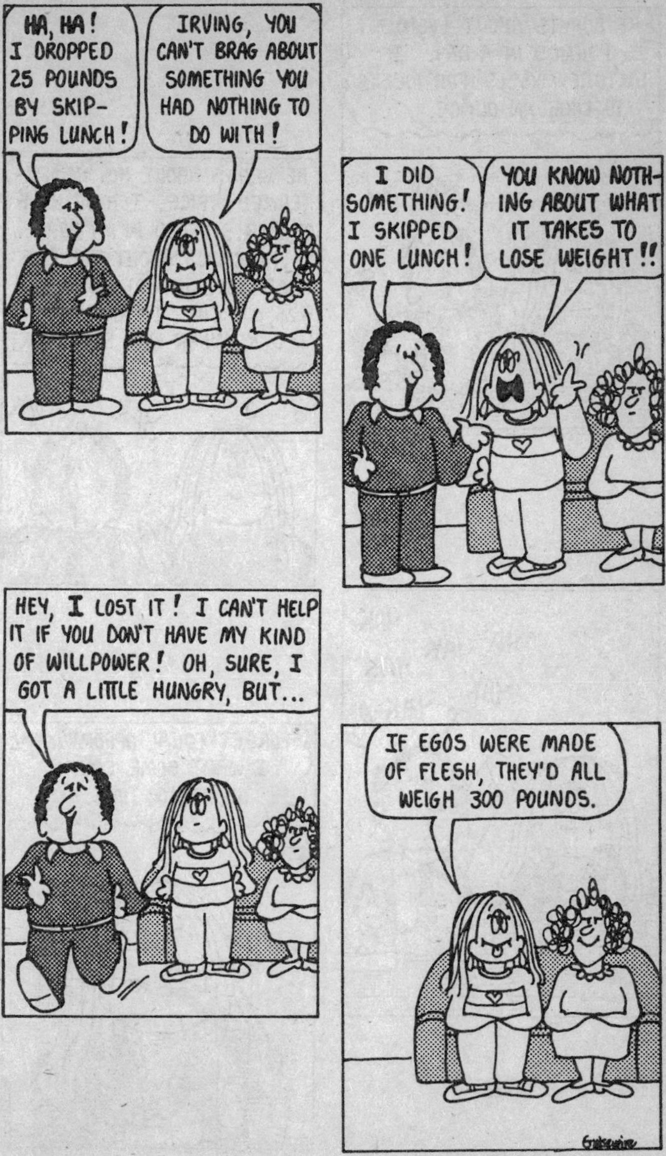
HA, HA! I DROPPED 25 POUNDS BY SKIPPING LUNCH!
IRVING, YOU CAN'T BRAG ABOUT SOMETHING YOU HAD NOTHING TO DO WITH!
I DID SOMETHING! I SKIPPED ONE LUNCH!
YOU KNOW NOTHING ABOUT WHAT IT TAKES TO LOSE WEIGHT!!
HEY, I LOST IT! I CAN'T HELP IT IF YOU DON'T HAVE MY KIND OF WILLPOWER! OH, SURE, I GOT A LITTLE HUNGRY, BUT...
IF EGOS WERE MADE OF FLESH, THEY'D ALL WEIGH 300 POUNDS.

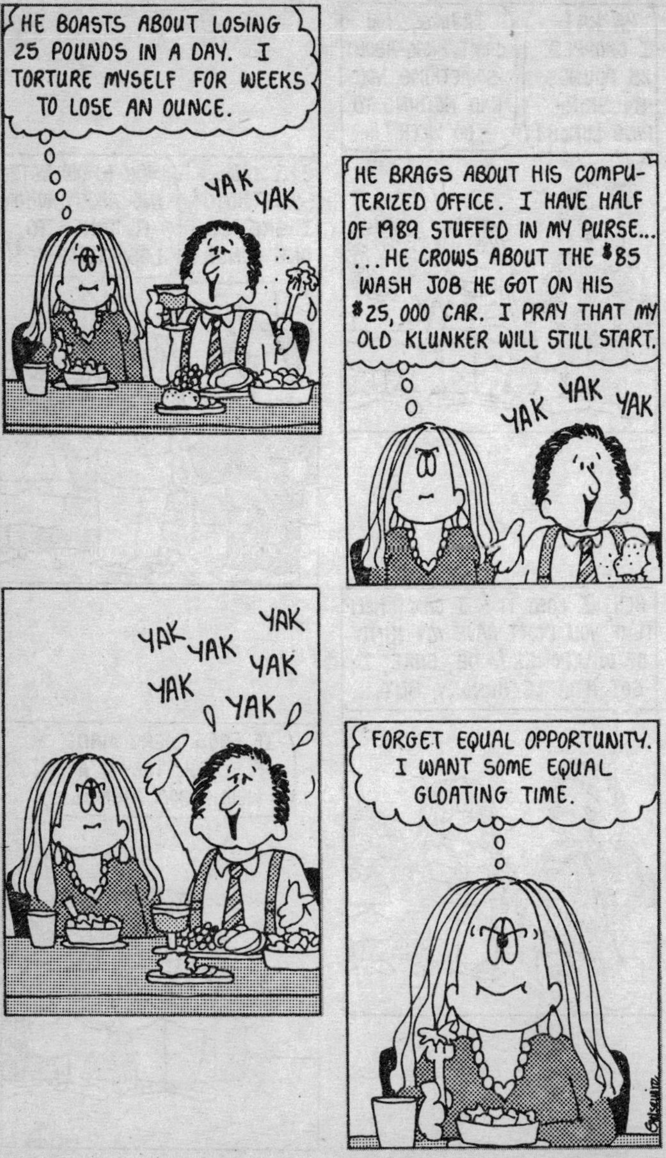
HE BOASTS ABOUT LOSING 25 POUNDS IN A DAY. I TORTURE MYSELF FOR WEEKS TO LOSE AN OUNCE.
YAK YAK
HE BRAGS ABOUT HIS COMPUTERIZED OFFICE. I HAVE HALF OF 1989 STUFFED IN MY PURSE... ...HE CROWS ABOUT THE $85 WASH JOB HE GOT ON HIS $25,000 CAR. I PRAY THAT MY OLD KLUNKER WILL STILL START.
YAK YAK YAK
YAK YAK YAK YAK YAK YAK
FORGET EQUAL OPPORTUNITY. I WANT SOME EQUAL GLOATING TIME.

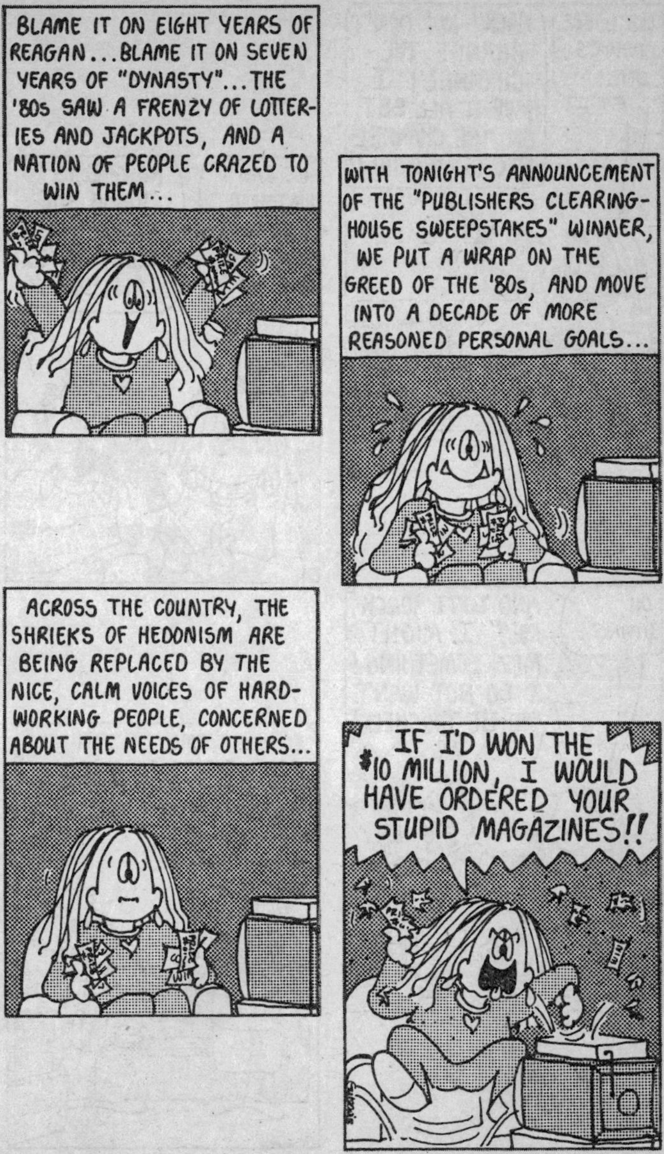
BLAME IT ON EIGHT YEARS OF REAGAN...BLAME IT ON SEVEN YEARS OF "DYNASTY"...THE '80s SAW A FRENZY OF LOTTERIES AND JACKPOTS, AND A NATION OF PEOPLE CRAZED TO WIN THEM...
WITH TONIGHT'S ANNOUNCEMENT OF THE "PUBLISHERS CLEARINGHOUSE SWEEPSTAKES" WINNER, WE PUT A WRAP ON THE GREED OF THE '80s, AND MOVE INTO A DECADE OF MORE REASONED PERSONAL GOALS...
ACROSS THE COUNTRY, THE SHRIEKS OF HEDONISM ARE BEING REPLACED BY THE NICE, CALM VOICES OF HARD-WORKING PEOPLE, CONCERNED ABOUT THE NEEDS OF OTHERS...
IF I'D WON THE $10 MILLION, I WOULD HAVE ORDERED YOUR STUPID MAGAZINES!!

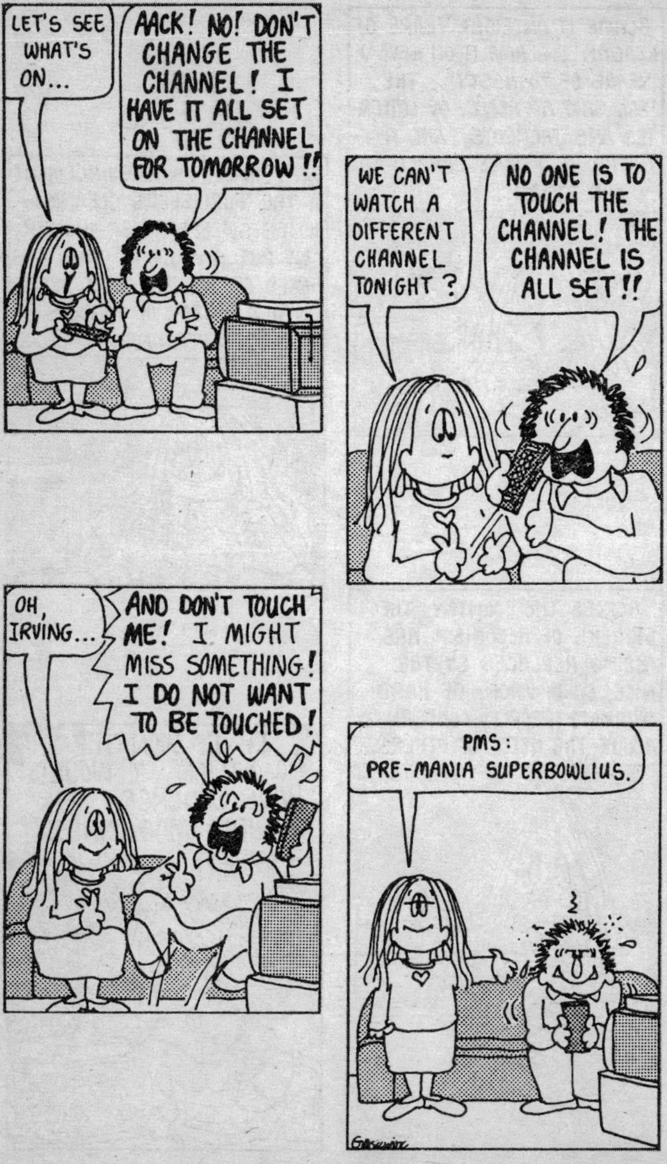
LET'S SEE WHAT'S ON...
AACK! NO! DON'T CHANGE THE CHANNEL! I HAVE IT ALL SET ON THE CHANNEL FOR TOMORROW!!
WE CAN'T WATCH A DIFFERENT CHANNEL TONIGHT?
NO ONE IS TO TOUCH THE CHANNEL! THE CHANNEL IS ALL SET!!
OH, IRVING...
AND DON'T TOUCH ME! I MIGHT MISS SOMETHING! I DO NOT WANT TO BE TOUCHED!
PMS: PRE-MANIA SUPERBOWLIUS.

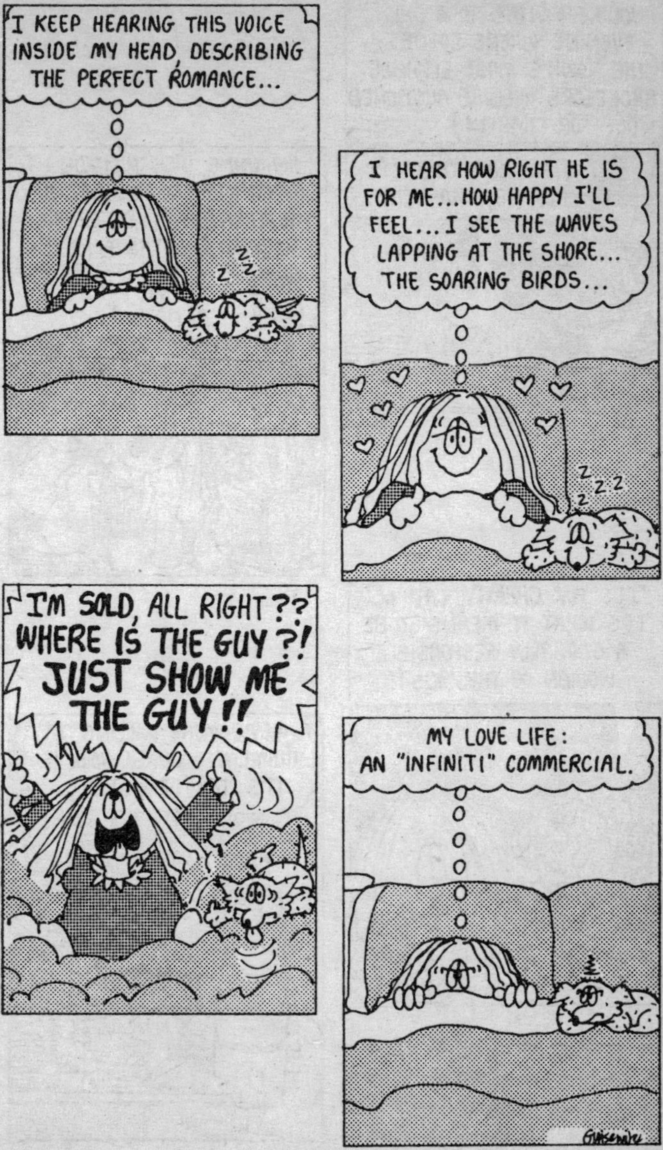
I KEEP HEARING THIS VOICE INSIDE MY HEAD, DESCRIBING THE PERFECT ROMANCE...
I HEAR HOW RIGHT HE IS FOR ME...HOW HAPPY I'LL FEEL... I SEE THE WAVES LAPPING AT THE SHORE... THE SOARING BIRDS...
I'M SOLD, ALL RIGHT?? WHERE IS THE GUY?! JUST SHOW ME THE GUY!!
MY LOVE LIFE: AN "INFINITI" COMMERCIAL.

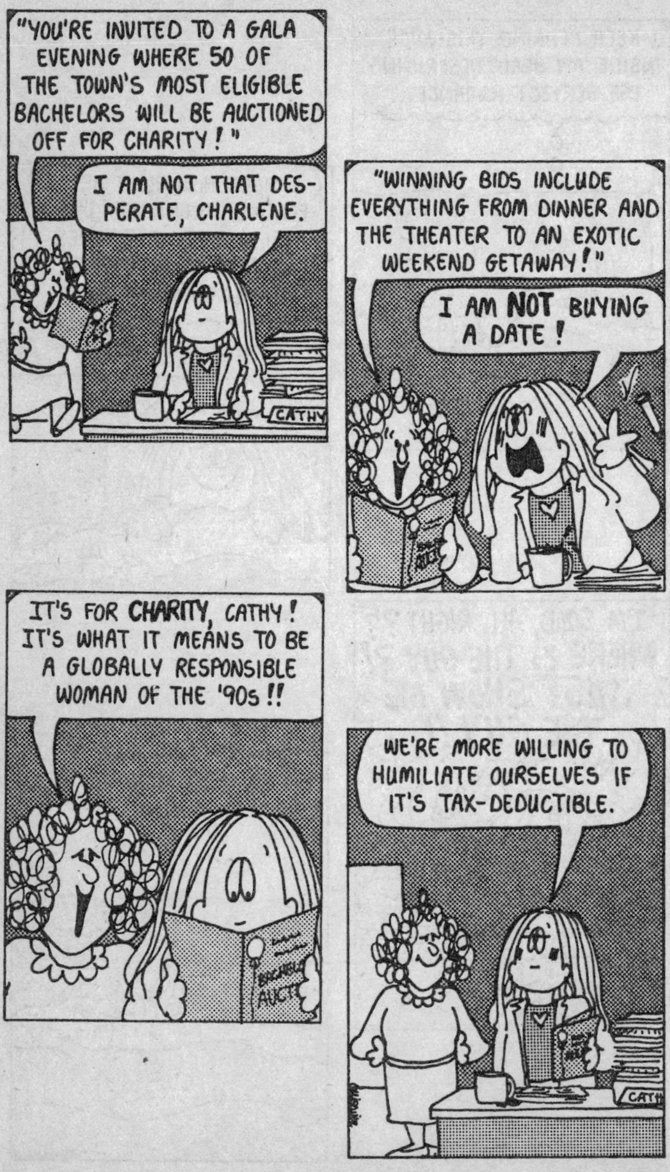
"YOU'RE INVITED TO A GALA EVENING WHERE 50 OF THE TOWN'S MOST ELIGIBLE BACHELORS WILL BE AUCTIONED OFF FOR CHARITY!"
I AM NOT THAT DES-PERATE, CHARLENE.
CATHY
"WINNING BIDS INCLUDE EVERYTHING FROM DINNER AND THE THEATER TO AN EXOTIC WEEKEND GETAWAY!"
I AM NOT BUYING A DATE!
IT'S FOR CHARITY, CATHY! IT'S WHAT IT MEANS TO BE A GLOBALLY RESPONSIBLE WOMAN OF THE '90s!!
WE'RE MORE WILLING TO HUMILIATE OURSELVES IF IT'S TAX-DEDUCTIBLE.

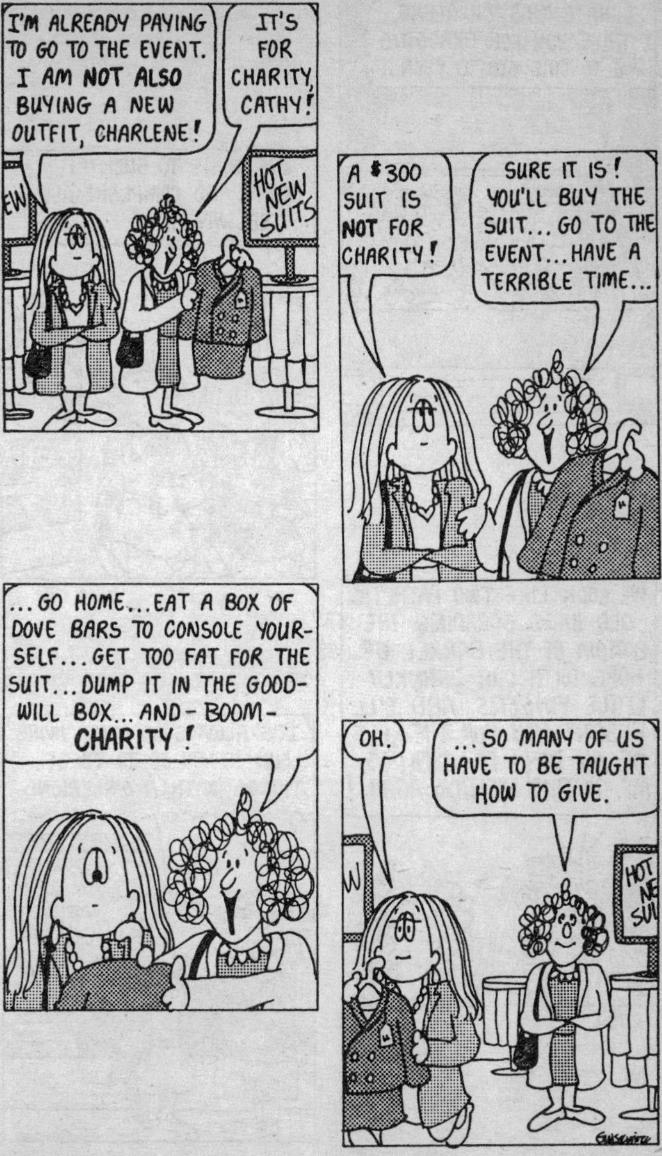
I'M ALREADY PAYING TO GO TO THE EVENT. I AM NOT ALSO BUYING A NEW OUTFIT, CHARLENE!
IT'S FOR CHARITY, CATHY!
HOT NEW SUITS
A $300 SUIT IS NOT FOR CHARITY!
SURE IT IS! YOU'LL BUY THE SUIT... GO TO THE EVENT... HAVE A TERRIBLE TIME...
...GO HOME...EAT A BOX OF DOVE BARS TO CONSOLE YOURSELF...GET TOO FAT FOR THE SUIT...DUMP IT IN THE GOODWILL BOX...AND-BOOM-CHARITY!
OH.
...SO MANY OF US HAVE TO BE TAUGHT HOW TO GIVE.

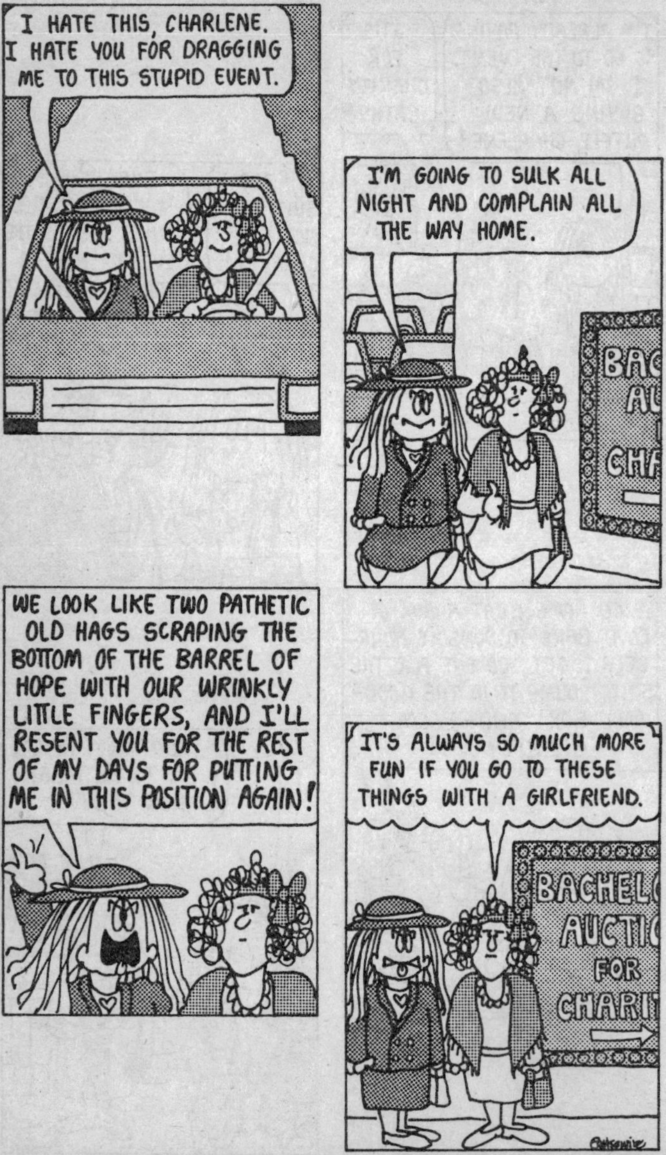
I HATE THIS, CHARLENE. I HATE YOU FOR DRAGGING ME TO THIS STUPID EVENT.
I'M GOING TO SULK ALL NIGHT AND COMPLAIN ALL THE WAY HOME.
WE LOOK LIKE TWO PATHETIC OLD HAGS SCRAPING THE BOTTOM OF THE BARREL OF HOPE WITH OUR WRINKLY LITTLE FINGERS, AND I'LL RESENT YOU FOR THE REST OF MY DAYS FOR PUTTING ME IN THIS POSITION AGAIN!
IT'S ALWAYS SO MUCH MORE FUN IF YOU GO TO THESE THINGS WITH A GIRLFRIEND.
FOR

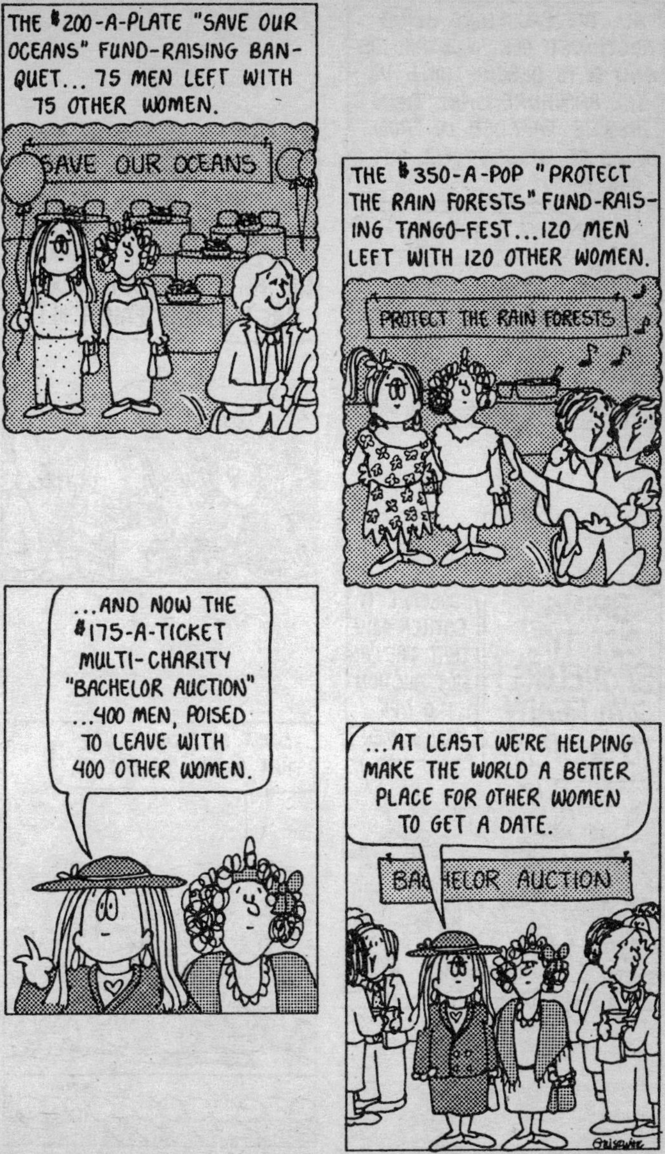
THE $200-A-PLATE "SAVE OUR OCEANS" FUND-RAISING BANQUET... 75 MEN LEFT WITH 75 OTHER WOMEN.
SAVE OUR OCEANS
THE $350-A-POP "PROTECT THE RAIN FORESTS" FUND-RAISING TANGO-FEST...120 MEN LEFT WITH 120 OTHER WOMEN.
PROTECT THE RAIN FORESTS
...AND NOW THE $175-A-TICKET MULTI-CHARITY "BACHELOR AUCTION" ...400 MEN, POISED TO LEAVE WITH 400 OTHER WOMEN.
...AT LEAST WE'RE HELPING MAKE THE WORLD A BETTER PLACE FOR OTHER WOMEN TO GET A DATE.
BACHELOR AUCTION
Guisewite

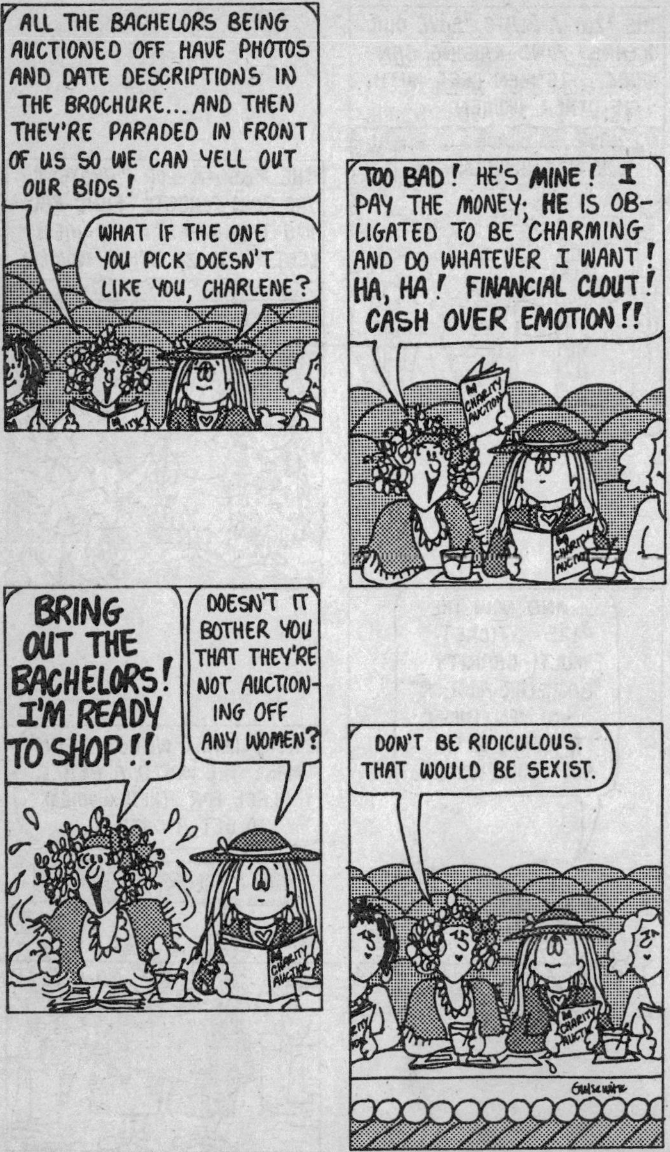
ALL THE BACHELORS BEING AUCTIONED OFF HAVE PHOTOS AND DATE DESCRIPTIONS IN THE BROCHURE... AND THEN THEY'RE PARADED IN FRONT OF US SO WE CAN YELL OUT OUR BIDS!
WHAT IF THE ONE YOU PICK DOESN'T LIKE YOU, CHARLENE?
TOO BAD! HE'S MINE! I PAY THE MONEY; HE IS OBLIGATED TO BE CHARMING AND DO WHATEVER I WANT! HA, HA! FINANCIAL CLOUT! CASH OVER EMOTION!!
CHARITY AUCTION
BRING OUT THE BACHELORS! I'M READY TO SHOP!!
DOESN'T IT BOTHER YOU THAT THEY'RE NOT AUCTIONING OFF ANY WOMEN?
DON'T BE RIDICULOUS. THAT WOULD BE SEXIST.
Guisewite

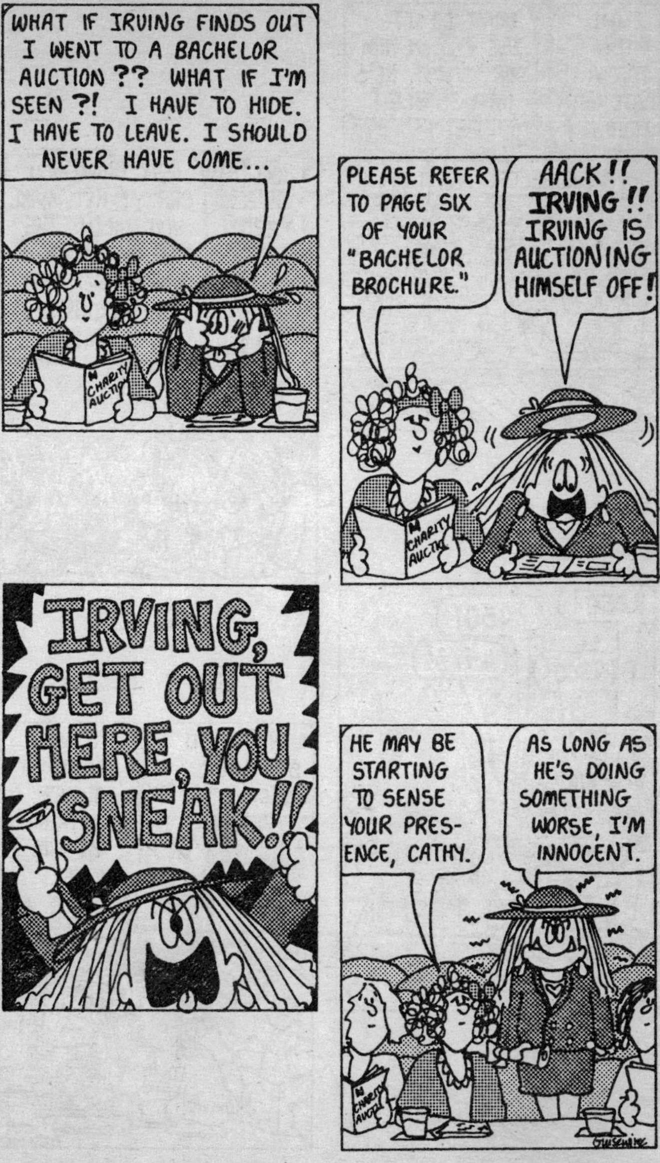
WHAT IF IRVING FINDS OUT I WENT TO A BACHELOR AUCTION?? WHAT IF I'M SEEN?! I HAVE TO HIDE. I HAVE TO LEAVE. I SHOULD NEVER HAVE COME...
PLEASE REFER TO PAGE SIX OF YOUR "BACHELOR BROCHURE."
AACK!! IRVING!! IRVING IS AUCTIONING HIMSELF OFF!
IRVING, GET OUT HERE, YOU SNEAK!!
HE MAY BE STARTING TO SENSE YOUR PRES-ENCE, CATHY.
AS LONG AS HE'S DOING SOMETHING WORSE, I'M INNOCENT.

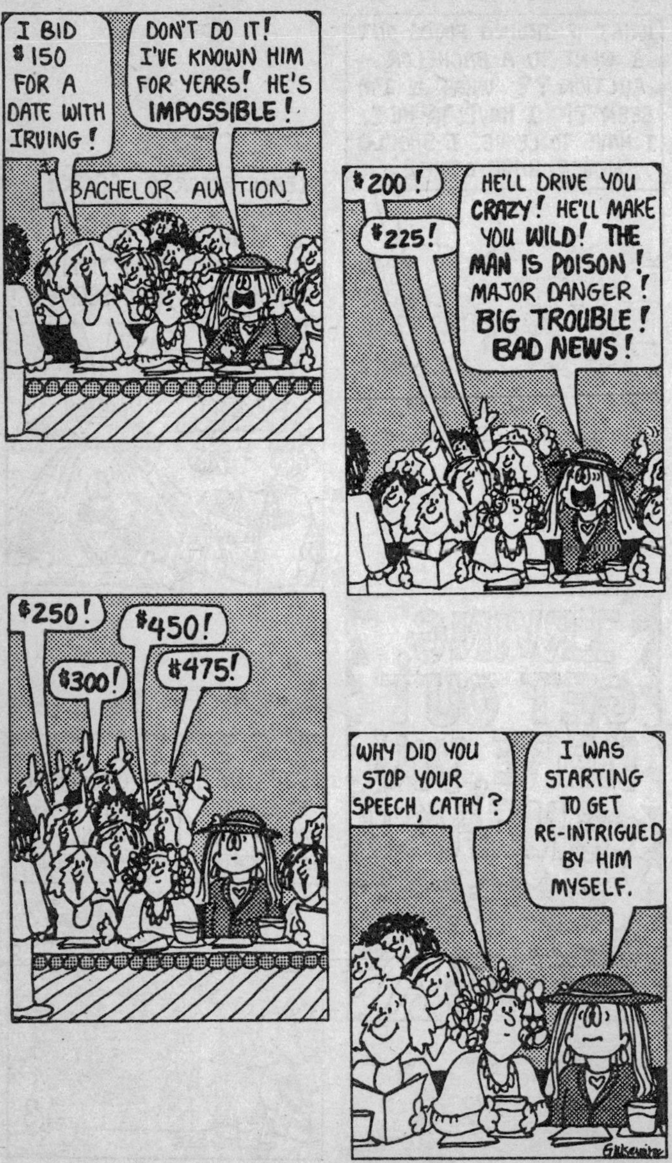
I BID $150 FOR A DATE WITH IRVING!
DON'T DO IT! I'VE KNOWN HIM FOR YEARS! HE'S IMPOSSIBLE!
BACHELOR AUCTION
$200!
$225!
HE'LL DRIVE YOU CRAZY! HE'LL MAKE YOU WILD! THE MAN IS POISON! MAJOR DANGER! BIG TROUBLE! BAD NEWS!
$250!
$300!
$450!
$475!
WHY DID YOU STOP YOUR SPEECH, CATHY?
I WAS STARTING TO GET RE-INTRIGUED BY HIM MYSELF.

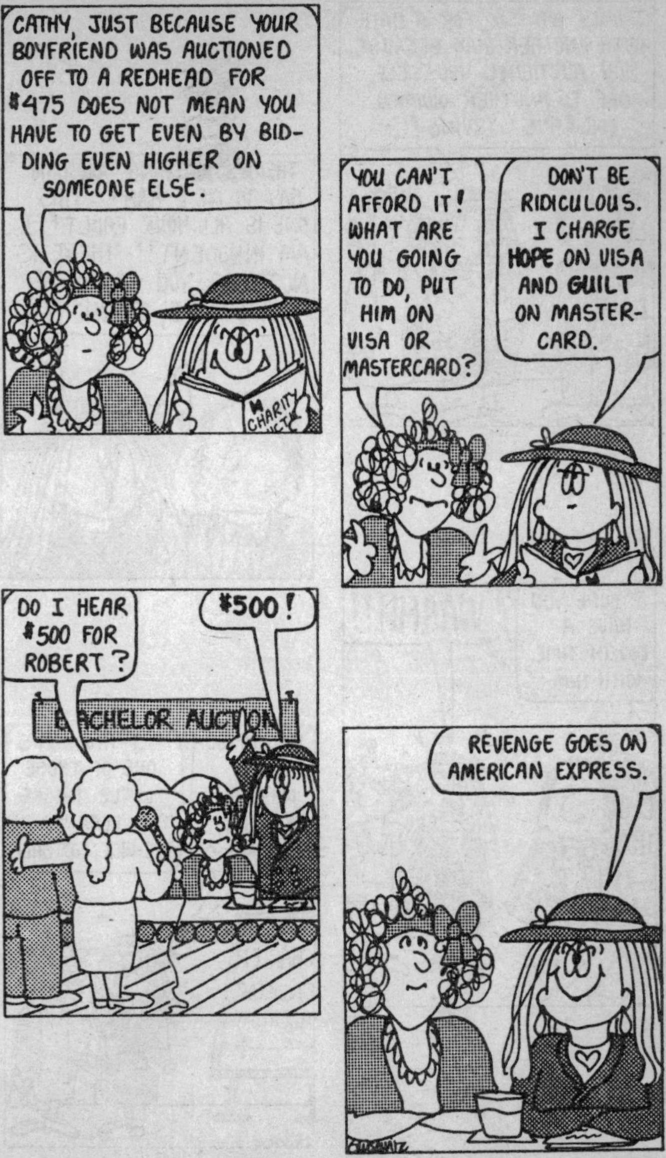
CATHY, JUST BECAUSE YOUR BOYFRIEND WAS AUCTIONED OFF TO A REDHEAD FOR $475 DOES NOT MEAN YOU HAVE TO GET EVEN BY BIDDING EVEN HIGHER ON SOMEONE ELSE.
YOU CAN'T AFFORD IT! WHAT ARE YOU GOING TO DO, PUT HIM ON VISA OR MASTERCARD?
DON'T BE RIDICULOUS. I CHARGE **HOPE** ON VISA AND **GUILT** ON MASTERCARD.
DO I HEAR $500 FOR ROBERT?
$500!
BACHELOR AUCTION
REVENGE GOES ON AMERICAN EXPRESS.

I ONLY BID $500 FOR A DATE WITH ANOTHER MAN BECAUSE YOU AUCTIONED YOURSELF OFF TO ANOTHER WOMAN FOR $475, IRVING!
THERE'S NOTHING YOU CAN SAY TO ME! HAH! THIS ONE IS ALL YOUR FAULT! I AM INNOCENT!! THERE IS NOTHING YOU CAN SAY THIS TIME, IRVING!!
I HOPE YOU HAVE A LOVELY TIME WITH HIM.
WAAHH!!
IF I'M SO RIGHT, WHY IS HE STILL WINNING?
I THINK IT'S ONE OF THOSE LITTLE TRICKS THEY LEARNED IN PEE-WEE FOOTBALL.
CHARITY BACHELOR AUCTION
Guisewite

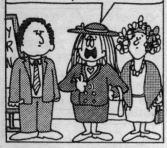

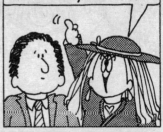

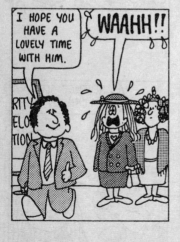

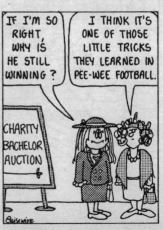

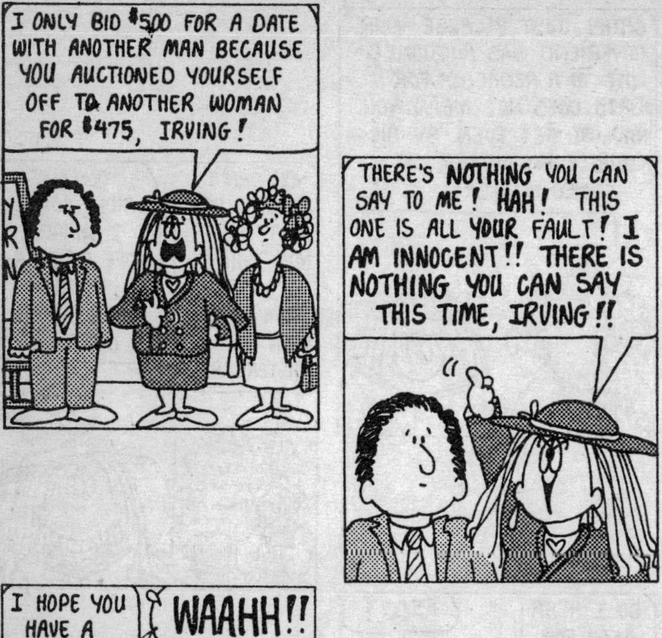

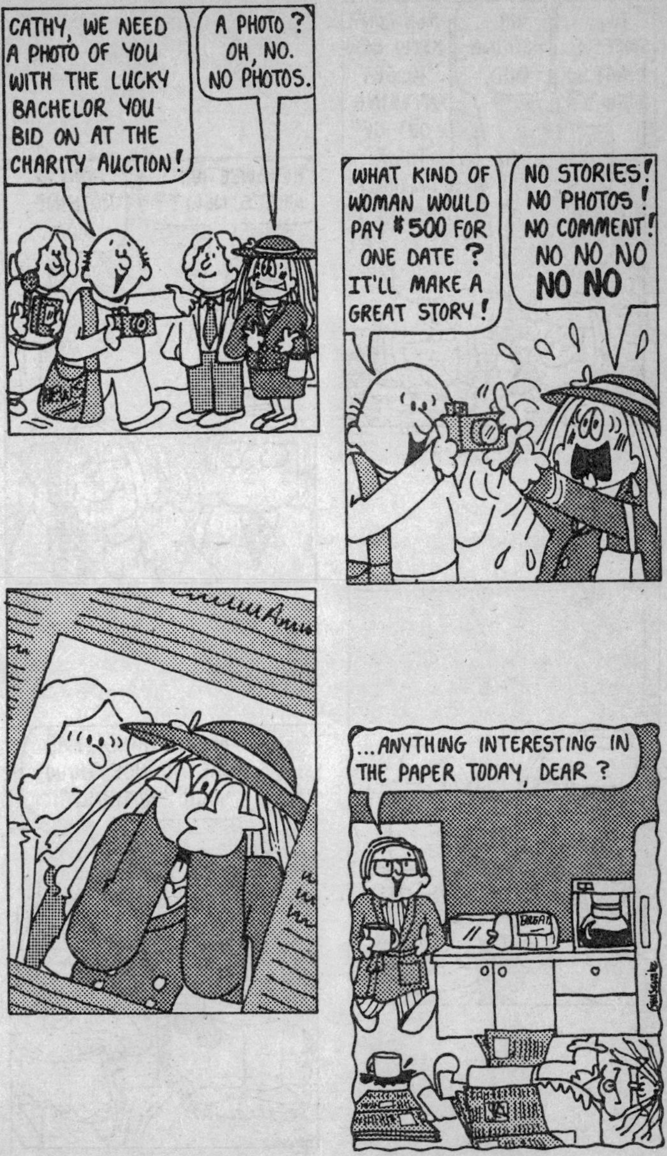
CATHY, WE NEED A PHOTO OF YOU WITH THE LUCKY BACHELOR YOU BID ON AT THE CHARITY AUCTION!
A PHOTO? OH, NO. NO PHOTOS.
WHAT KIND OF WOMAN WOULD PAY $500 FOR ONE DATE? IT'LL MAKE A GREAT STORY!
NO STORIES! NO PHOTOS! NO COMMENT! NO NO NO NO NO
...ANYTHING INTERESTING IN THE PAPER TODAY, DEAR?

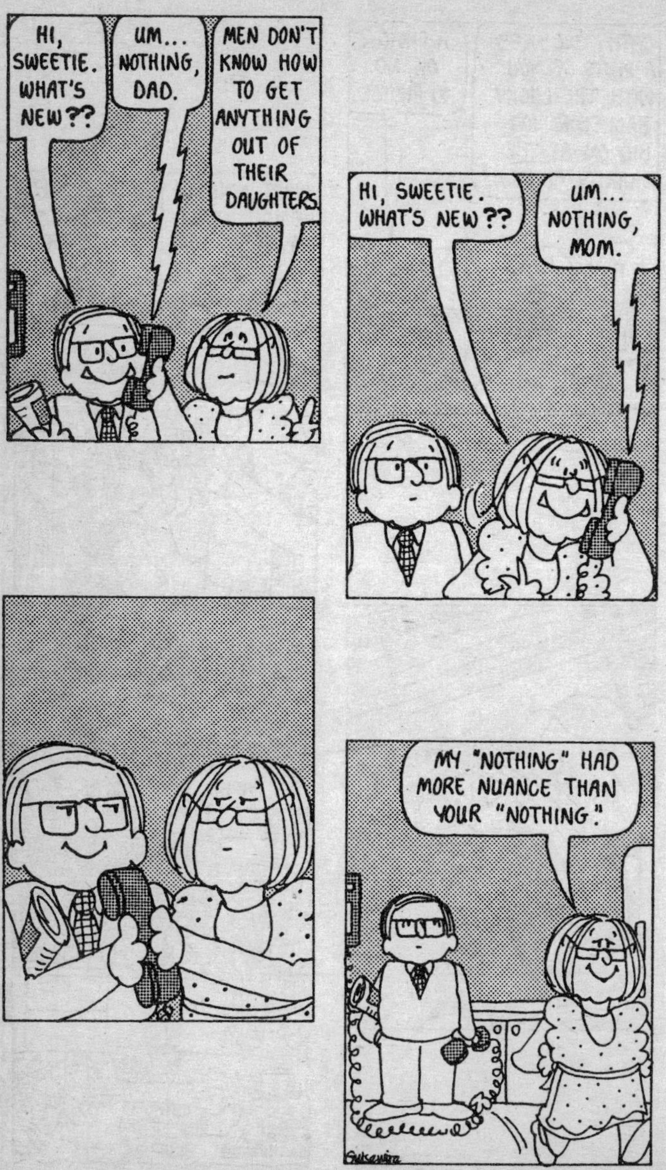
HI, SWEETIE. WHAT'S NEW??
UM... NOTHING, DAD.
MEN DON'T KNOW HOW TO GET ANYTHING OUT OF THEIR DAUGHTERS.
HI, SWEETIE. WHAT'S NEW??
UM... NOTHING, MOM.
MY "NOTHING" HAD MORE NUANCE THAN YOUR "NOTHING."

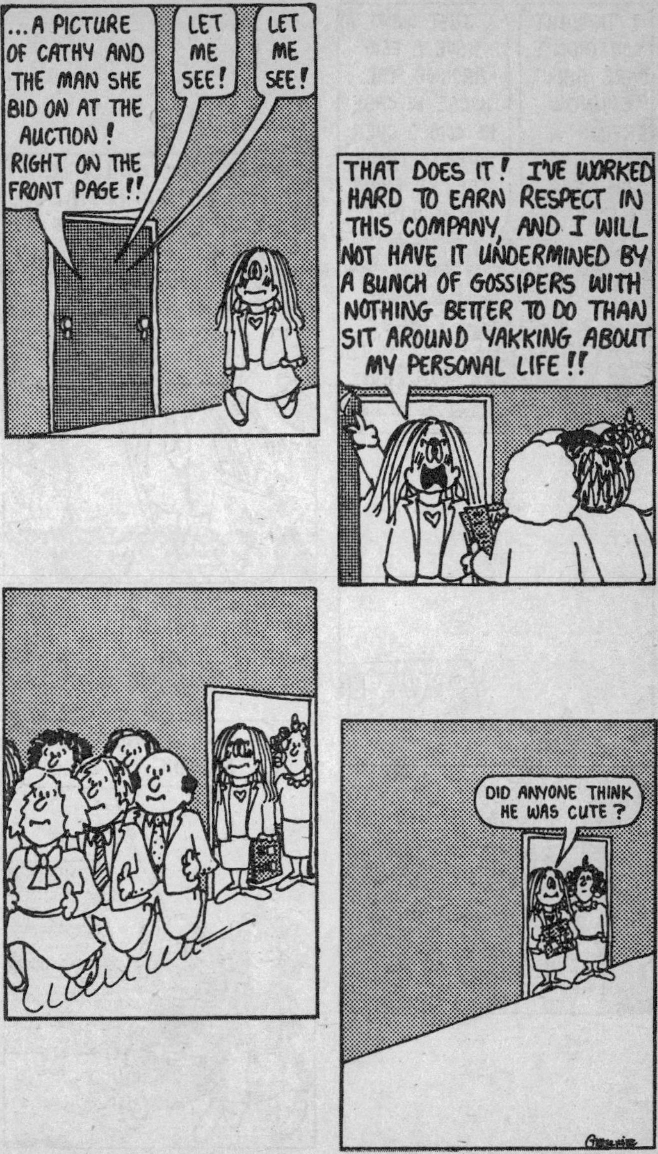
...A PICTURE OF CATHY AND THE MAN SHE BID ON AT THE AUCTION! RIGHT ON THE FRONT PAGE!!
LET ME SEE!
LET ME SEE!
THAT DOES IT! I'VE WORKED HARD TO EARN RESPECT IN THIS COMPANY, AND I WILL NOT HAVE IT UNDERMINED BY A BUNCH OF GOSSIPERS WITH NOTHING BETTER TO DO THAN SIT AROUND YAKKING ABOUT MY PERSONAL LIFE!!
DID ANYONE THINK HE WAS CUTE?

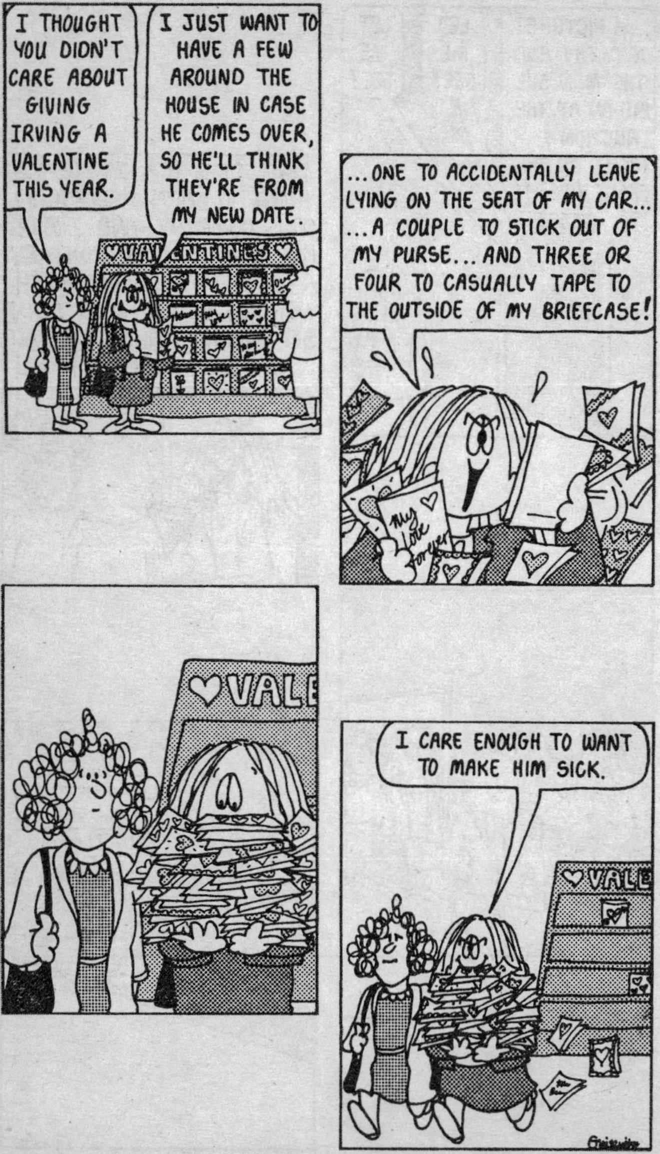
I THOUGHT YOU DIDN'T CARE ABOUT GIVING IRVING A VALENTINE THIS YEAR.
I JUST WANT TO HAVE A FEW AROUND THE HOUSE IN CASE HE COMES OVER, SO HE'LL THINK THEY'RE FROM MY NEW DATE.
...ONE TO ACCIDENTALLY LEAVE LYING ON THE SEAT OF MY CAR... ...A COUPLE TO STICK OUT OF MY PURSE... AND THREE OR FOUR TO CASUALLY TAPE TO THE OUTSIDE OF MY BRIEFCASE!
My Love Forever
I CARE ENOUGH TO WANT TO MAKE HIM SICK.

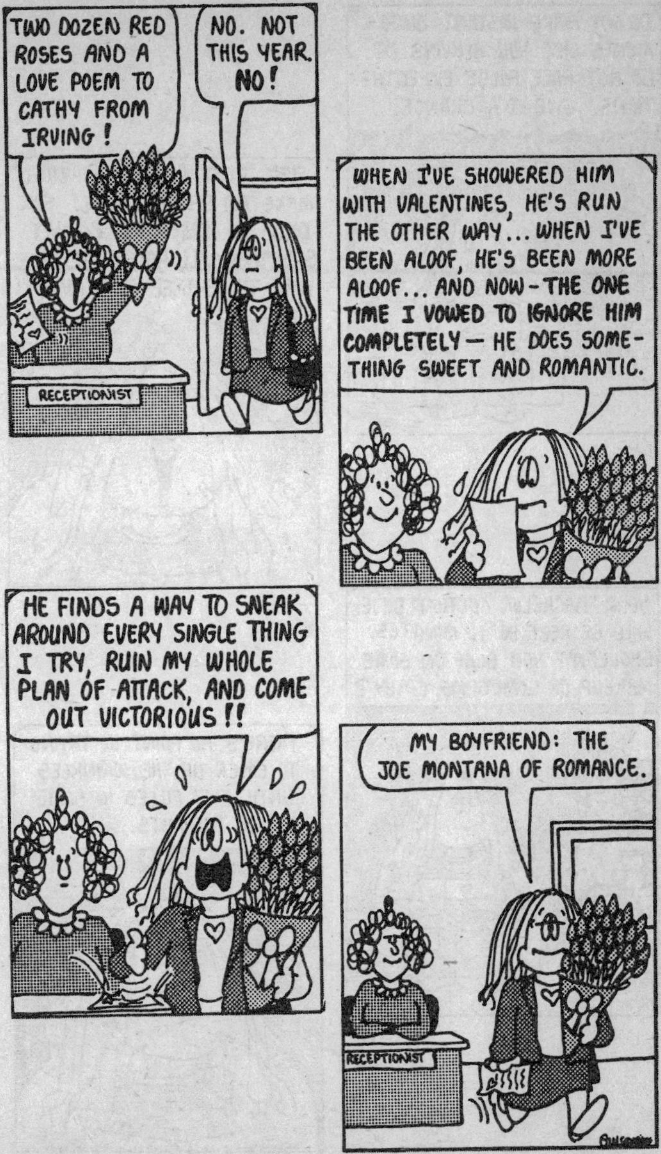
TWO DOZEN RED ROSES AND A LOVE POEM TO CATHY FROM IRVING !
NO. NOT THIS YEAR. NO!
RECEPTIONIST
WHEN I'VE SHOWERED HIM WITH VALENTINES, HE'S RUN THE OTHER WAY... WHEN I'VE BEEN ALOOF, HE'S BEEN MORE ALOOF... AND NOW - THE ONE TIME I VOWED TO IGNORE HIM COMPLETELY - HE DOES SOME-THING SWEET AND ROMANTIC.
HE FINDS A WAY TO SNEAK AROUND EVERY SINGLE THING I TRY, RUIN MY WHOLE PLAN OF ATTACK, AND COME OUT VICTORIOUS !!
MY BOYFRIEND: THE JOE MONTANA OF ROMANCE.
RECEPTIONIST

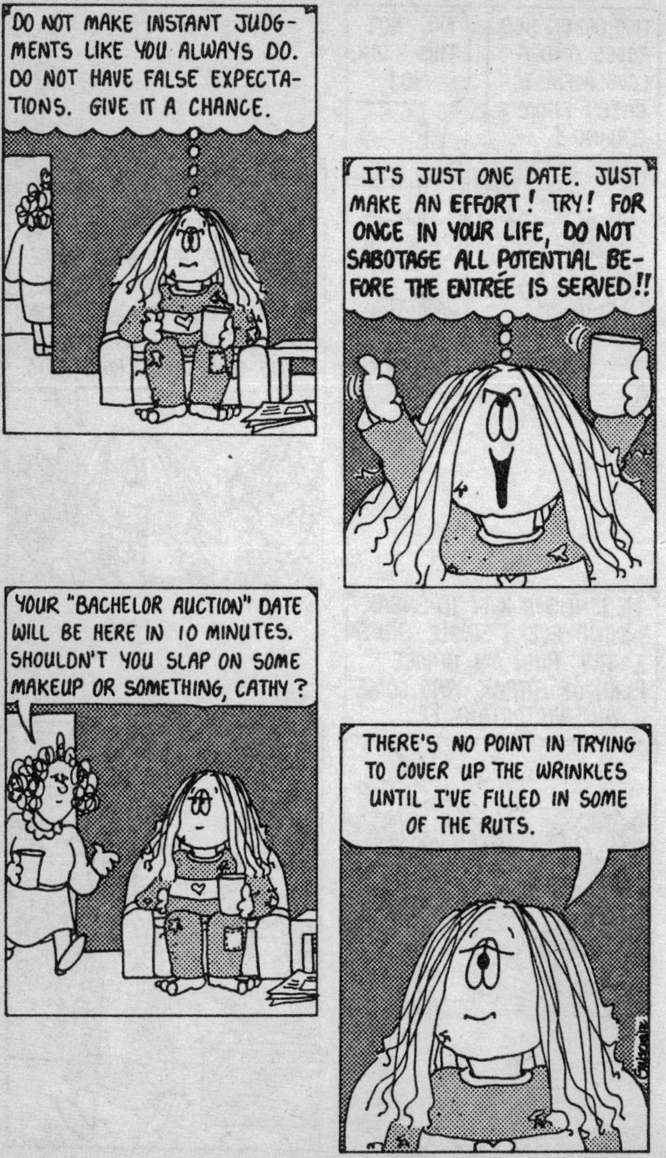
DO NOT MAKE INSTANT JUDGMENTS LIKE YOU ALWAYS DO. DO NOT HAVE FALSE EXPECTATIONS. GIVE IT A CHANCE.
IT'S JUST ONE DATE. JUST MAKE AN EFFORT! TRY! FOR ONCE IN YOUR LIFE, DO NOT SABOTAGE ALL POTENTIAL BEFORE THE ENTRÉE IS SERVED!!
YOUR "BACHELOR AUCTION" DATE WILL BE HERE IN 10 MINUTES. SHOULDN'T YOU SLAP ON SOME MAKEUP OR SOMETHING, CATHY?
THERE'S NO POINT IN TRYING TO COVER UP THE WRINKLES UNTIL I'VE FILLED IN SOME OF THE RUTS.

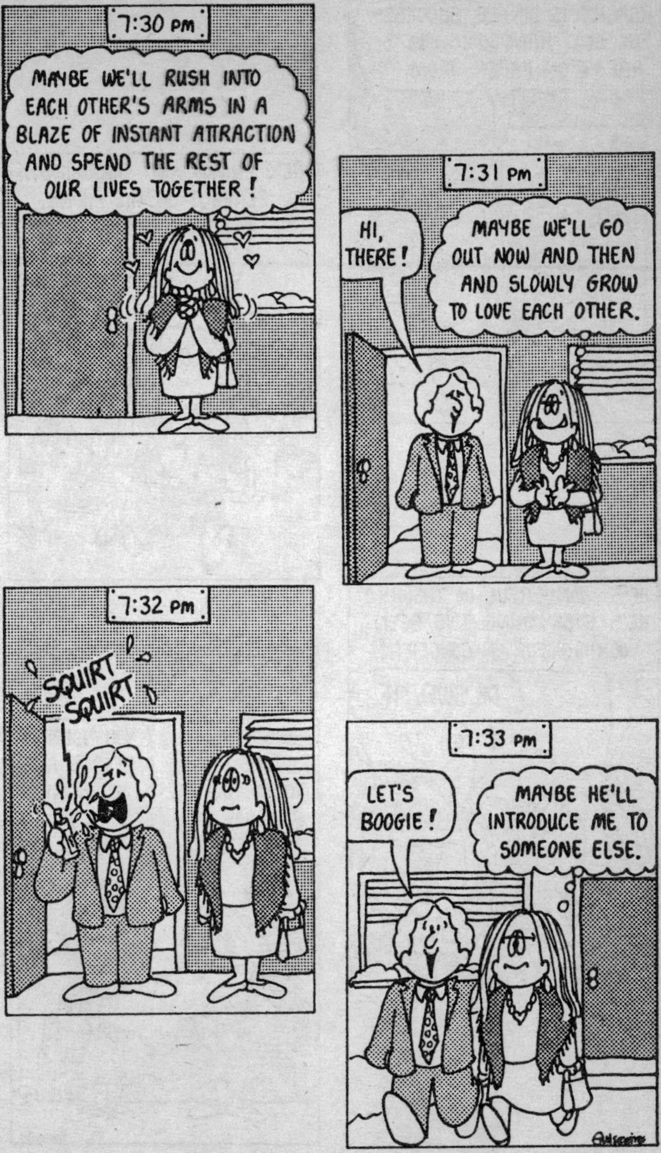
7:30 PM
MAYBE WE'LL RUSH INTO EACH OTHER'S ARMS IN A BLAZE OF INSTANT ATTRACTION AND SPEND THE REST OF OUR LIVES TOGETHER!
7:31 PM
HI, THERE!
MAYBE WE'LL GO OUT NOW AND THEN AND SLOWLY GROW TO LOVE EACH OTHER.
7:32 PM
SQUIRT SQUIRT
7:33 PM
LET'S BOOGIE!
MAYBE HE'LL INTRODUCE ME TO SOMEONE ELSE.

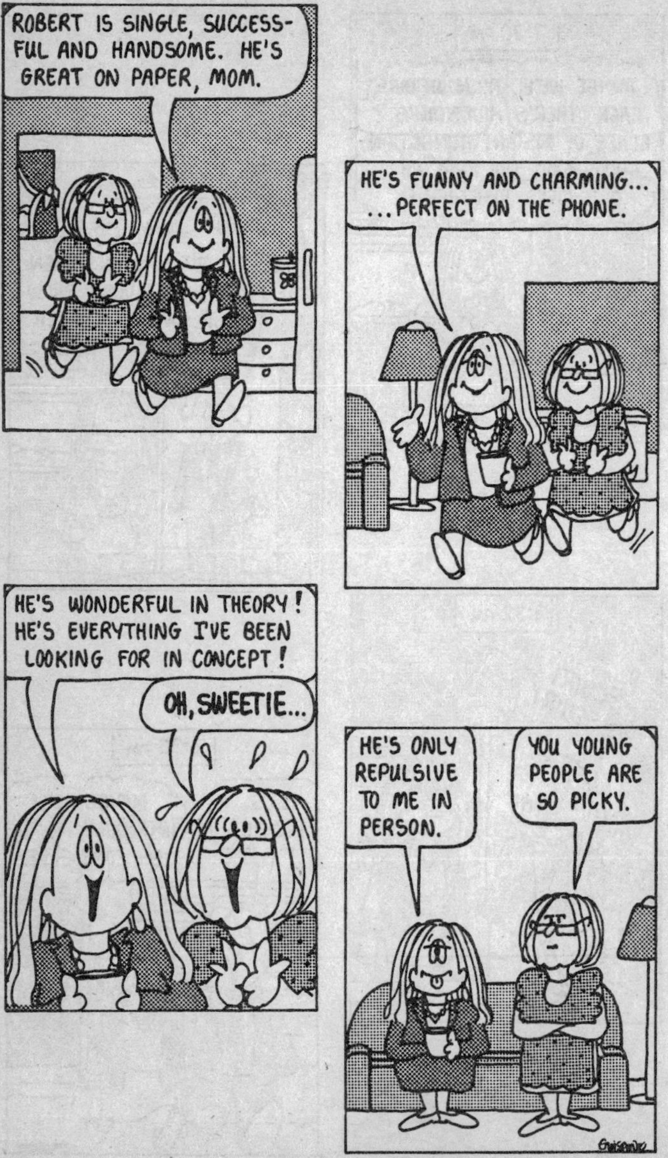
ROBERT IS SINGLE, SUCCESSFUL AND HANDSOME. HE'S GREAT ON PAPER, MOM.
HE'S FUNNY AND CHARMING...
...PERFECT ON THE PHONE.
HE'S WONDERFUL IN THEORY! HE'S EVERYTHING I'VE BEEN LOOKING FOR IN CONCEPT!
OH, SWEETIE...
HE'S ONLY REPULSIVE TO ME IN PERSON.
YOU YOUNG PEOPLE ARE SO PICKY.
GUISEWITE

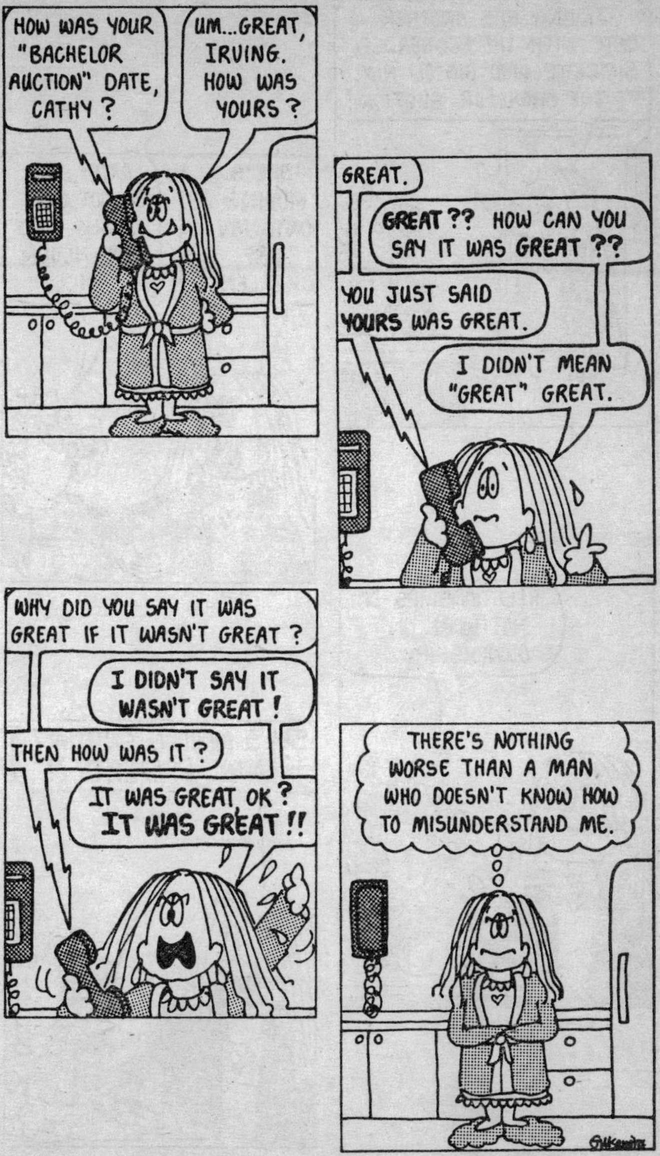
HOW WAS YOUR "BACHELOR AUCTION" DATE, CATHY?
UM...GREAT, IRVING. HOW WAS YOURS?
GREAT.
GREAT?? HOW CAN YOU SAY IT WAS GREAT??
YOU JUST SAID YOURS WAS GREAT.
I DIDN'T MEAN "GREAT" GREAT.
WHY DID YOU SAY IT WAS GREAT IF IT WASN'T GREAT?
I DIDN'T SAY IT WASN'T GREAT!
THEN HOW WAS IT?
IT WAS GREAT, OK? IT WAS GREAT!!
THERE'S NOTHING WORSE THAN A MAN WHO DOESN'T KNOW HOW TO MISUNDERSTAND ME.

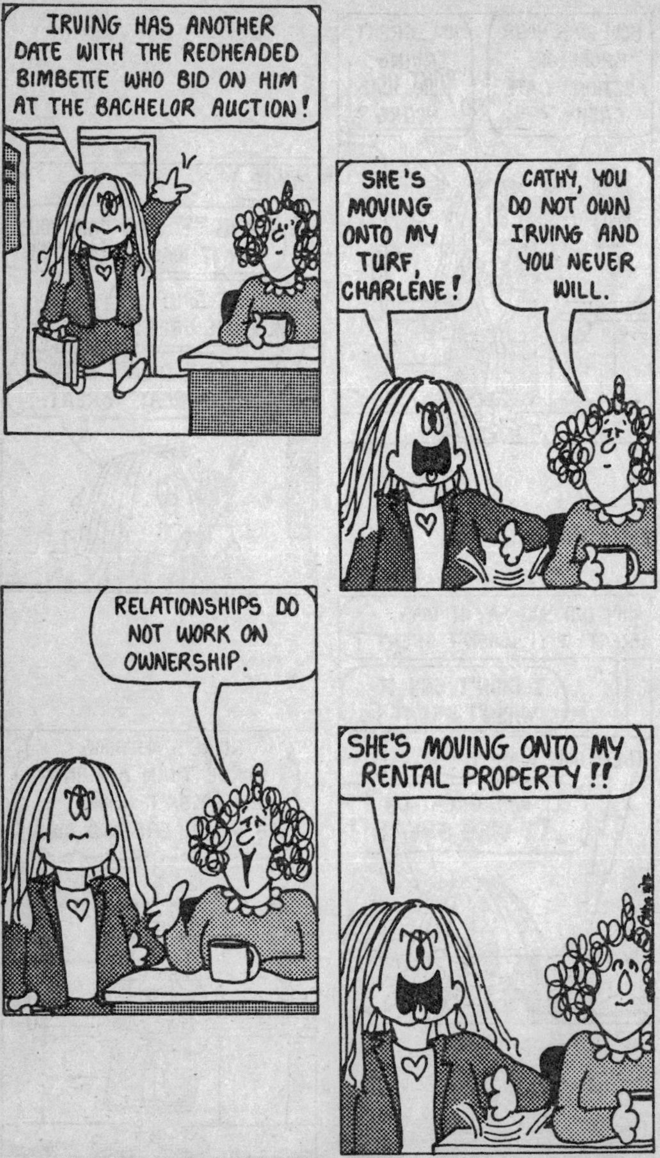
IRVING HAS ANOTHER DATE WITH THE REDHEADED BIMBETTE WHO BID ON HIM AT THE BACHELOR AUCTION!
SHE'S MOVING ONTO MY TURF, CHARLENE!
CATHY, YOU DO NOT OWN IRVING AND YOU NEVER WILL.
RELATIONSHIPS DO NOT WORK ON OWNERSHIP.
SHE'S MOVING ONTO MY RENTAL PROPERTY!!

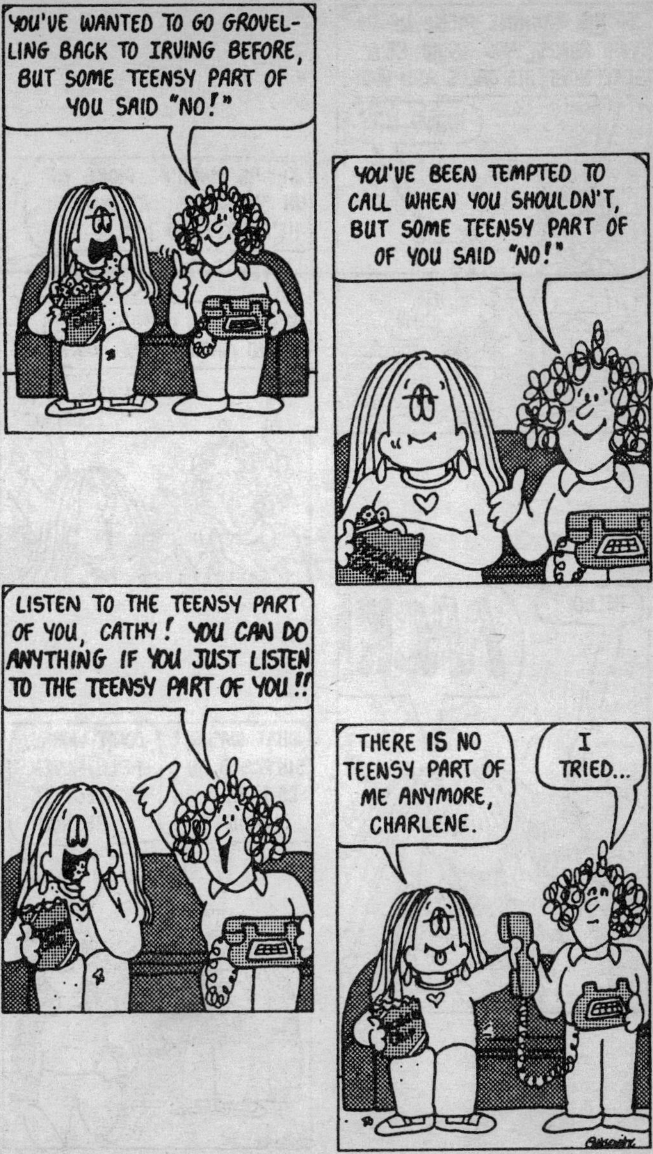
YOU'VE WANTED TO GO GROVELLING BACK TO IRVING BEFORE, BUT SOME TEENSY PART OF YOU SAID "NO!"
YOU'VE BEEN TEMPTED TO CALL WHEN YOU SHOULDN'T, BUT SOME TEENSY PART OF OF YOU SAID "NO!"
LISTEN TO THE TEENSY PART OF YOU, CATHY! YOU CAN DO ANYTHING IF YOU JUST LISTEN TO THE TEENSY PART OF YOU!!
THERE IS NO TEENSY PART OF ME ANYMORE, CHARLENE.
I TRIED...

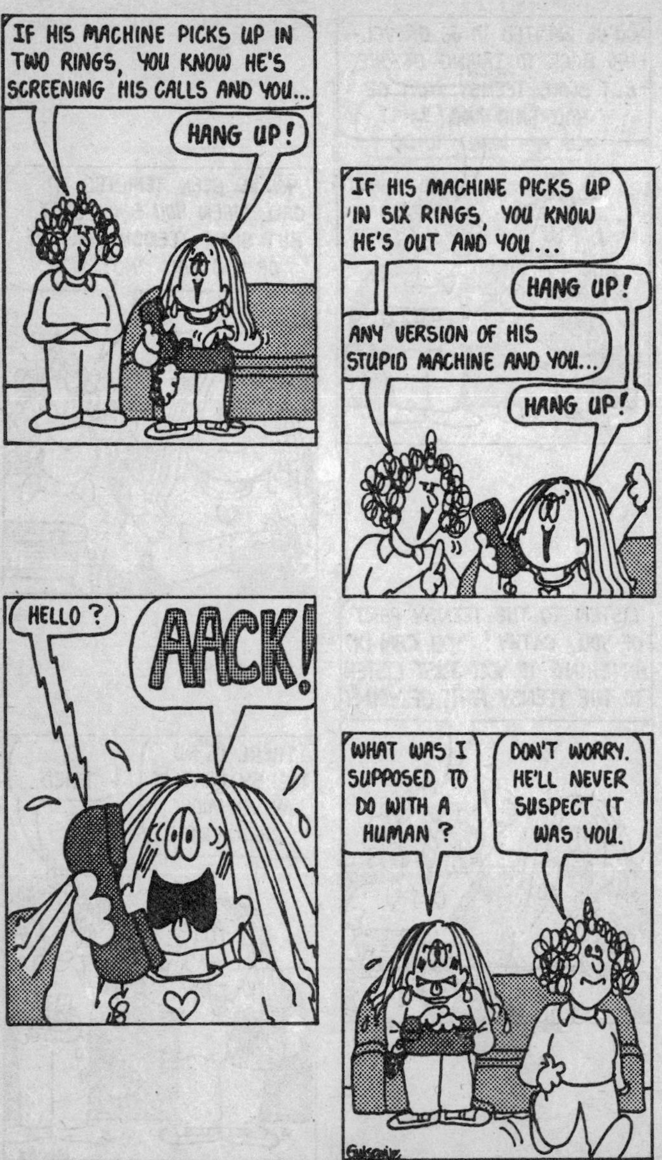

IF HIS MACHINE PICKS UP IN TWO RINGS, YOU KNOW HE'S SCREENING HIS CALLS AND YOU...
HANG UP!
IF HIS MACHINE PICKS UP IN SIX RINGS, YOU KNOW HE'S OUT AND YOU...
HANG UP!
ANY VERSION OF HIS STUPID MACHINE AND YOU...
HANG UP!
HELLO?
AACK!
WHAT WAS I SUPPOSED TO DO WITH A HUMAN?
DON'T WORRY. HE'LL NEVER SUSPECT IT WAS YOU.

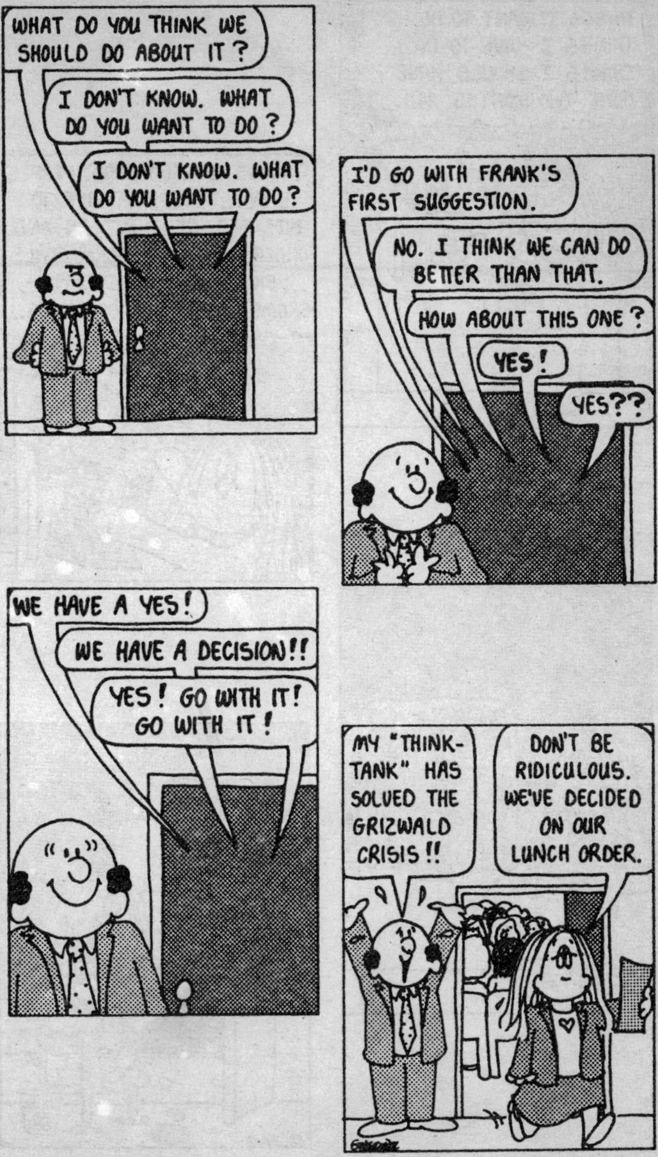
WHAT DO YOU THINK WE SHOULD DO ABOUT IT?
I DON'T KNOW. WHAT DO YOU WANT TO DO?
I DON'T KNOW. WHAT DO YOU WANT TO DO?
I'D GO WITH FRANK'S FIRST SUGGESTION.
NO. I THINK WE CAN DO BETTER THAN THAT.
HOW ABOUT THIS ONE?
YES!
YES??
WE HAVE A YES!
WE HAVE A DECISION!!
YES! GO WITH IT! GO WITH IT!
MY "THINK-TANK" HAS SOLVED THE GRIZWALD CRISIS!!
DON'T BE RIDICULOUS. WE'VE DECIDED ON OUR LUNCH ORDER.

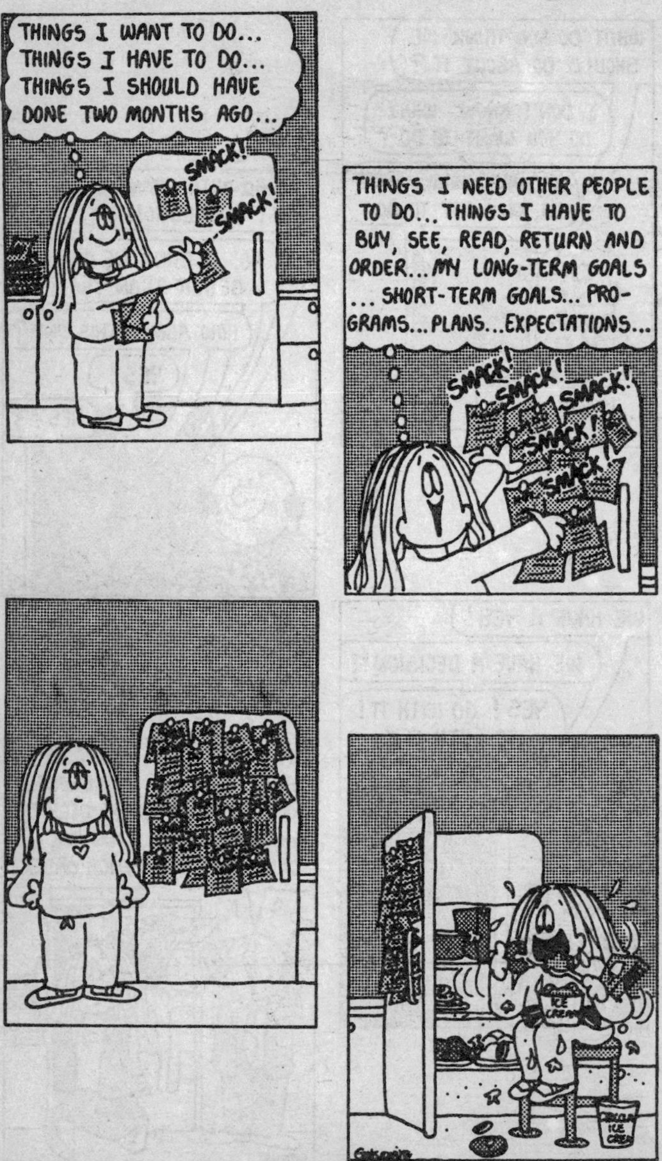
THINGS I WANT TO DO... THINGS I HAVE TO DO... THINGS I SHOULD HAVE DONE TWO MONTHS AGO...
SMACK!
SMACK!
THINGS I NEED OTHER PEOPLE TO DO... THINGS I HAVE TO BUY, SEE, READ, RETURN AND ORDER... MY LONG-TERM GOALS ... SHORT-TERM GOALS... PROGRAMS... PLANS... EXPECTATIONS...
SMACK!
SMACK!
SMACK!
SMACK!
SMACK!
ICE CREAM

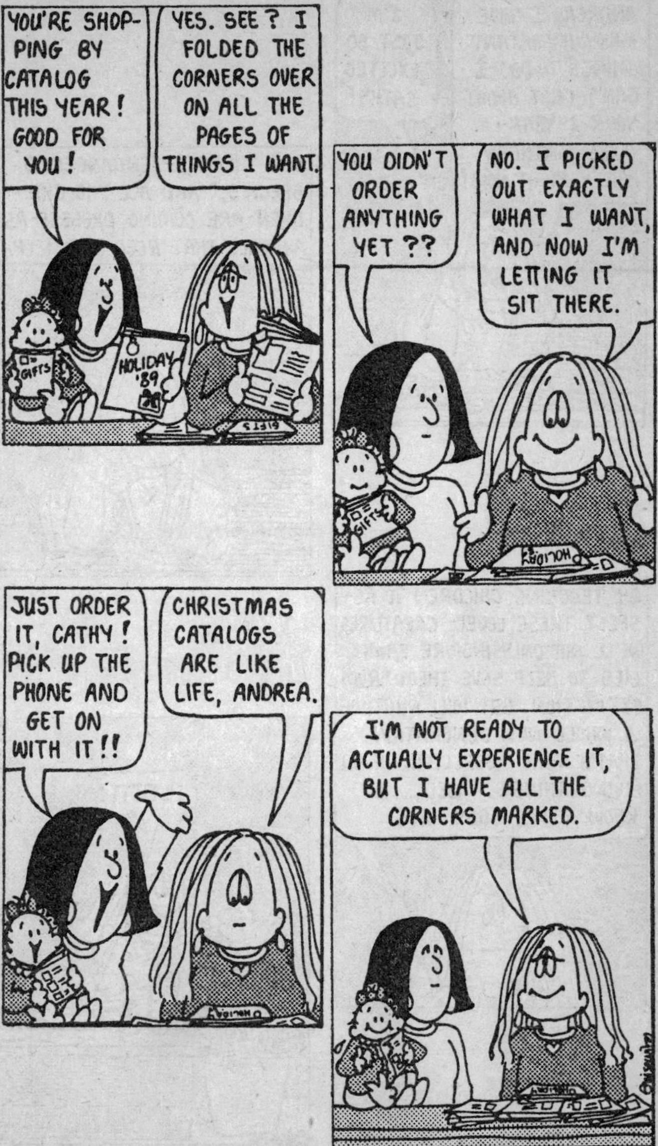
YOU'RE SHOPPING BY CATALOG THIS YEAR! GOOD FOR YOU!
YES. SEE? I FOLDED THE CORNERS OVER ON ALL THE PAGES OF THINGS I WANT.
GIFTS
HOLIDAY '89
YOU DIDN'T ORDER ANYTHING YET??
NO. I PICKED OUT EXACTLY WHAT I WANT, AND NOW I'M LETTING IT SIT THERE.
JUST ORDER IT, CATHY! PICK UP THE PHONE AND GET ON WITH IT!!
CHRISTMAS CATALOGS ARE LIKE LIFE, ANDREA.
I'M NOT READY TO ACTUALLY EXPERIENCE IT, BUT I HAVE ALL THE CORNERS MARKED.

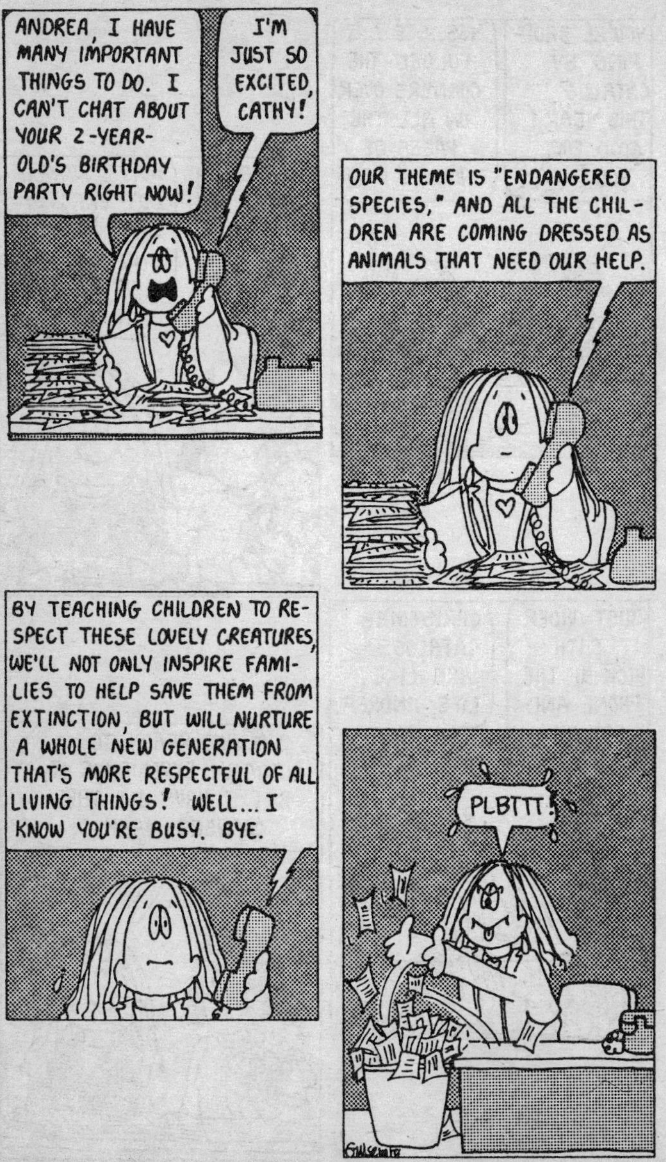
ANDREA, I HAVE MANY IMPORTANT THINGS TO DO. I CAN'T CHAT ABOUT YOUR 2-YEAR-OLD'S BIRTHDAY PARTY RIGHT NOW!
I'M JUST SO EXCITED, CATHY!
OUR THEME IS "ENDANGERED SPECIES," AND ALL THE CHILDREN ARE COMING DRESSED AS ANIMALS THAT NEED OUR HELP.
BY TEACHING CHILDREN TO RESPECT THESE LOVELY CREATURES, WE'LL NOT ONLY INSPIRE FAMILIES TO HELP SAVE THEM FROM EXTINCTION, BUT WILL NURTURE A WHOLE NEW GENERATION THAT'S MORE RESPECTFUL OF ALL LIVING THINGS! WELL... I KNOW YOU'RE BUSY. BYE.
PLBTTT!

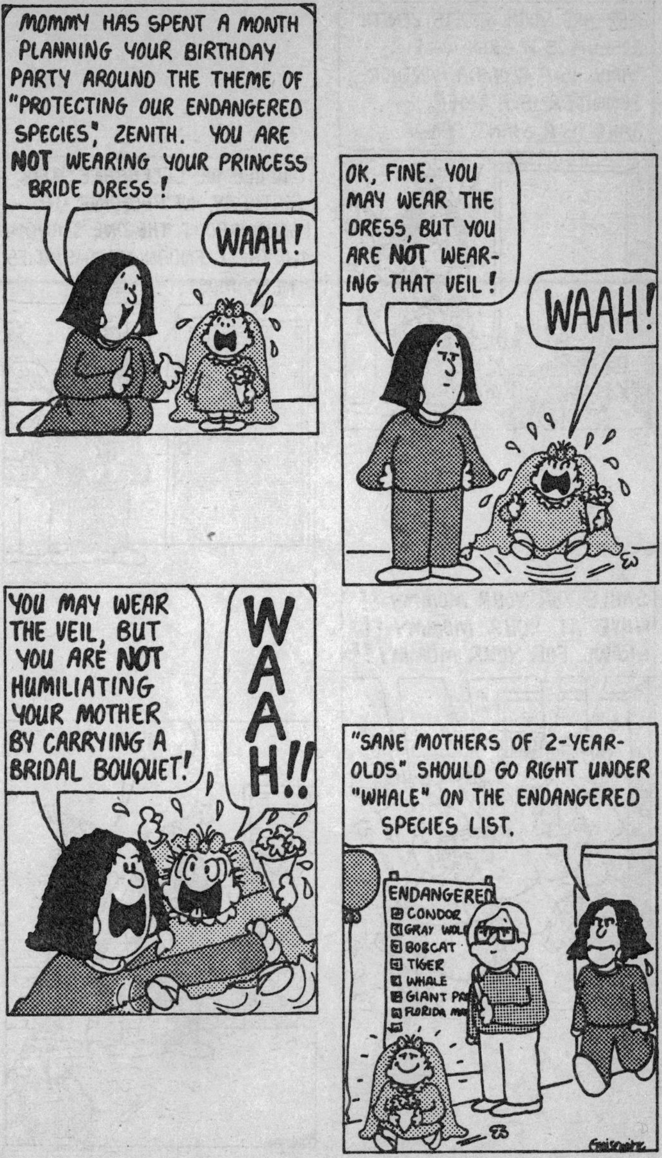
MOMMY HAS SPENT A MONTH PLANNING YOUR BIRTHDAY PARTY AROUND THE THEME OF "PROTECTING OUR ENDANGERED SPECIES," ZENITH. YOU ARE NOT WEARING YOUR PRINCESS BRIDE DRESS!
WAAH!
OK, FINE. YOU MAY WEAR THE DRESS, BUT YOU ARE NOT WEARING THAT VEIL!
WAAH!
YOU MAY WEAR THE VEIL, BUT YOU ARE NOT HUMILIATING YOUR MOTHER BY CARRYING A BRIDAL BOUQUET!
WAAH!!
"SANE MOTHERS OF 2-YEAR-OLDS" SHOULD GO RIGHT UNDER "WHALE" ON THE ENDANGERED SPECIES LIST.
ENDANGERED
CONDOR
BOBCAT
TIGER
WHALE

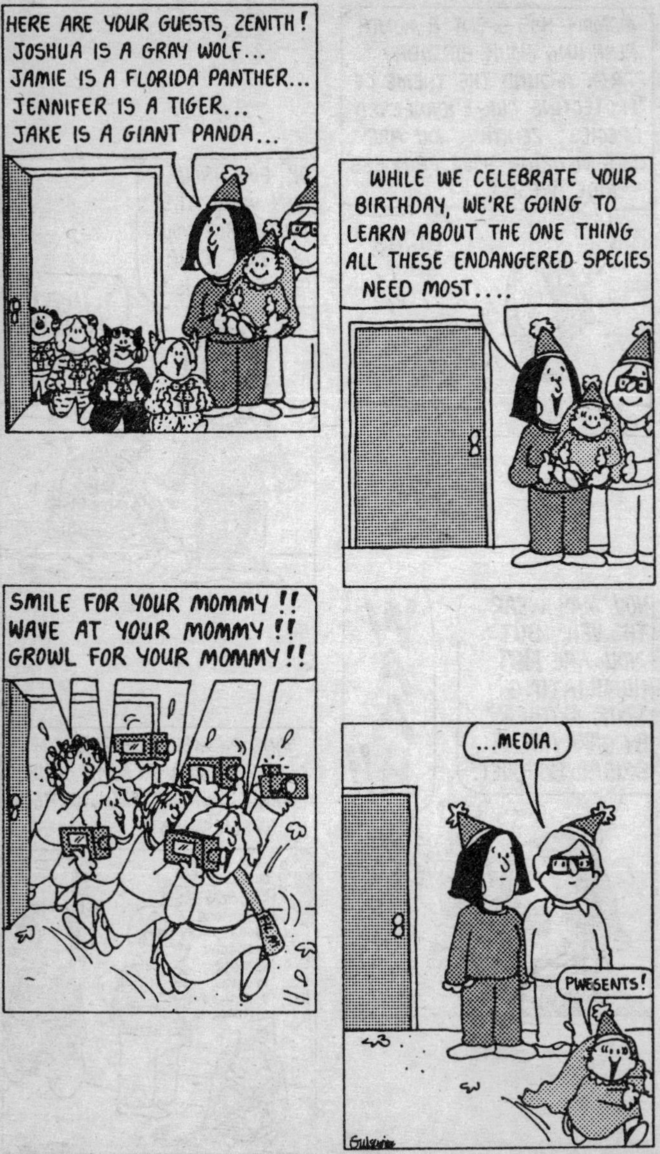
HERE ARE YOUR GUESTS, ZENITH! JOSHUA IS A GRAY WOLF... JAMIE IS A FLORIDA PANTHER... JENNIFER IS A TIGER... JAKE IS A GIANT PANDA...
WHILE WE CELEBRATE YOUR BIRTHDAY, WE'RE GOING TO LEARN ABOUT THE ONE THING ALL THESE ENDANGERED SPECIES NEED MOST....
SMILE FOR YOUR MOMMY!! WAVE AT YOUR MOMMY!! GROWL FOR YOUR MOMMY!!
...MEDIA.
PWESENTS!

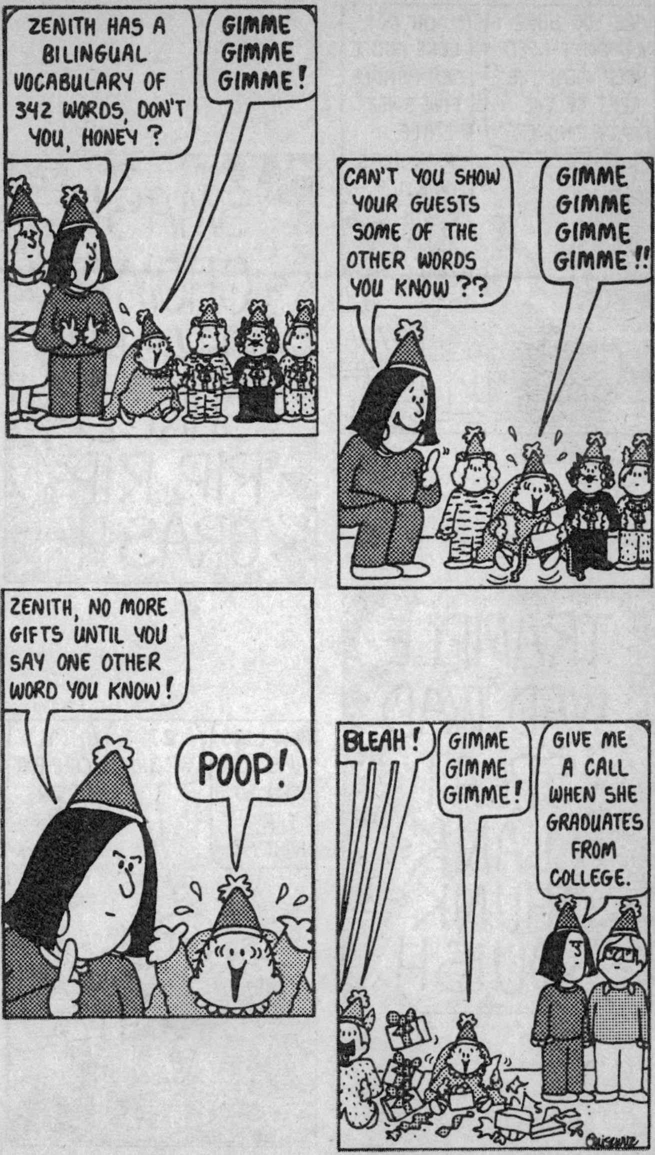

ZENITH HAS A BILINGUAL VOCABULARY OF 342 WORDS, DON'T YOU, HONEY ?
GIMME GIMME GIMME!
CAN'T YOU SHOW YOUR GUESTS SOME OF THE OTHER WORDS YOU KNOW ??
GIMME GIMME GIMME GIMME !!
ZENITH, NO MORE GIFTS UNTIL YOU SAY ONE OTHER WORD YOU KNOW!
POOP!
BLEAH!
GIMME GIMME GIMME!
GIVE ME A CALL WHEN SHE GRADUATES FROM COLLEGE.

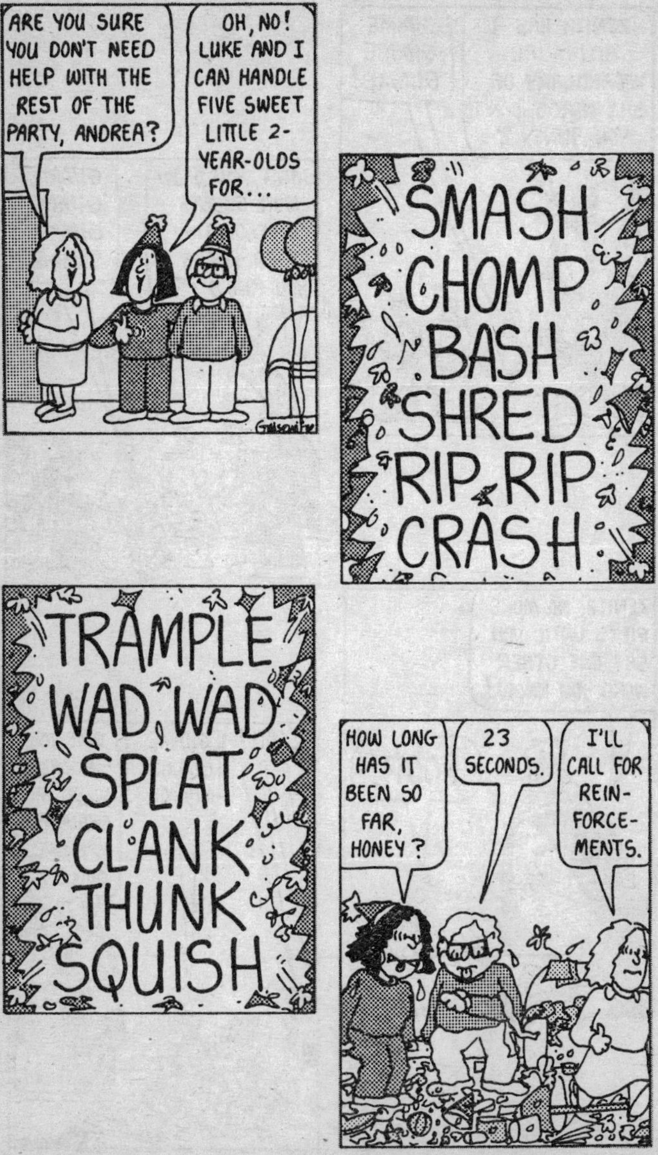
ARE YOU SURE YOU DON'T NEED HELP WITH THE REST OF THE PARTY, ANDREA?
OH, NO! LUKE AND I CAN HANDLE FIVE SWEET LITTLE 2-YEAR-OLDS FOR...
SMASH CHOMP BASH SHRED RIP RIP CRASH
TRAMPLE WAD WAD SPLAT CLANK THUNK SQUISH
HOW LONG HAS IT BEEN SO FAR, HONEY?
23 SECONDS.
I'LL CALL FOR REIN-FORCE-MENTS.

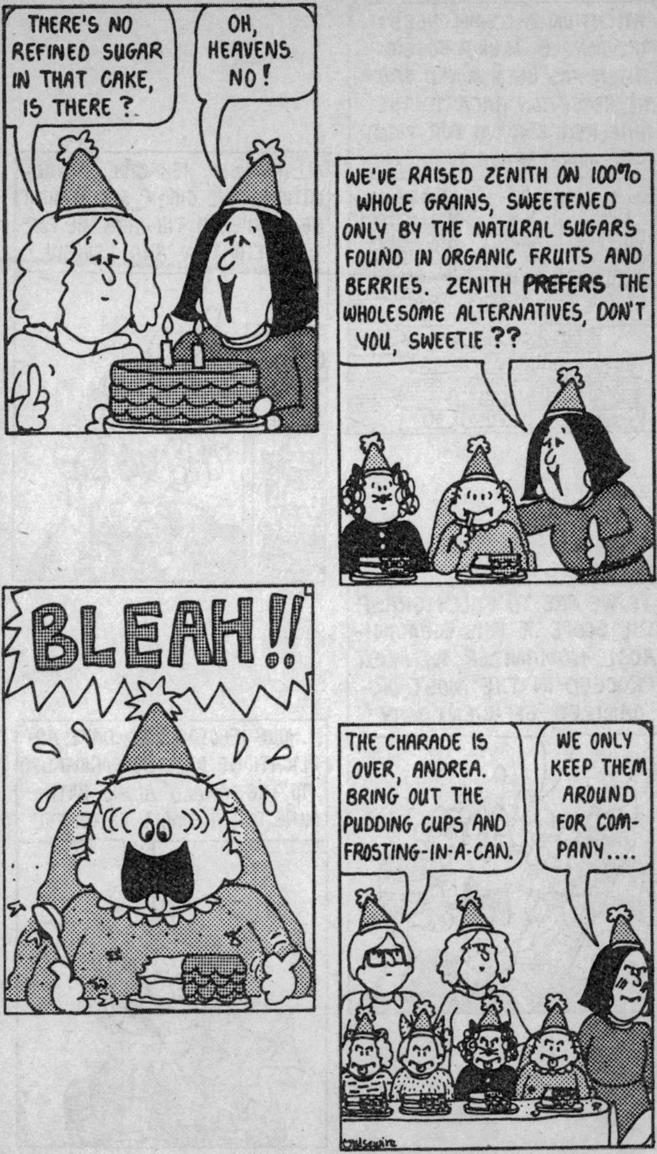
THERE'S NO REFINED SUGAR IN THAT CAKE, IS THERE ?
OH, HEAVENS NO !
WE'VE RAISED ZENITH ON 100% WHOLE GRAINS, SWEETENED ONLY BY THE NATURAL SUGARS FOUND IN ORGANIC FRUITS AND BERRIES. ZENITH PREFERS THE WHOLESOME ALTERNATIVES, DON'T YOU, SWEETIE ??
BLEAH !!
THE CHARADE IS OVER, ANDREA. BRING OUT THE PUDDING CUPS AND FROSTING-IN-A-CAN.
WE ONLY KEEP THEM AROUND FOR COM-PANY....

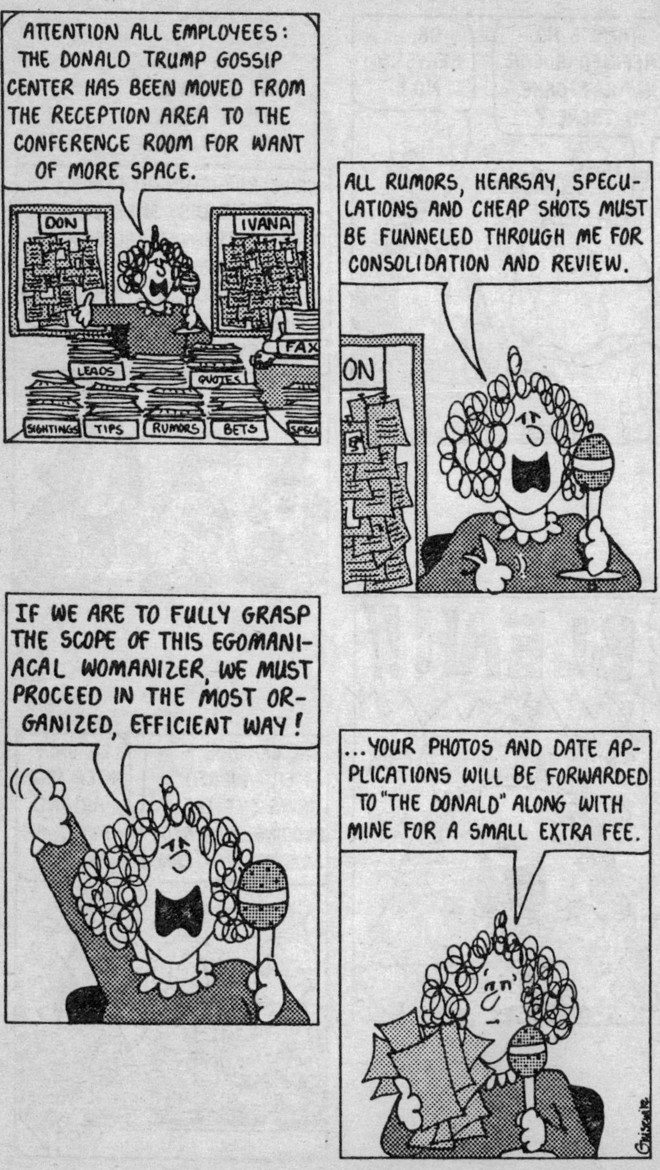
ATTENTION ALL EMPLOYEES: THE DONALD TRUMP GOSSIP CENTER HAS BEEN MOVED FROM THE RECEPTION AREA TO THE CONFERENCE ROOM FOR WANT OF MORE SPACE.
DON
IVANA
FAX
LEADS
QUOTES
SIGHTINGS
TIPS
RUMORS
BETS
ALL RUMORS, HEARSAY, SPECULATIONS AND CHEAP SHOTS MUST BE FUNNELED THROUGH ME FOR CONSOLIDATION AND REVIEW.
ON
IF WE ARE TO FULLY GRASP THE SCOPE OF THIS EGOMANIACAL WOMANIZER, WE MUST PROCEED IN THE MOST ORGANIZED, EFFICIENT WAY!
...YOUR PHOTOS AND DATE APPLICATIONS WILL BE FORWARDED TO "THE DONALD" ALONG WITH MINE FOR A SMALL EXTRA FEE.
Guisewite

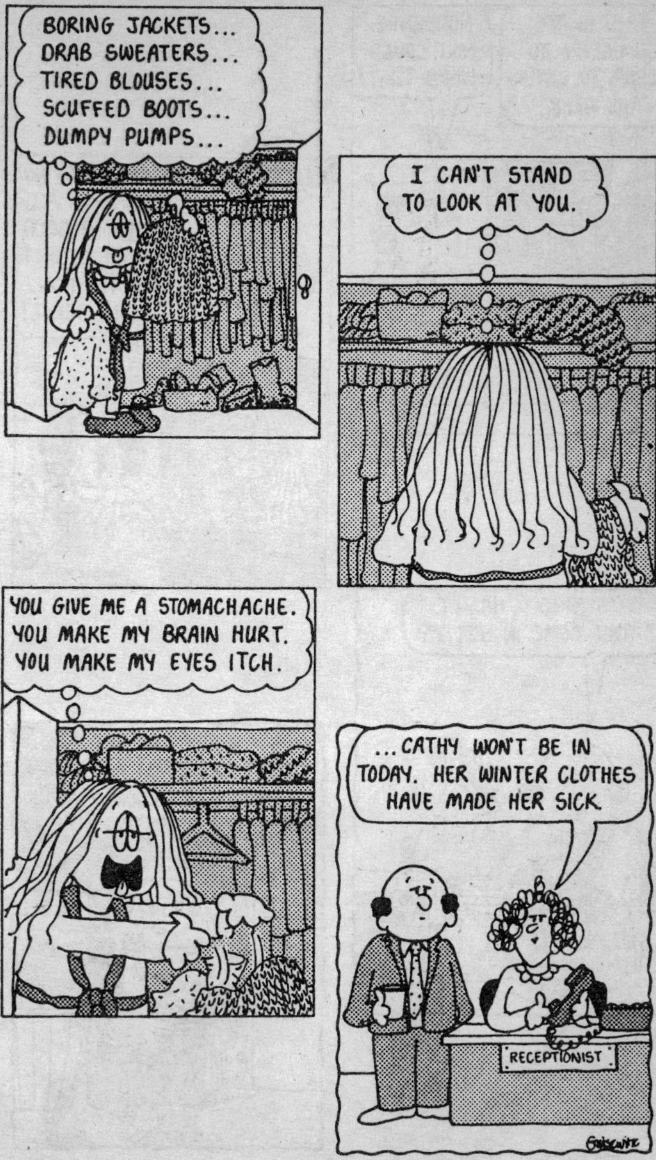
BORING JACKETS... DRAB SWEATERS... TIRED BLOUSES... SCUFFED BOOTS... DUMPY PUMPS...
I CAN'T STAND TO LOOK AT YOU.
YOU GIVE ME A STOMACHACHE. YOU MAKE MY BRAIN HURT. YOU MAKE MY EYES ITCH.
...CATHY WON'T BE IN TODAY. HER WINTER CLOTHES HAVE MADE HER SICK.
RECEPTIONIST

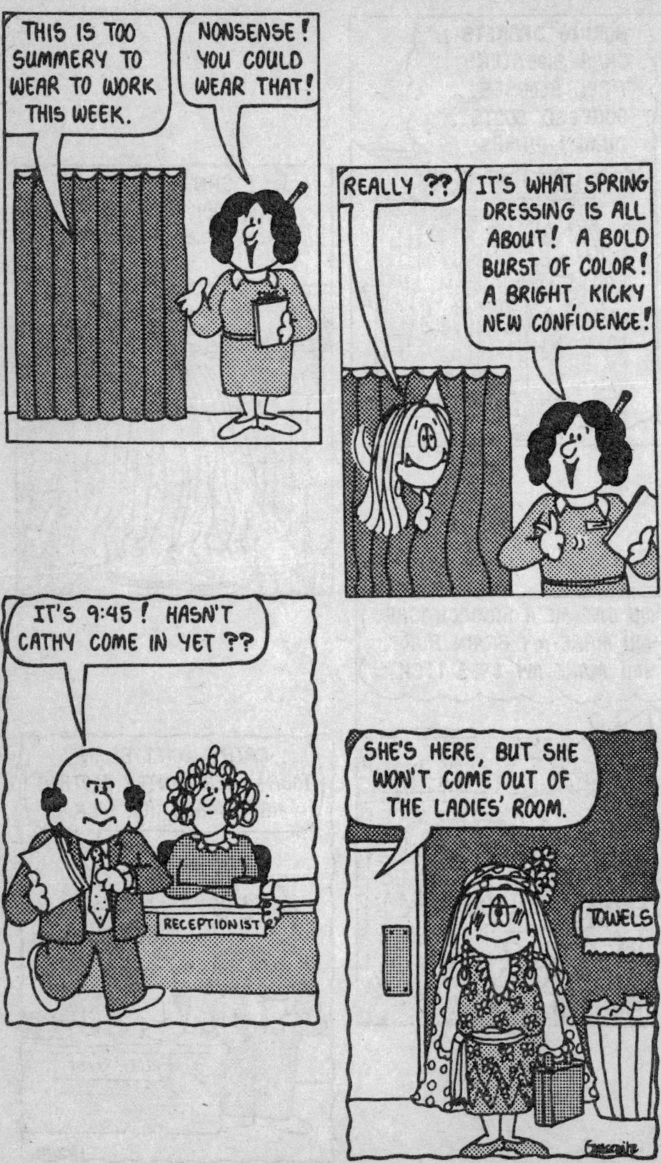
THIS IS TOO SUMMERY TO WEAR TO WORK THIS WEEK.
NONSENSE! YOU COULD WEAR THAT!
REALLY ??
IT'S WHAT SPRING DRESSING IS ALL ABOUT! A BOLD BURST OF COLOR! A BRIGHT, KICKY NEW CONFIDENCE!
IT'S 9:45! HASN'T CATHY COME IN YET ??
RECEPTIONIST
SHE'S HERE, BUT SHE WON'T COME OUT OF THE LADIES' ROOM.
TOWELS

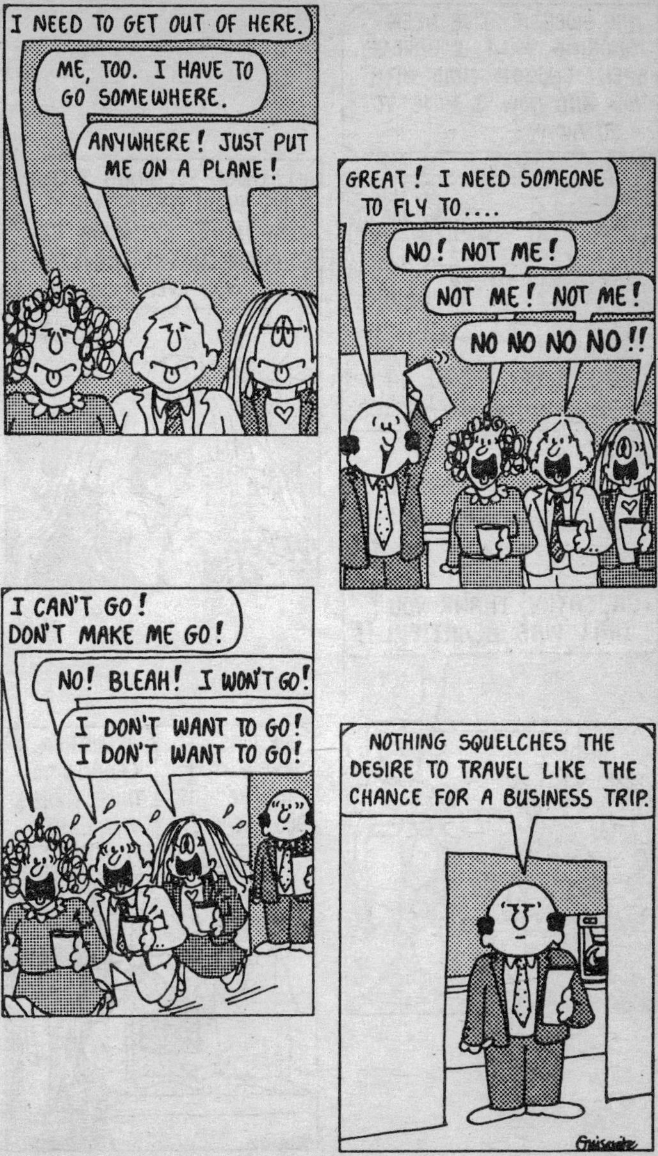
I NEED TO GET OUT OF HERE.
ME, TOO. I HAVE TO GO SOMEWHERE.
ANYWHERE! JUST PUT ME ON A PLANE!
GREAT! I NEED SOMEONE TO FLY TO....
NO! NOT ME!
NOT ME! NOT ME!
NO NO NO NO!!
I CAN'T GO! DON'T MAKE ME GO!
NO! BLEAH! I WON'T GO!
I DON'T WANT TO GO! I DON'T WANT TO GO!
NOTHING SQUELCHES THE DESIRE TO TRAVEL LIKE THE CHANCE FOR A BUSINESS TRIP.

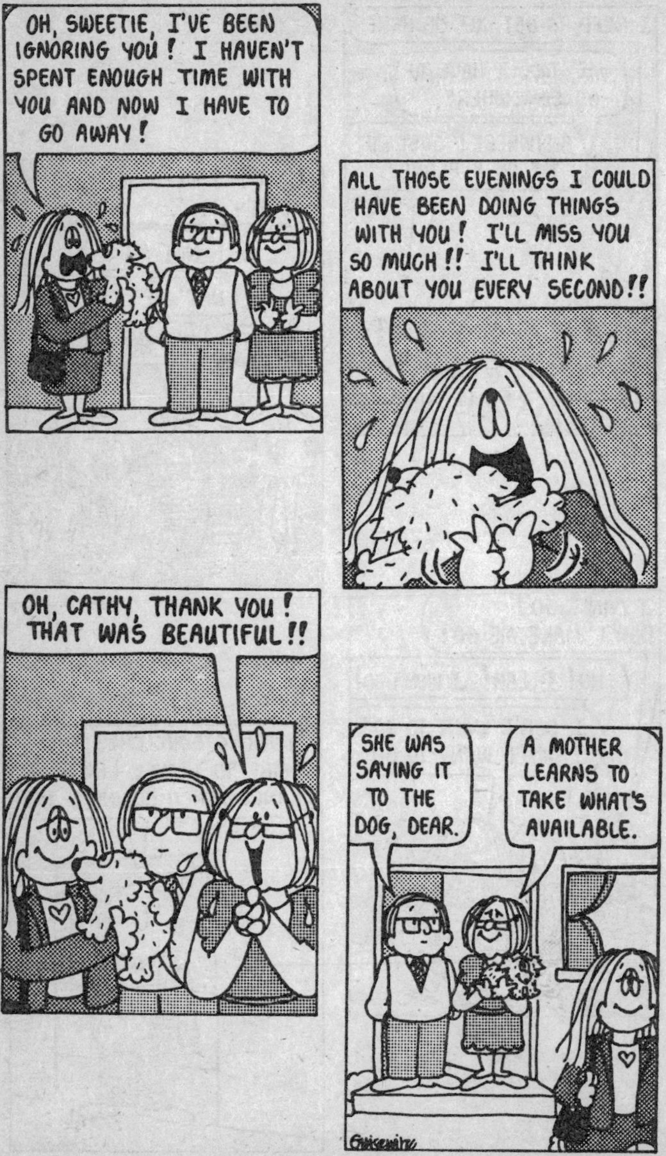
OH, SWEETIE, I'VE BEEN IGNORING YOU! I HAVEN'T SPENT ENOUGH TIME WITH YOU AND NOW I HAVE TO GO AWAY!
ALL THOSE EVENINGS I COULD HAVE BEEN DOING THINGS WITH YOU! I'LL MISS YOU SO MUCH!! I'LL THINK ABOUT YOU EVERY SECOND!!
OH, CATHY, THANK YOU! THAT WAS BEAUTIFUL!!
SHE WAS SAYING IT TO THE DOG, DEAR.
A MOTHER LEARNS TO TAKE WHAT'S AVAILABLE.

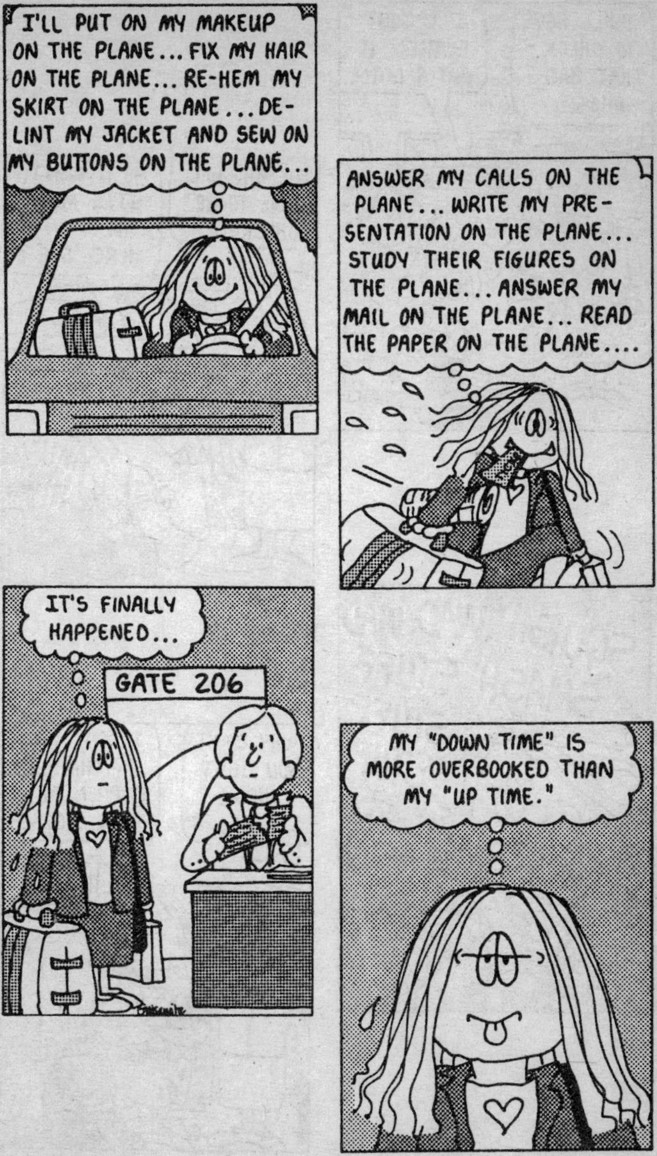
I'LL PUT ON MY MAKEUP ON THE PLANE... FIX MY HAIR ON THE PLANE... RE-HEM MY SKIRT ON THE PLANE... DE-LINT MY JACKET AND SEW ON MY BUTTONS ON THE PLANE...
ANSWER MY CALLS ON THE PLANE... WRITE MY PRESENTATION ON THE PLANE... STUDY THEIR FIGURES ON THE PLANE... ANSWER MY MAIL ON THE PLANE... READ THE PAPER ON THE PLANE....
IT'S FINALLY HAPPENED...
GATE 206
MY "DOWN TIME" IS MORE OVERBOOKED THAN MY "UP TIME."

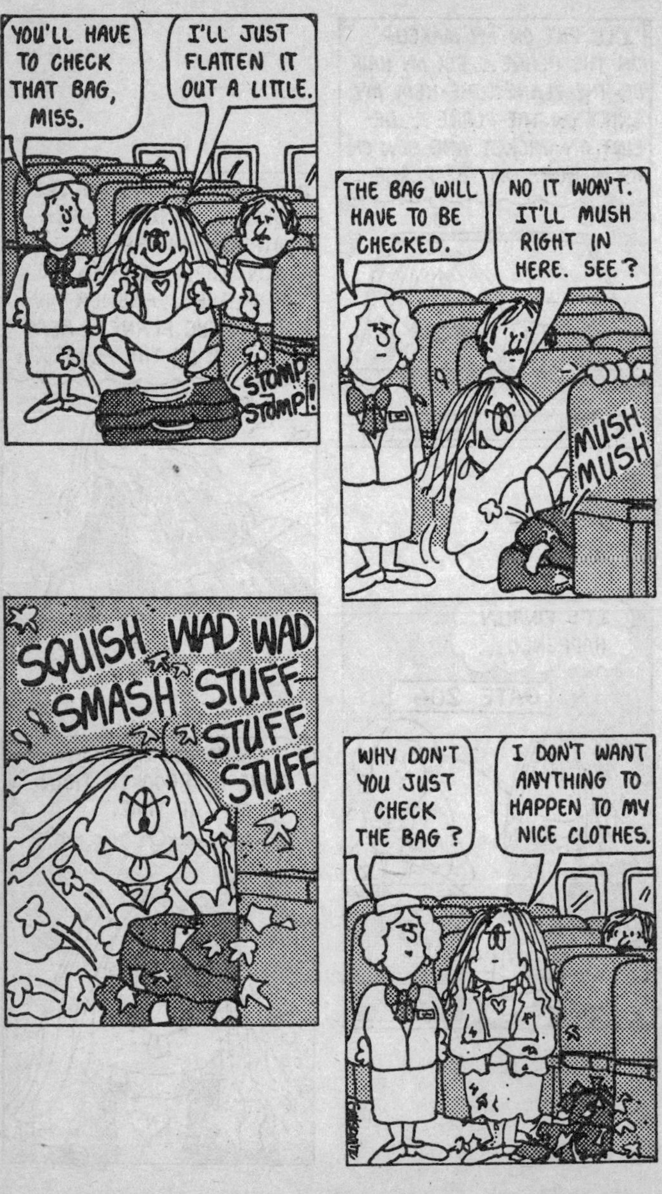

YOU'LL HAVE TO CHECK THAT BAG, MISS.
I'LL JUST FLATTEN IT OUT A LITTLE.
STOMP STOMP!!
THE BAG WILL HAVE TO BE CHECKED.
NO IT WON'T. IT'LL MUSH RIGHT IN HERE. SEE?
MUSH MUSH
SQUISH WAD WAD SMASH STUFF STUFF STUFF
WHY DON'T YOU JUST CHECK THE BAG?
I DON'T WANT ANYTHING TO HAPPEN TO MY NICE CLOTHES.

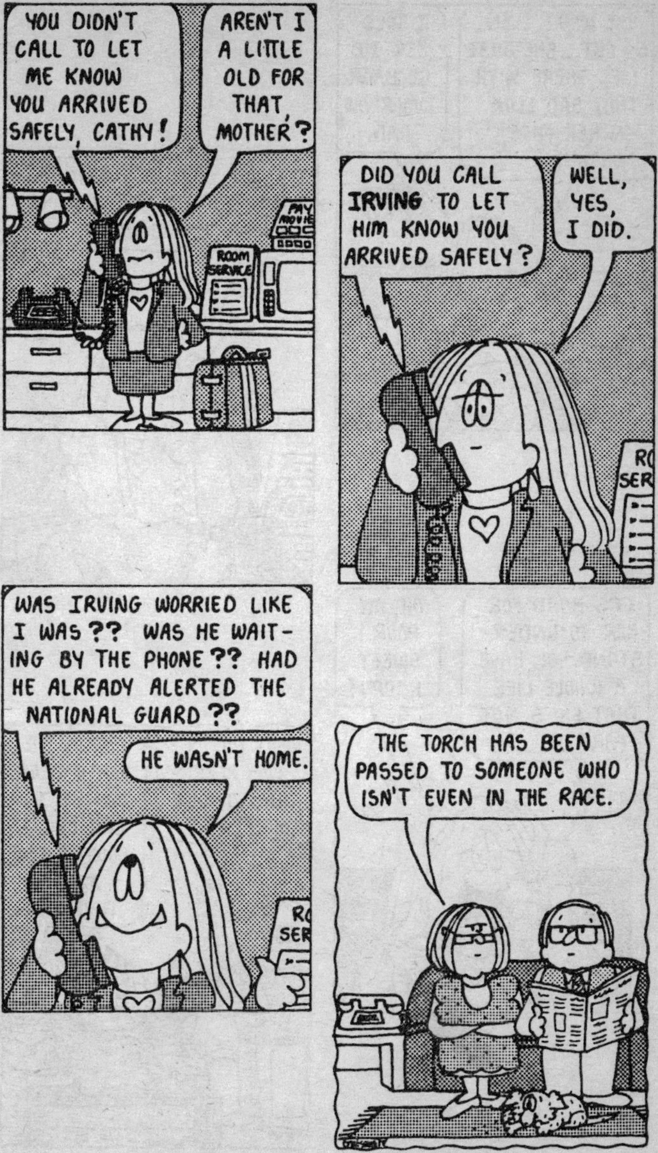
YOU DIDN'T CALL TO LET ME KNOW YOU ARRIVED SAFELY, CATHY!
AREN'T I A LITTLE OLD FOR THAT, MOTHER?
ROOM SERVICE
DID YOU CALL IRVING TO LET HIM KNOW YOU ARRIVED SAFELY?
WELL, YES, I DID.
WAS IRVING WORRIED LIKE I WAS?? WAS HE WAITING BY THE PHONE?? HAD HE ALREADY ALERTED THE NATIONAL GUARD??
HE WASN'T HOME.
THE TORCH HAS BEEN PASSED TO SOMEONE WHO ISN'T EVEN IN THE RACE.

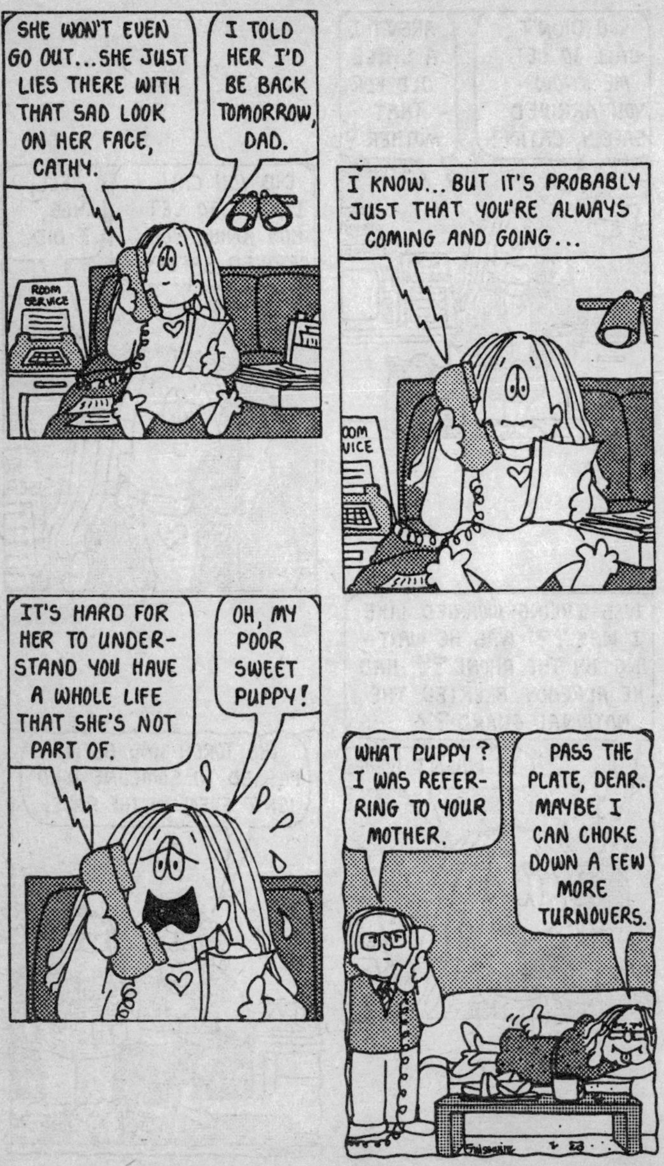
SHE WON'T EVEN GO OUT...SHE JUST LIES THERE WITH THAT SAD LOOK ON HER FACE, CATHY.
I TOLD HER I'D BE BACK TOMORROW, DAD.
ROOM SERVICE
I KNOW... BUT IT'S PROBABLY JUST THAT YOU'RE ALWAYS COMING AND GOING...
IT'S HARD FOR HER TO UNDER-STAND YOU HAVE A WHOLE LIFE THAT SHE'S NOT PART OF.
OH, MY POOR SWEET PUPPY!
WHAT PUPPY? I WAS REFER-RING TO YOUR MOTHER.
PASS THE PLATE, DEAR. MAYBE I CAN CHOKE DOWN A FEW MORE TURNOVERS.

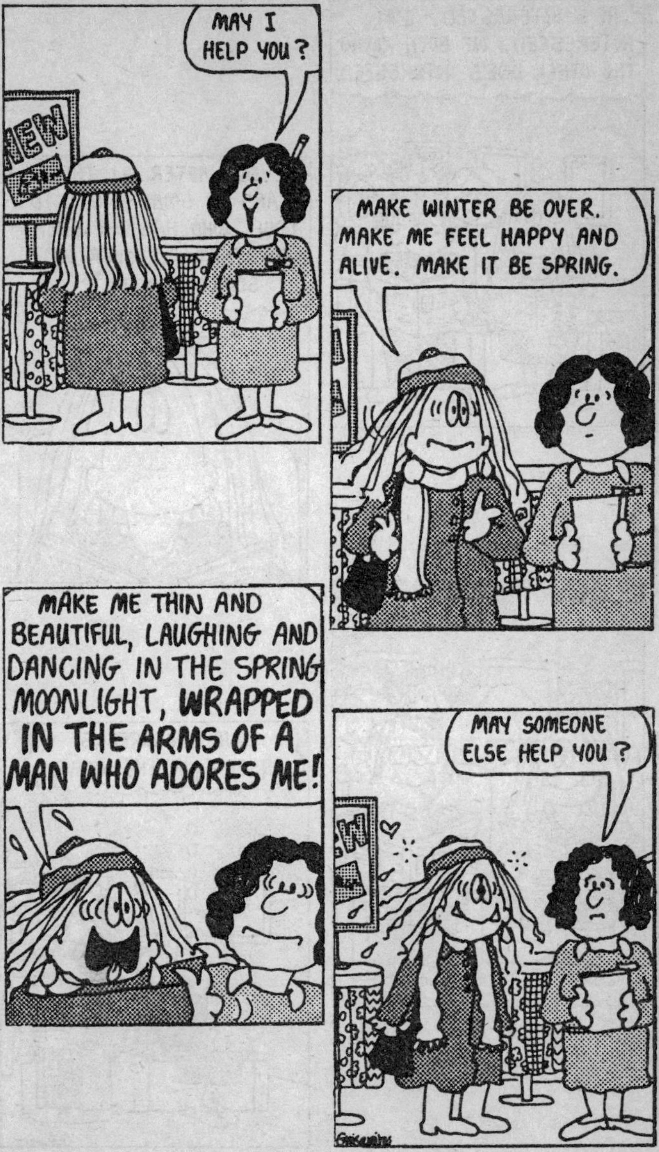
MAY I HELP YOU?
MAKE WINTER BE OVER. MAKE ME FEEL HAPPY AND ALIVE. MAKE IT BE SPRING.
MAKE ME THIN AND BEAUTIFUL, LAUGHING AND DANCING IN THE SPRING MOONLIGHT, WRAPPED IN THE ARMS OF A MAN WHO ADORES ME!
MAY SOMEONE ELSE HELP YOU?

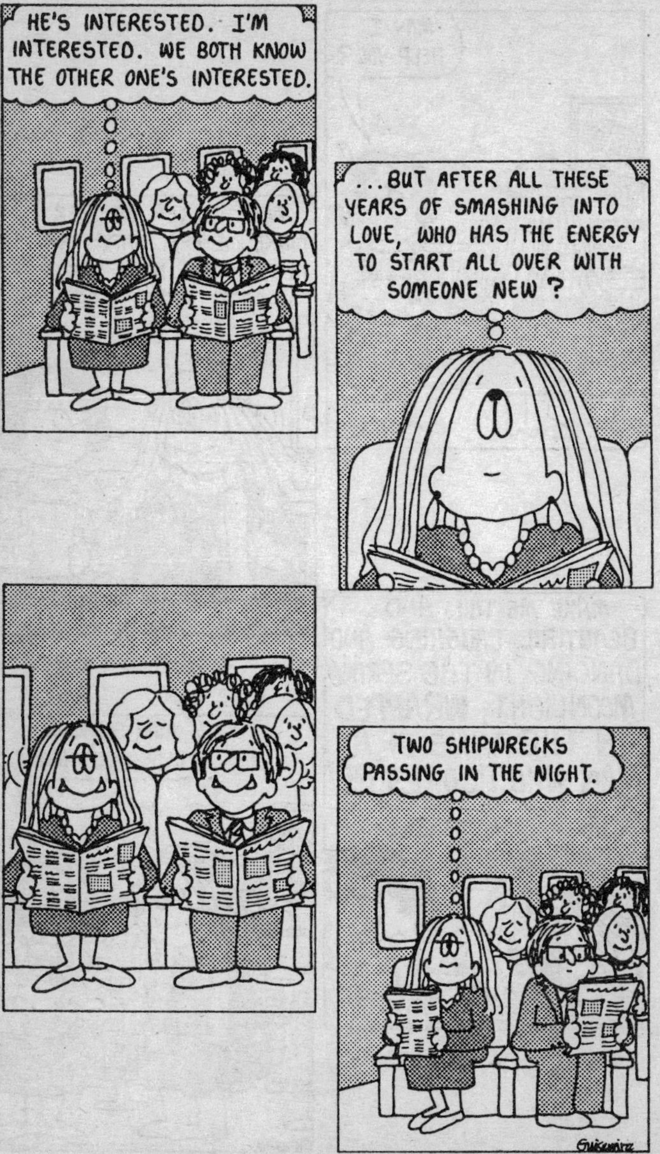
HE'S INTERESTED. I'M INTERESTED. WE BOTH KNOW THE OTHER ONE'S INTERESTED.
...BUT AFTER ALL THESE YEARS OF SMASHING INTO LOVE, WHO HAS THE ENERGY TO START ALL OVER WITH SOMEONE NEW?
TWO SHIPWRECKS PASSING IN THE NIGHT.
Guisewite

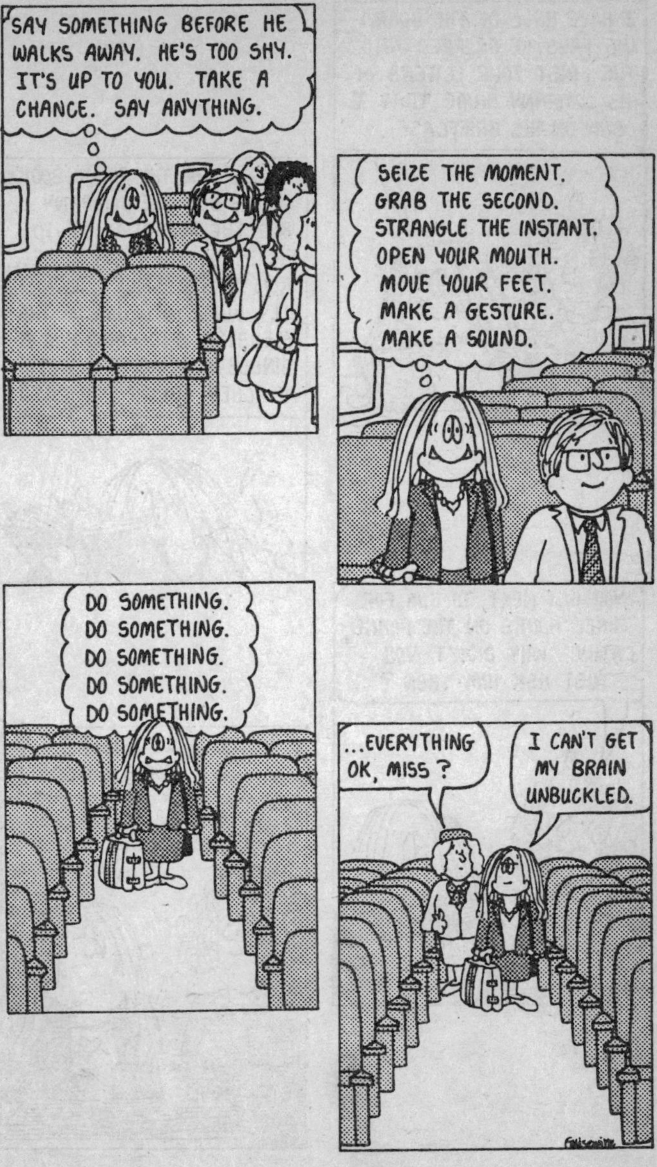
SAY SOMETHING BEFORE HE WALKS AWAY. HE'S TOO SHY. IT'S UP TO YOU. TAKE A CHANCE. SAY ANYTHING.
SEIZE THE MOMENT. GRAB THE SECOND. STRANGLE THE INSTANT. OPEN YOUR MOUTH. MOVE YOUR FEET. MAKE A GESTURE. MAKE A SOUND.
DO SOMETHING. DO SOMETHING. DO SOMETHING. DO SOMETHING. DO SOMETHING.
...EVERYTHING OK, MISS?
I CAN'T GET MY BRAIN UNBUCKLED.

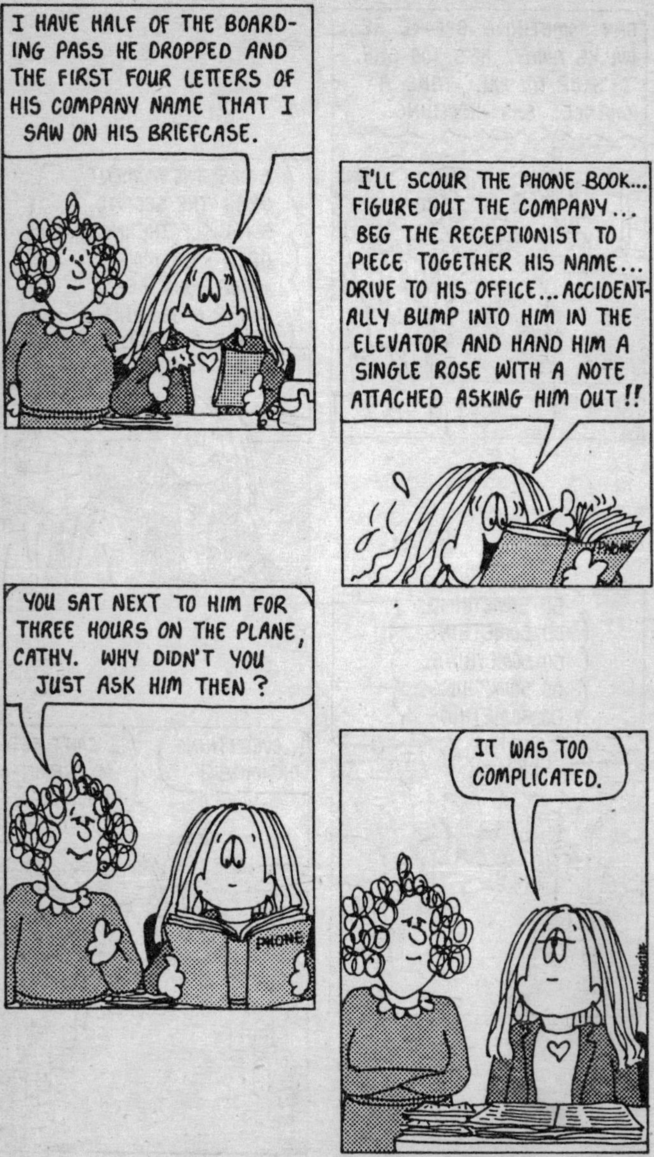
I HAVE HALF OF THE BOARDING PASS HE DROPPED AND THE FIRST FOUR LETTERS OF HIS COMPANY NAME THAT I SAW ON HIS BRIEFCASE.
I'LL SCOUR THE PHONE BOOK... FIGURE OUT THE COMPANY... BEG THE RECEPTIONIST TO PIECE TOGETHER HIS NAME... DRIVE TO HIS OFFICE... ACCIDENTALLY BUMP INTO HIM IN THE ELEVATOR AND HAND HIM A SINGLE ROSE WITH A NOTE ATTACHED ASKING HIM OUT!!
PHONE
YOU SAT NEXT TO HIM FOR THREE HOURS ON THE PLANE, CATHY. WHY DIDN'T YOU JUST ASK HIM THEN?
PHONE
IT WAS TOO COMPLICATED.

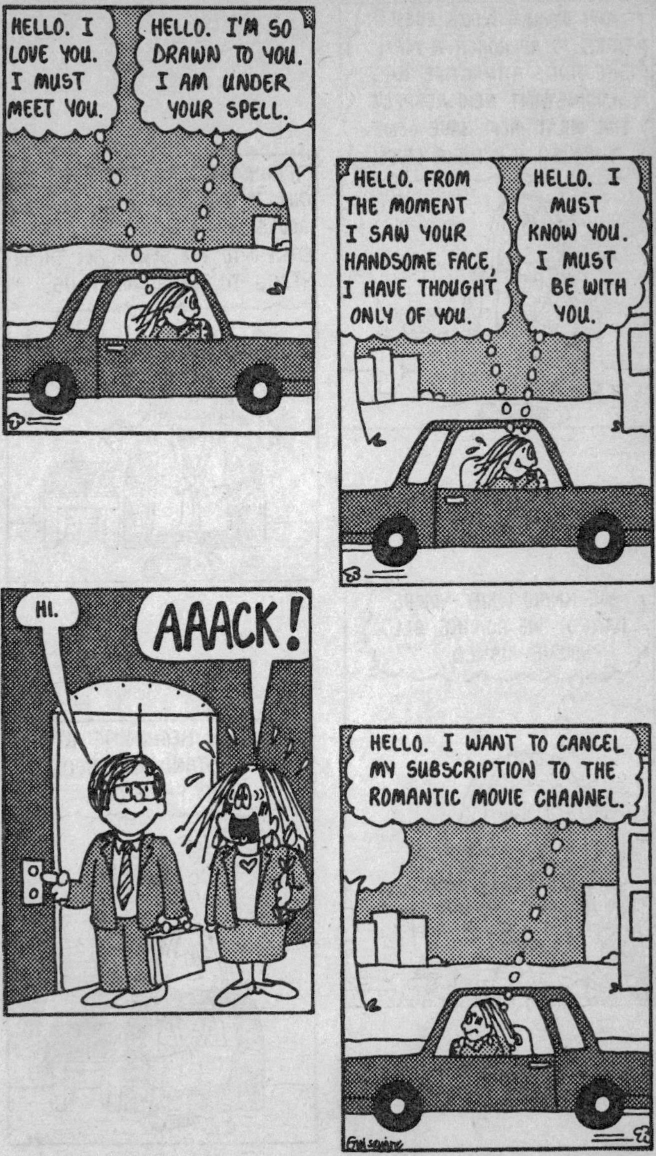
HELLO. I LOVE YOU. I MUST MEET YOU.
HELLO. I'M SO DRAWN TO YOU. I AM UNDER YOUR SPELL.
HELLO. FROM THE MOMENT I SAW YOUR HANDSOME FACE, I HAVE THOUGHT ONLY OF YOU.
HELLO. I MUST KNOW YOU. I MUST BE WITH YOU.
HI.
AAACK!
HELLO. I WANT TO CANCEL MY SUBSCRIPTION TO THE ROMANTIC MOVIE CHANNEL.

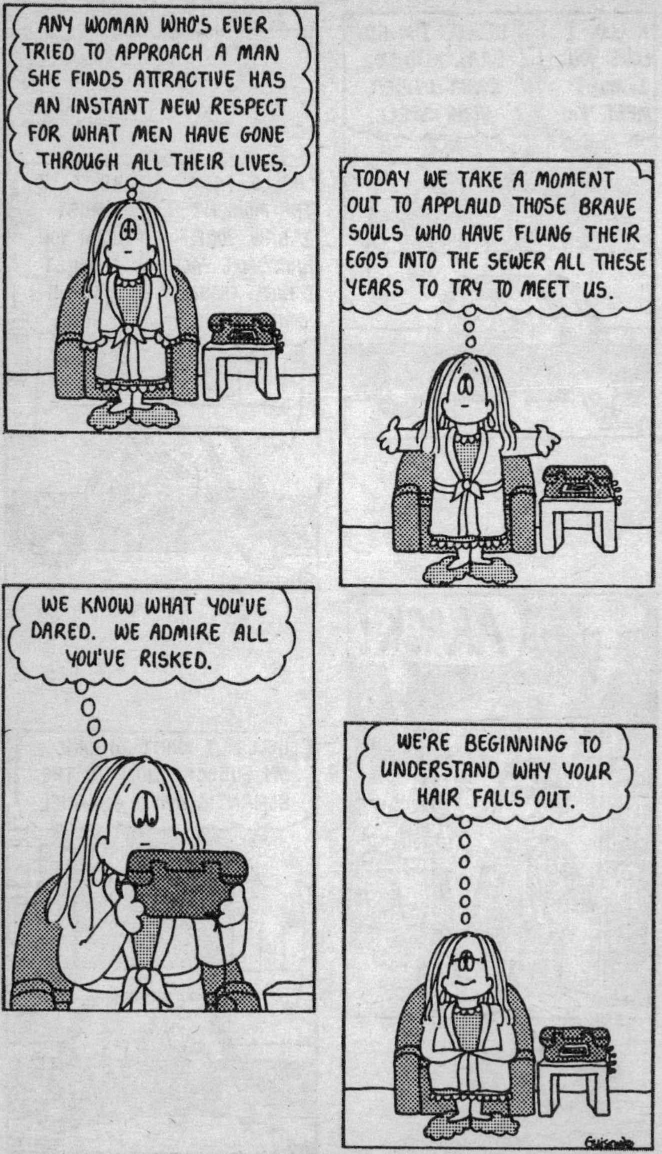
ANY WOMAN WHO'S EVER TRIED TO APPROACH A MAN SHE FINDS ATTRACTIVE HAS AN INSTANT NEW RESPECT FOR WHAT MEN HAVE GONE THROUGH ALL THEIR LIVES.
TODAY WE TAKE A MOMENT OUT TO APPLAUD THOSE BRAVE SOULS WHO HAVE FLUNG THEIR EGOS INTO THE SEWER ALL THESE YEARS TO TRY TO MEET US.
WE KNOW WHAT YOU'VE DARED. WE ADMIRE ALL YOU'VE RISKED.
WE'RE BEGINNING TO UNDERSTAND WHY YOUR HAIR FALLS OUT.

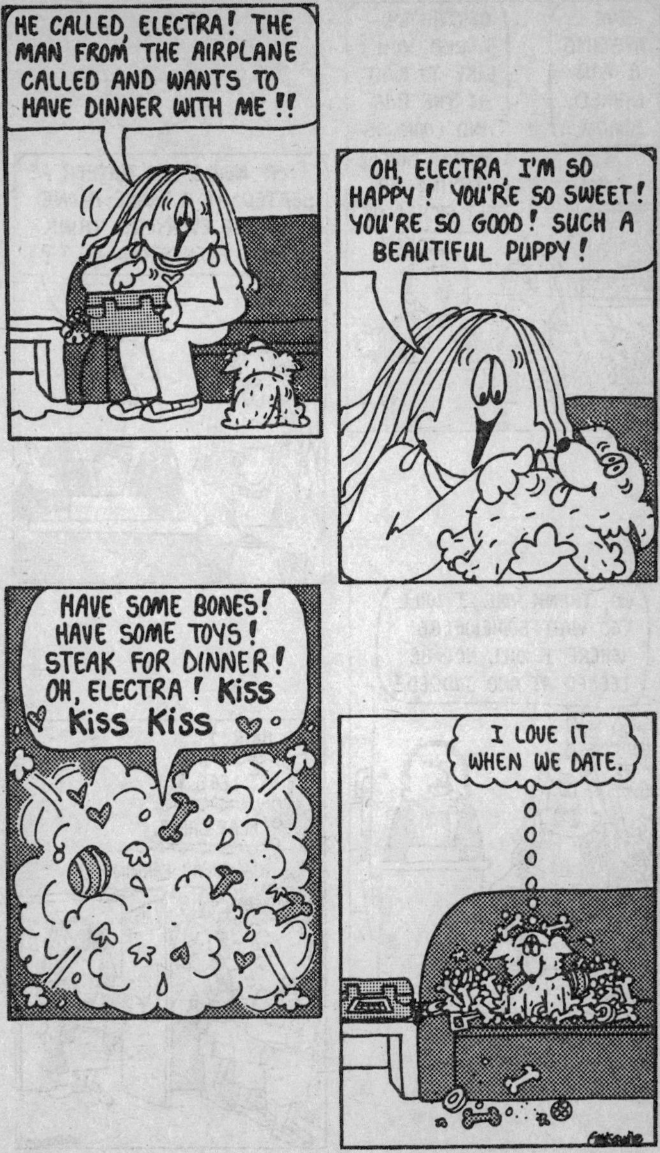
HE CALLED, ELECTRA! THE MAN FROM THE AIRPLANE CALLED AND WANTS TO HAVE DINNER WITH ME !!
OH, ELECTRA, I'M SO HAPPY ! YOU'RE SO SWEET! YOU'RE SO GOOD! SUCH A BEAUTIFUL PUPPY !
HAVE SOME BONES! HAVE SOME TOYS! STEAK FOR DINNER! OH, ELECTRA! Kiss Kiss Kiss
I LOVE IT WHEN WE DATE.

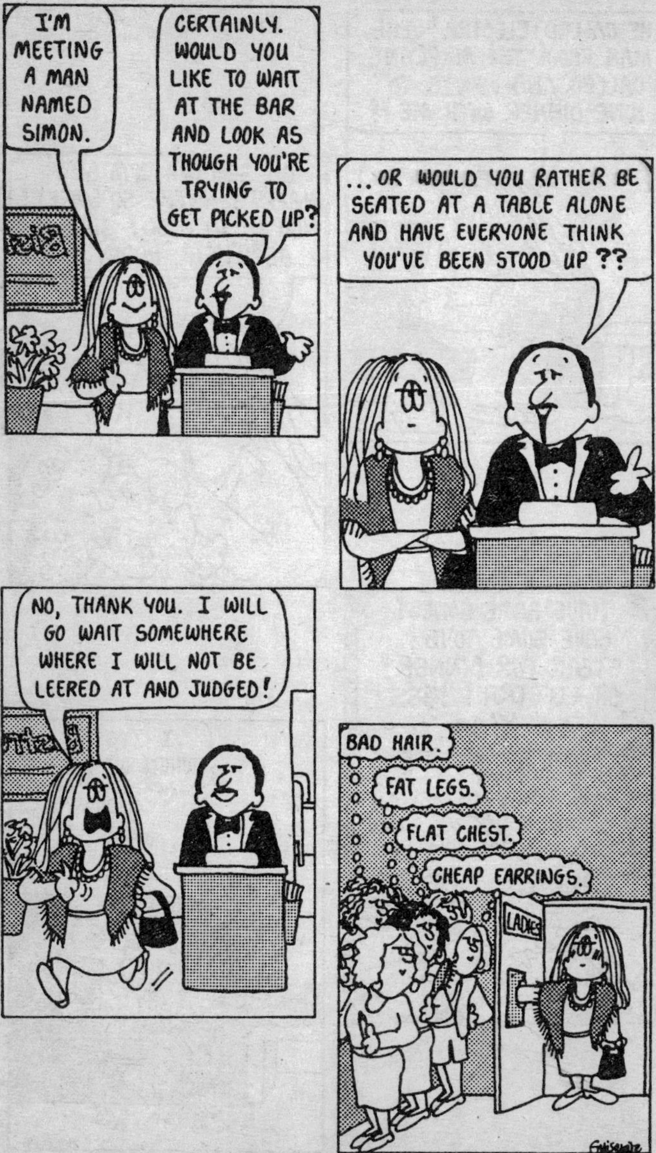

I'M MEETING A MAN NAMED SIMON.
CERTAINLY. WOULD YOU LIKE TO WAIT AT THE BAR AND LOOK AS THOUGH YOU'RE TRYING TO GET PICKED UP?
...OR WOULD YOU RATHER BE SEATED AT A TABLE ALONE AND HAVE EVERYONE THINK YOU'VE BEEN STOOD UP??
NO, THANK YOU. I WILL GO WAIT SOMEWHERE WHERE I WILL NOT BE LEERED AT AND JUDGED!
BAD HAIR.
FAT LEGS.
FLAT CHEST.
CHEAP EARRINGS.
LADIES

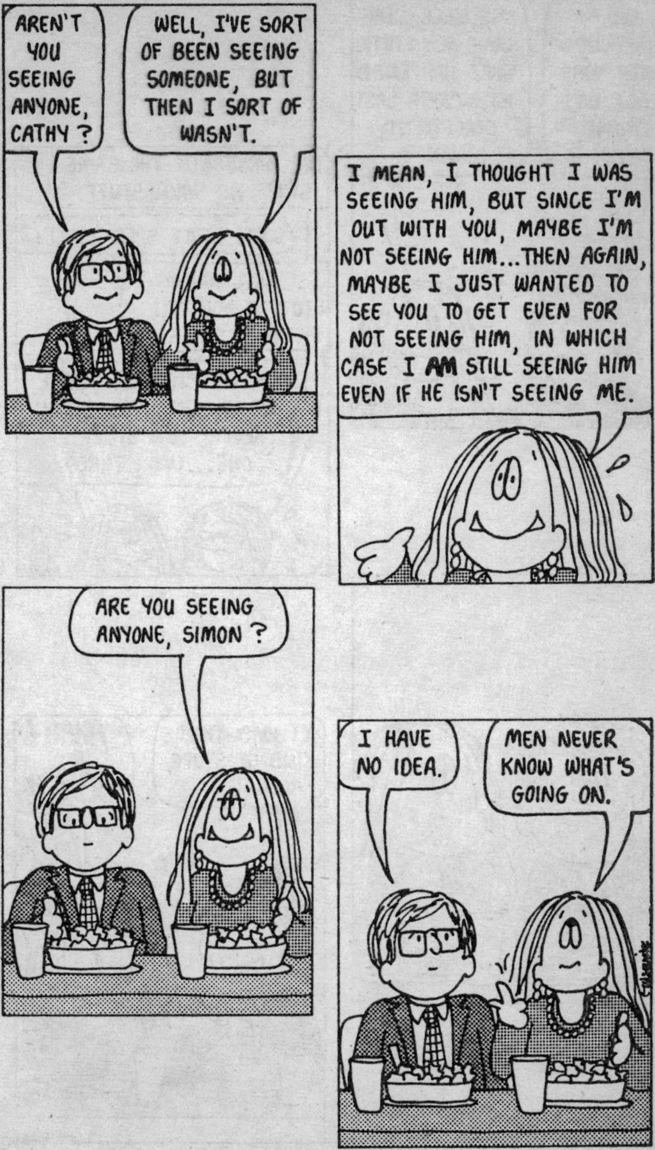
AREN'T YOU SEEING ANYONE, CATHY ?
WELL, I'VE SORT OF BEEN SEEING SOMEONE, BUT THEN I SORT OF WASN'T.
I MEAN, I THOUGHT I WAS SEEING HIM, BUT SINCE I'M OUT WITH YOU, MAYBE I'M NOT SEEING HIM... THEN AGAIN, MAYBE I JUST WANTED TO SEE YOU TO GET EVEN FOR NOT SEEING HIM, IN WHICH CASE I AM STILL SEEING HIM EVEN IF HE ISN'T SEEING ME.
ARE YOU SEEING ANYONE, SIMON ?
I HAVE NO IDEA.
MEN NEVER KNOW WHAT'S GOING ON.

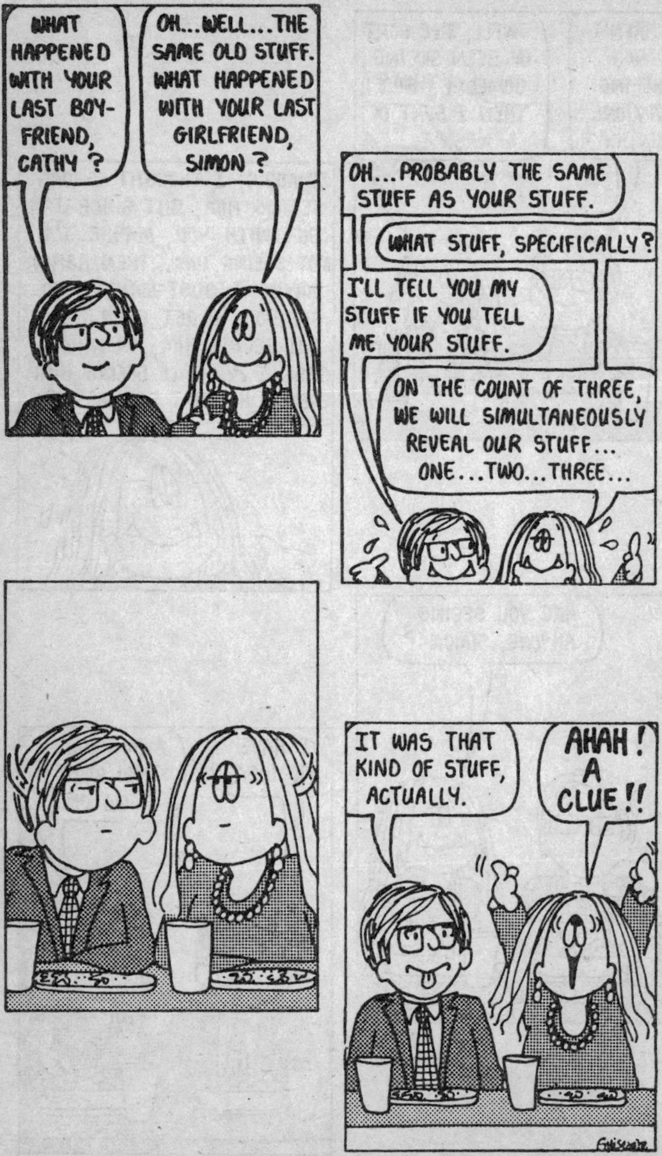
WHAT HAPPENED WITH YOUR LAST BOY-FRIEND, CATHY ?
OH...WELL...THE SAME OLD STUFF. WHAT HAPPENED WITH YOUR LAST GIRLFRIEND, SIMON ?
OH...PROBABLY THE SAME STUFF AS YOUR STUFF.
WHAT STUFF, SPECIFICALLY?
I'LL TELL YOU MY STUFF IF YOU TELL ME YOUR STUFF.
ON THE COUNT OF THREE, WE WILL SIMULTANEOUSLY REVEAL OUR STUFF... ONE...TWO...THREE...
IT WAS THAT KIND OF STUFF, ACTUALLY.
AHAH! A CLUE!!

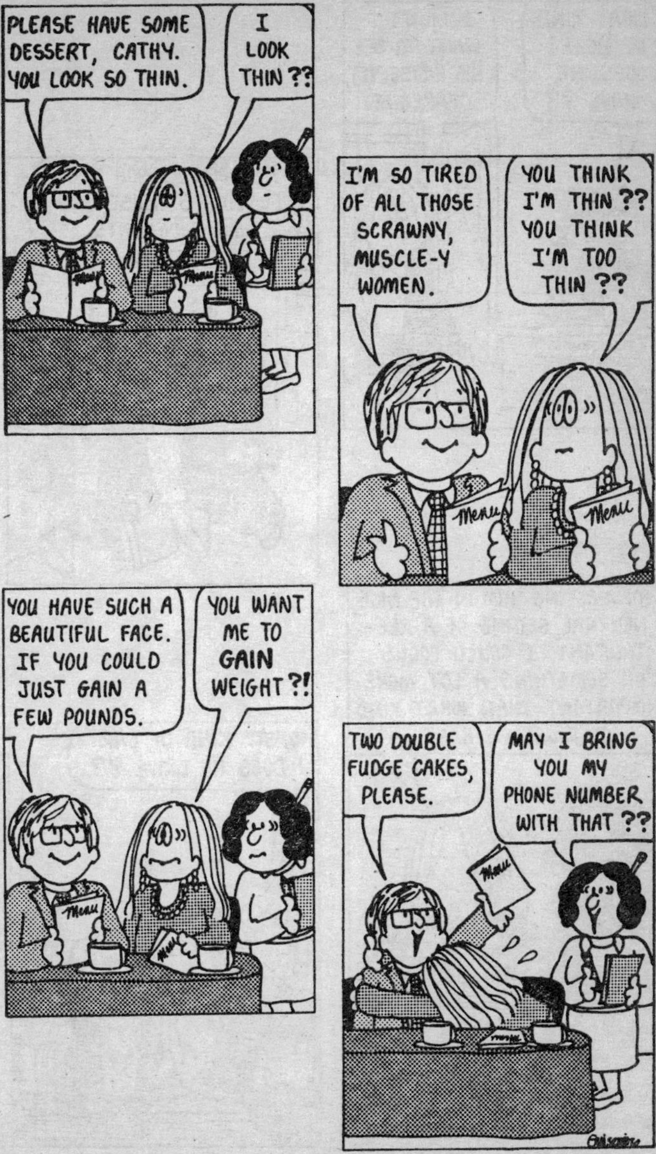
PLEASE HAVE SOME DESSERT, CATHY. YOU LOOK SO THIN.
I LOOK THIN??
I'M SO TIRED OF ALL THOSE SCRAWNY, MUSCLE-Y WOMEN.
YOU THINK I'M THIN?? YOU THINK I'M TOO THIN??
YOU HAVE SUCH A BEAUTIFUL FACE. IF YOU COULD JUST GAIN A FEW POUNDS.
YOU WANT ME TO GAIN WEIGHT?!
TWO DOUBLE FUDGE CAKES, PLEASE.
MAY I BRING YOU MY PHONE NUMBER WITH THAT??

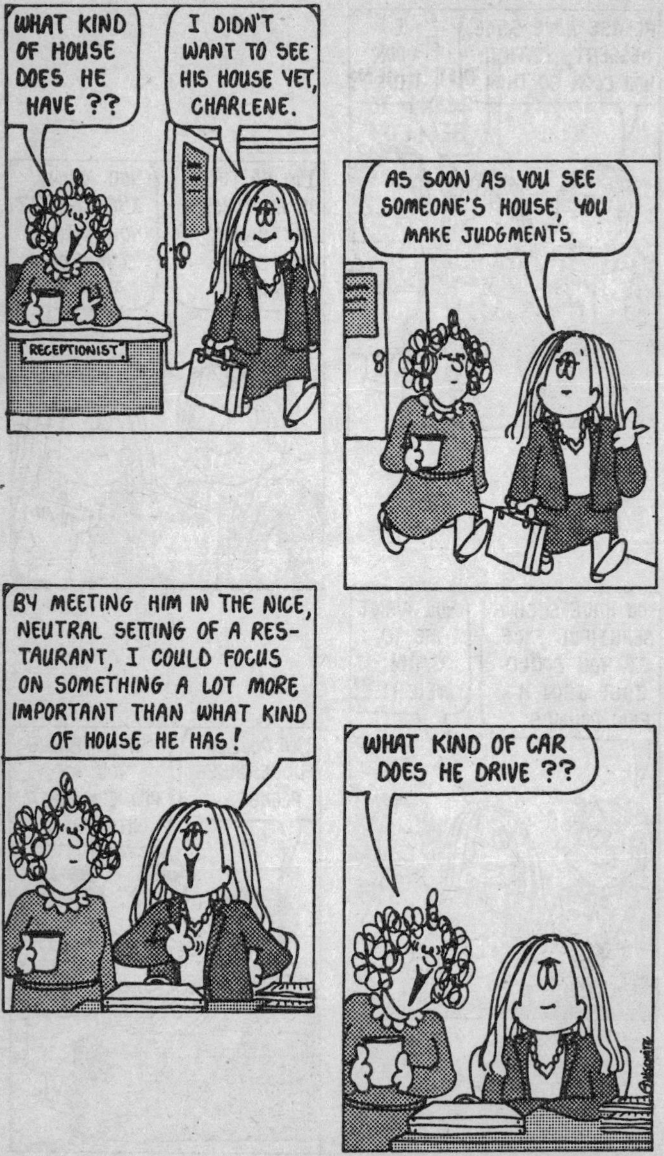
WHAT KIND OF HOUSE DOES HE HAVE ??
I DIDN'T WANT TO SEE HIS HOUSE YET, CHARLENE.
RECEPTIONIST
AS SOON AS YOU SEE SOMEONE'S HOUSE, YOU MAKE JUDGMENTS.
BY MEETING HIM IN THE NICE, NEUTRAL SETTING OF A RESTAURANT, I COULD FOCUS ON SOMETHING A LOT MORE IMPORTANT THAN WHAT KIND OF HOUSE HE HAS!
WHAT KIND OF CAR DOES HE DRIVE ??

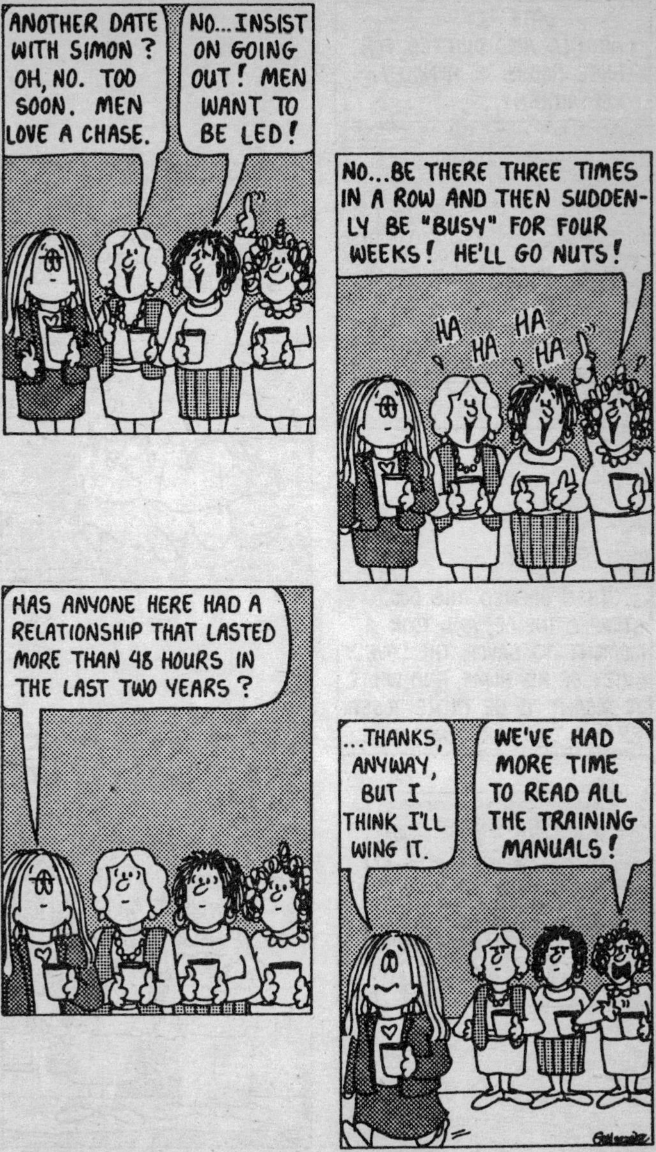
ANOTHER DATE WITH SIMON? OH, NO. TOO SOON. MEN LOVE A CHASE.
NO...INSIST ON GOING OUT! MEN WANT TO BE LED!
NO...BE THERE THREE TIMES IN A ROW AND THEN SUDDEN-LY BE "BUSY" FOR FOUR WEEKS! HE'LL GO NUTS!
HA HA HA HA
HAS ANYONE HERE HAD A RELATIONSHIP THAT LASTED MORE THAN 48 HOURS IN THE LAST TWO YEARS?
...THANKS, ANYWAY, BUT I THINK I'LL WING IT.
WE'VE HAD MORE TIME TO READ ALL THE TRAINING MANUALS!

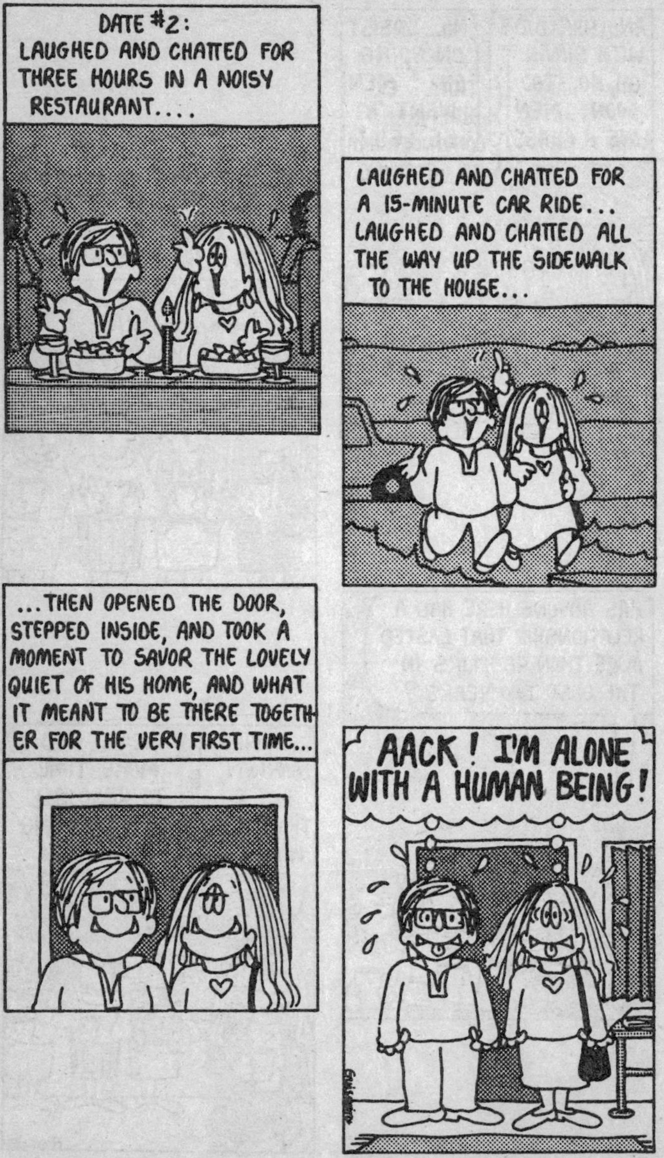
DATE #2:
LAUGHED AND CHATTED FOR THREE HOURS IN A NOISY RESTAURANT....
LAUGHED AND CHATTED FOR A 15-MINUTE CAR RIDE... LAUGHED AND CHATTED ALL THE WAY UP THE SIDEWALK TO THE HOUSE...
...THEN OPENED THE DOOR, STEPPED INSIDE, AND TOOK A MOMENT TO SAVOR THE LOVELY QUIET OF HIS HOME, AND WHAT IT MEANT TO BE THERE TOGETHER FOR THE VERY FIRST TIME...
AACK! I'M ALONE WITH A HUMAN BEING!

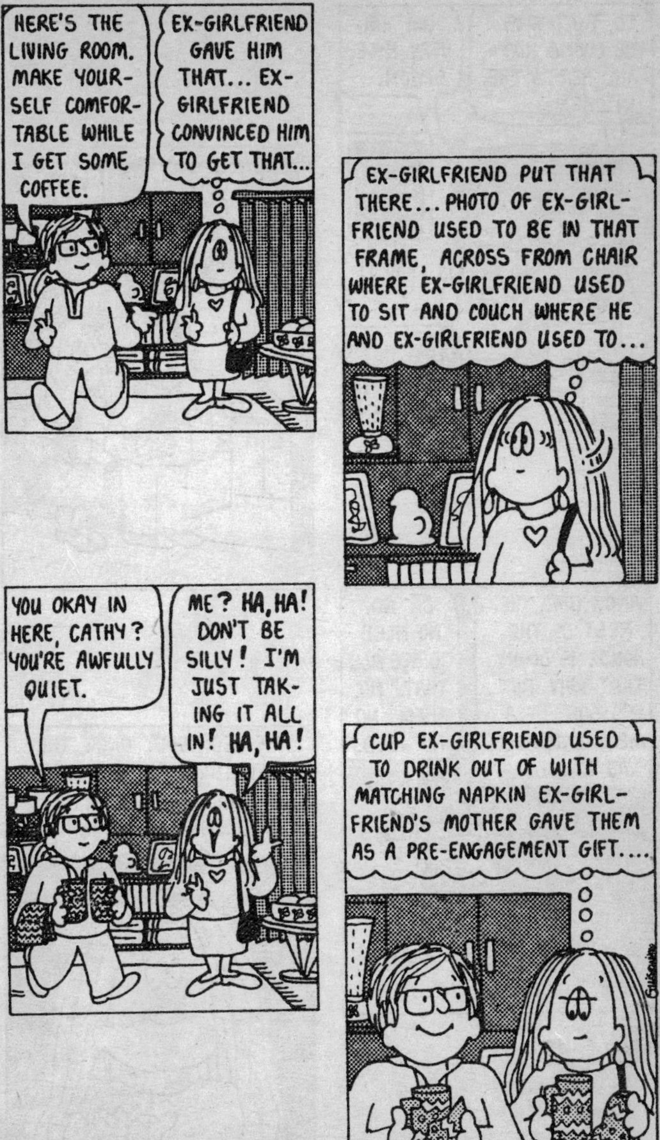
HERE'S THE LIVING ROOM. MAKE YOURSELF COMFORTABLE WHILE I GET SOME COFFEE.
EX-GIRLFRIEND GAVE HIM THAT... EX-GIRLFRIEND CONVINCED HIM TO GET THAT...
EX-GIRLFRIEND PUT THAT THERE... PHOTO OF EX-GIRLFRIEND USED TO BE IN THAT FRAME, ACROSS FROM CHAIR WHERE EX-GIRLFRIEND USED TO SIT AND COUCH WHERE HE AND EX-GIRLFRIEND USED TO...
YOU OKAY IN HERE, CATHY? YOU'RE AWFULLY QUIET.
ME? HA, HA! DON'T BE SILLY! I'M JUST TAKING IT ALL IN! HA, HA!
CUP EX-GIRLFRIEND USED TO DRINK OUT OF WITH MATCHING NAPKIN EX-GIRLFRIEND'S MOTHER GAVE THEM AS A PRE-ENGAGEMENT GIFT....

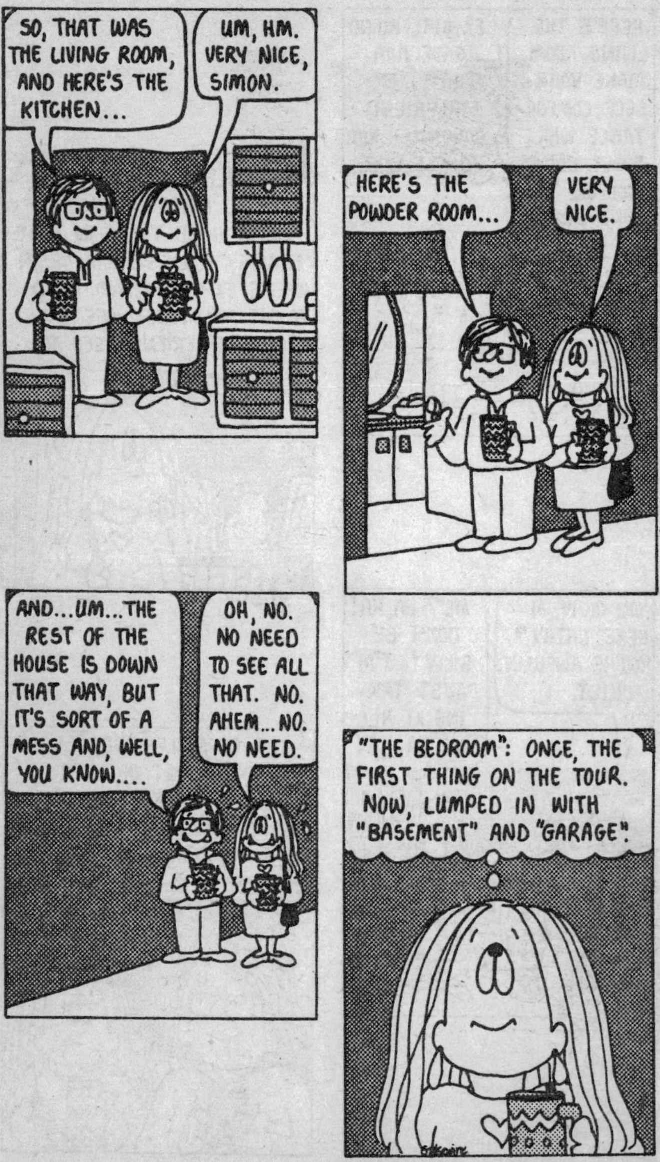
SO, THAT WAS THE LIVING ROOM, AND HERE'S THE KITCHEN...
UM, HM. VERY NICE, SIMON.
HERE'S THE POWDER ROOM...
VERY NICE.
AND...UM...THE REST OF THE HOUSE IS DOWN THAT WAY, BUT IT'S SORT OF A MESS AND, WELL, YOU KNOW....
OH, NO. NO NEED TO SEE ALL THAT. NO. AHEM...NO. NO NEED.
"THE BEDROOM": ONCE, THE FIRST THING ON THE TOUR. NOW, LUMPED IN WITH "BASEMENT" AND "GARAGE".

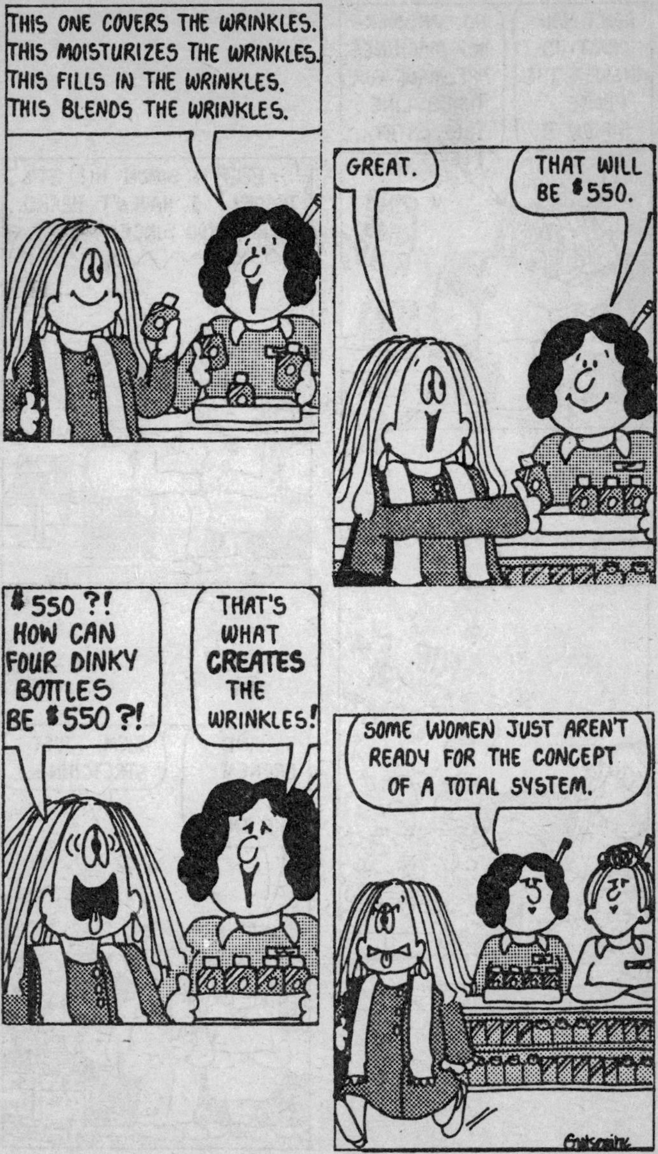
THIS ONE COVERS THE WRINKLES. THIS MOISTURIZES THE WRINKLES. THIS FILLS IN THE WRINKLES. THIS BLENDS THE WRINKLES.
GREAT.
THAT WILL BE $550.
$550 ?! HOW CAN FOUR DINKY BOTTLES BE $550 ?!
THAT'S WHAT CREATES THE WRINKLES!
SOME WOMEN JUST AREN'T READY FOR THE CONCEPT OF A TOTAL SYSTEM.

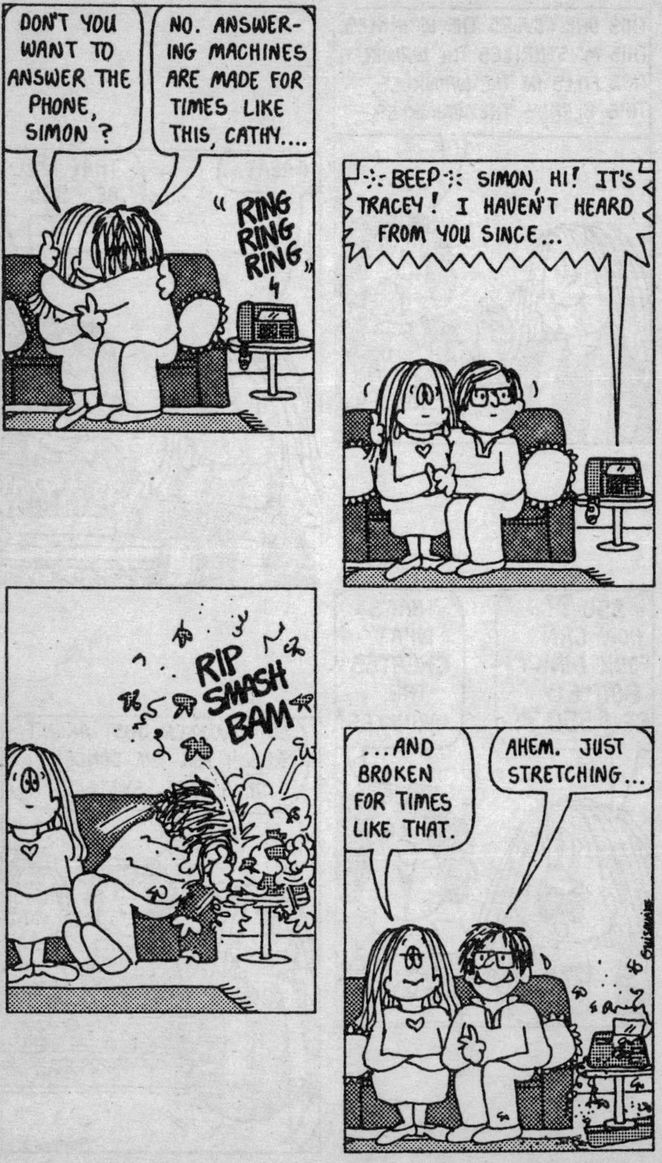
DON'T YOU WANT TO ANSWER THE PHONE, SIMON?
NO. ANSWERING MACHINES ARE MADE FOR TIMES LIKE THIS, CATHY....
"RING RING RING"
BEEP SIMON, HI! IT'S TRACEY! I HAVEN'T HEARD FROM YOU SINCE...
RIP SMASH BAM
...AND BROKEN FOR TIMES LIKE THAT.
AHEM. JUST STRETCHING...
Guisewite

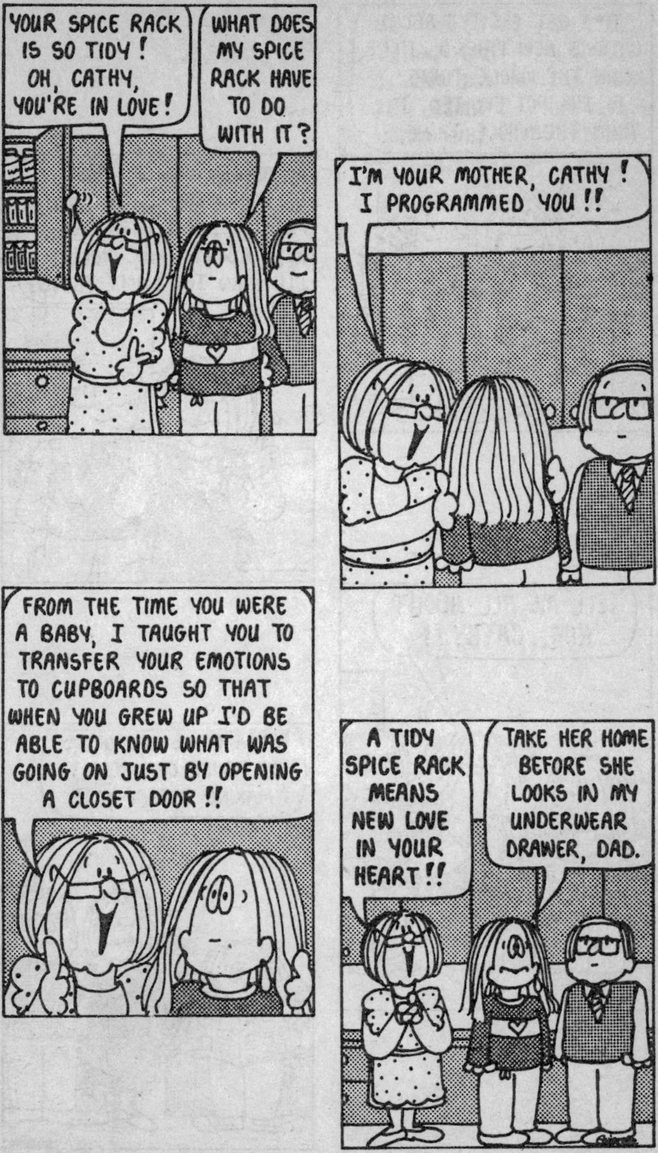
YOUR SPICE RACK IS SO TIDY! OH, CATHY, YOU'RE IN LOVE!
WHAT DOES MY SPICE RACK HAVE TO DO WITH IT?
I'M YOUR MOTHER, CATHY! I PROGRAMMED YOU!!
FROM THE TIME YOU WERE A BABY, I TAUGHT YOU TO TRANSFER YOUR EMOTIONS TO CUPBOARDS SO THAT WHEN YOU GREW UP I'D BE ABLE TO KNOW WHAT WAS GOING ON JUST BY OPENING A CLOSET DOOR!!
A TIDY SPICE RACK MEANS NEW LOVE IN YOUR HEART!!
TAKE HER HOME BEFORE SHE LOOKS IN MY UNDERWEAR DRAWER, DAD.

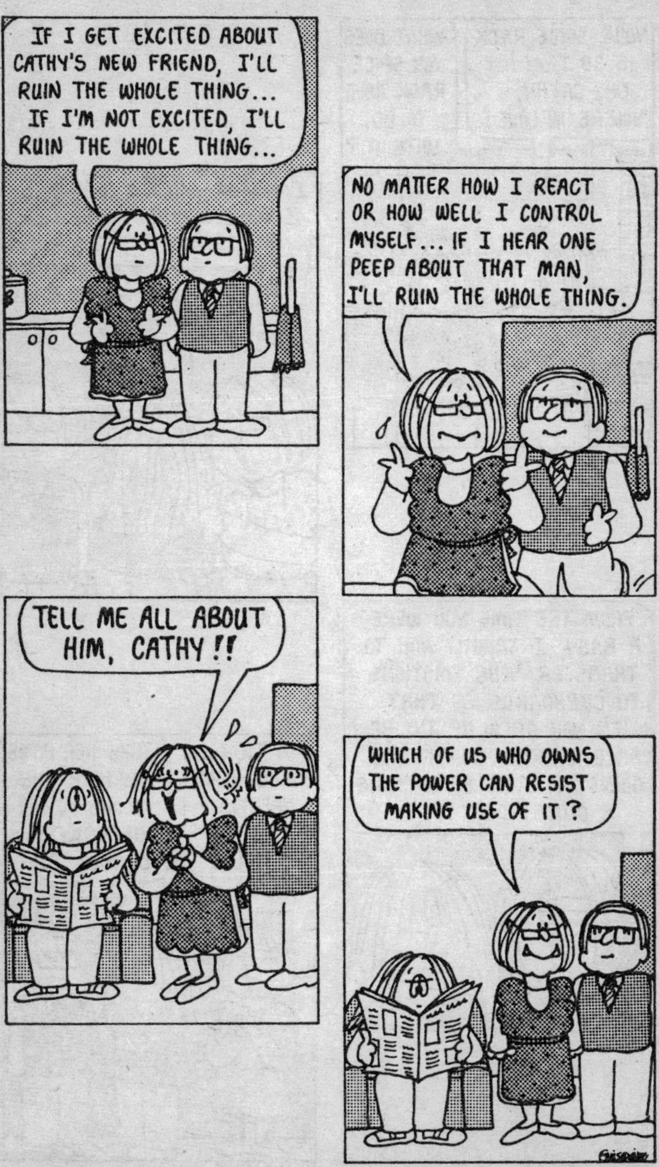
IF I GET EXCITED ABOUT CATHY'S NEW FRIEND, I'LL RUIN THE WHOLE THING... IF I'M NOT EXCITED, I'LL RUIN THE WHOLE THING...
NO MATTER HOW I REACT OR HOW WELL I CONTROL MYSELF... IF I HEAR ONE PEEP ABOUT THAT MAN, I'LL RUIN THE WHOLE THING.
TELL ME ALL ABOUT HIM, CATHY!!
WHICH OF US WHO OWNS THE POWER CAN RESIST MAKING USE OF IT?

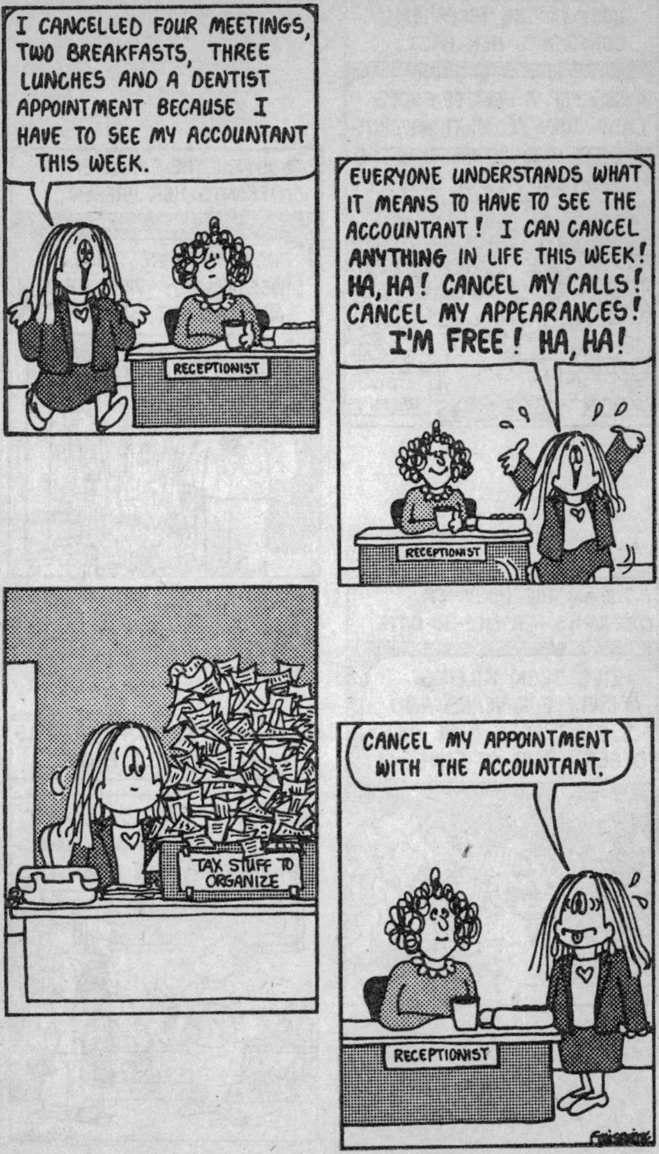
I CANCELLED FOUR MEETINGS, TWO BREAKFASTS, THREE LUNCHES AND A DENTIST APPOINTMENT BECAUSE I HAVE TO SEE MY ACCOUNTANT THIS WEEK.
RECEPTIONIST
EVERYONE UNDERSTANDS WHAT IT MEANS TO HAVE TO SEE THE ACCOUNTANT! I CAN CANCEL ANYTHING IN LIFE THIS WEEK! HA, HA! CANCEL MY CALLS! CANCEL MY APPEARANCES! I'M FREE! HA, HA!
RECEPTIONIST
TAX STUFF TO ORGANIZE
CANCEL MY APPOINTMENT WITH THE ACCOUNTANT.
RECEPTIONIST

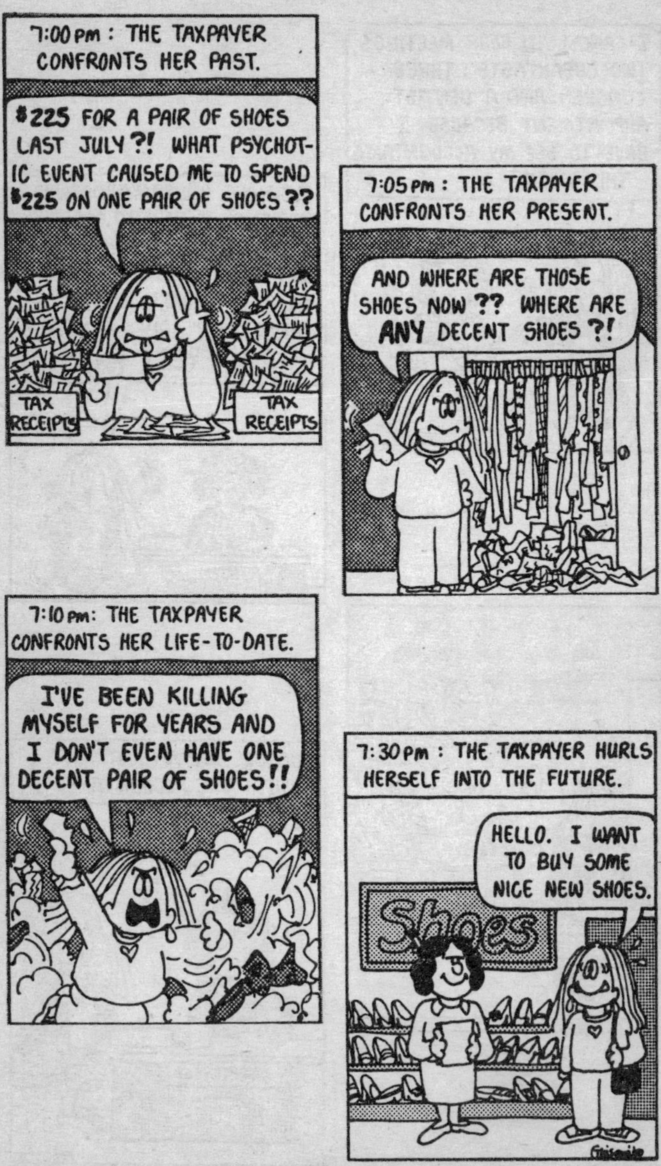
7:00 pm : THE TAXPAYER CONFRONTS HER PAST.
$225 FOR A PAIR OF SHOES LAST JULY ?! WHAT PSYCHOTIC EVENT CAUSED ME TO SPEND $225 ON ONE PAIR OF SHOES ??
TAX RECEIPTS
TAX RECEIPTS
7:05 pm : THE TAXPAYER CONFRONTS HER PRESENT.
AND WHERE ARE THOSE SHOES NOW ?? WHERE ARE ANY DECENT SHOES ?!
7:10 pm: THE TAXPAYER CONFRONTS HER LIFE-TO-DATE.
I'VE BEEN KILLING MYSELF FOR YEARS AND I DON'T EVEN HAVE ONE DECENT PAIR OF SHOES !!
7:30 pm : THE TAXPAYER HURLS HERSELF INTO THE FUTURE.
Shoes
HELLO. I WANT TO BUY SOME NICE NEW SHOES.

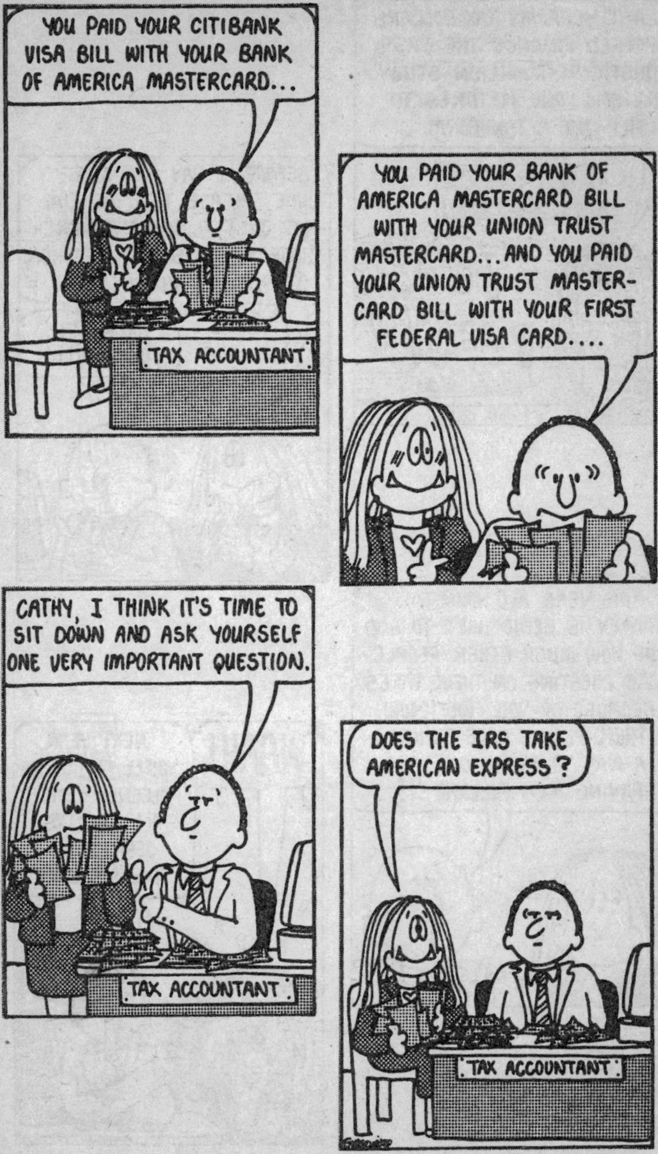
YOU PAID YOUR CITIBANK VISA BILL WITH YOUR BANK OF AMERICA MASTERCARD...
TAX ACCOUNTANT
YOU PAID YOUR BANK OF AMERICA MASTERCARD BILL WITH YOUR UNION TRUST MASTERCARD...AND YOU PAID YOUR UNION TRUST MASTER-CARD BILL WITH YOUR FIRST FEDERAL VISA CARD....
CATHY, I THINK IT'S TIME TO SIT DOWN AND ASK YOURSELF ONE VERY IMPORTANT QUESTION.
TAX ACCOUNTANT
DOES THE IRS TAKE AMERICAN EXPRESS?
TAX ACCOUNTANT

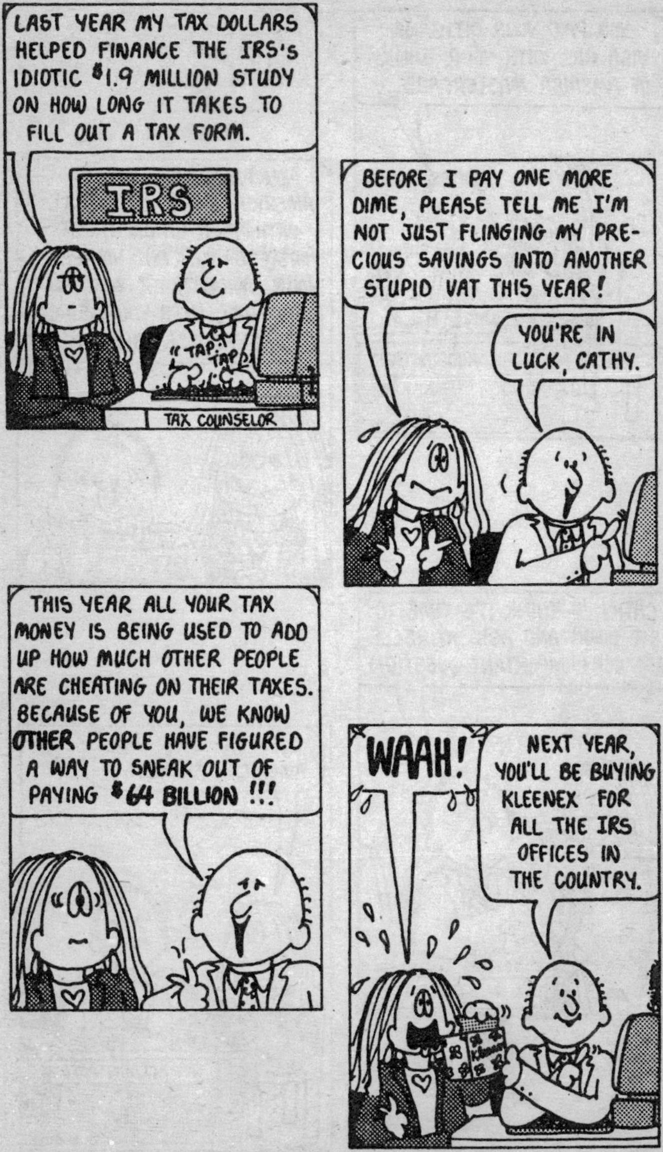
LAST YEAR MY TAX DOLLARS HELPED FINANCE THE IRS's IDIOTIC $1.9 MILLION STUDY ON HOW LONG IT TAKES TO FILL OUT A TAX FORM.
IRS
"TAP TAP"
TAX COUNSELOR
BEFORE I PAY ONE MORE DIME, PLEASE TELL ME I'M NOT JUST FLINGING MY PRECIOUS SAVINGS INTO ANOTHER STUPID VAT THIS YEAR!
YOU'RE IN LUCK, CATHY.
THIS YEAR ALL YOUR TAX MONEY IS BEING USED TO ADD UP HOW MUCH OTHER PEOPLE ARE CHEATING ON THEIR TAXES. BECAUSE OF YOU, WE KNOW OTHER PEOPLE HAVE FIGURED A WAY TO SNEAK OUT OF PAYING $64 BILLION !!!
WAAH!
NEXT YEAR, YOU'LL BE BUYING KLEENEX FOR ALL THE IRS OFFICES IN THE COUNTRY.

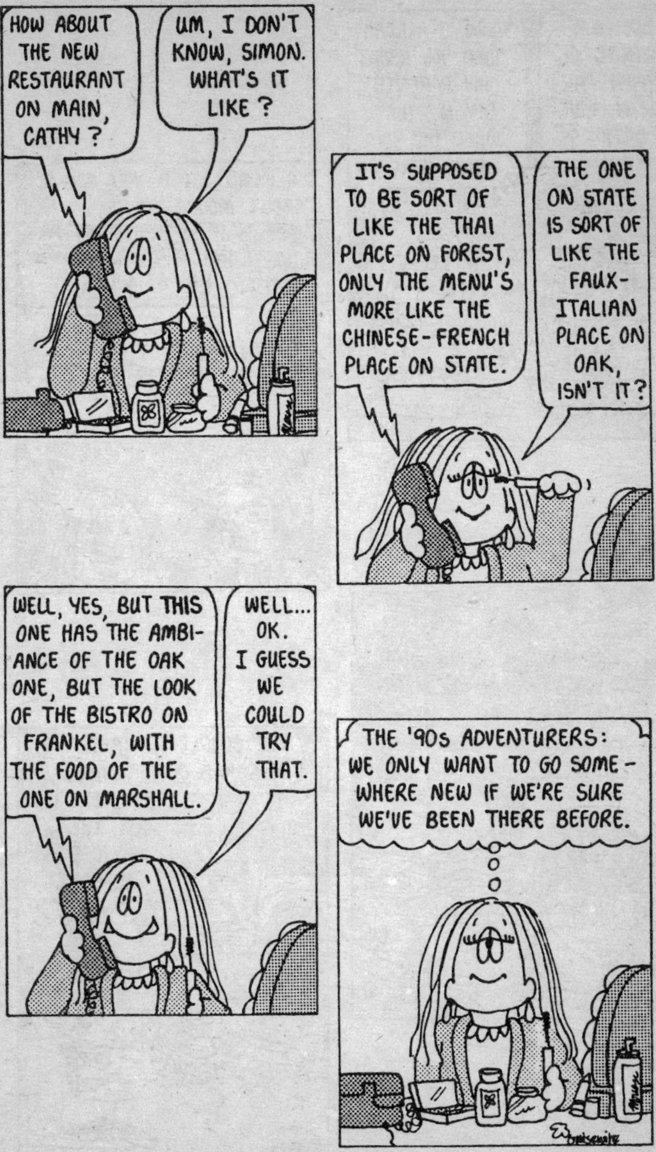

HOW ABOUT THE NEW RESTAURANT ON MAIN, CATHY ?
UM, I DON'T KNOW, SIMON. WHAT'S IT LIKE ?
IT'S SUPPOSED TO BE SORT OF LIKE THE THAI PLACE ON FOREST, ONLY THE MENU'S MORE LIKE THE CHINESE-FRENCH PLACE ON STATE.
THE ONE ON STATE IS SORT OF LIKE THE FAUX-ITALIAN PLACE ON OAK, ISN'T IT ?
WELL, YES, BUT THIS ONE HAS THE AMBIANCE OF THE OAK ONE, BUT THE LOOK OF THE BISTRO ON FRANKEL, WITH THE FOOD OF THE ONE ON MARSHALL.
WELL... OK. I GUESS WE COULD TRY THAT.
THE '90s ADVENTURERS: WE ONLY WANT TO GO SOMEWHERE NEW IF WE'RE SURE WE'VE BEEN THERE BEFORE.

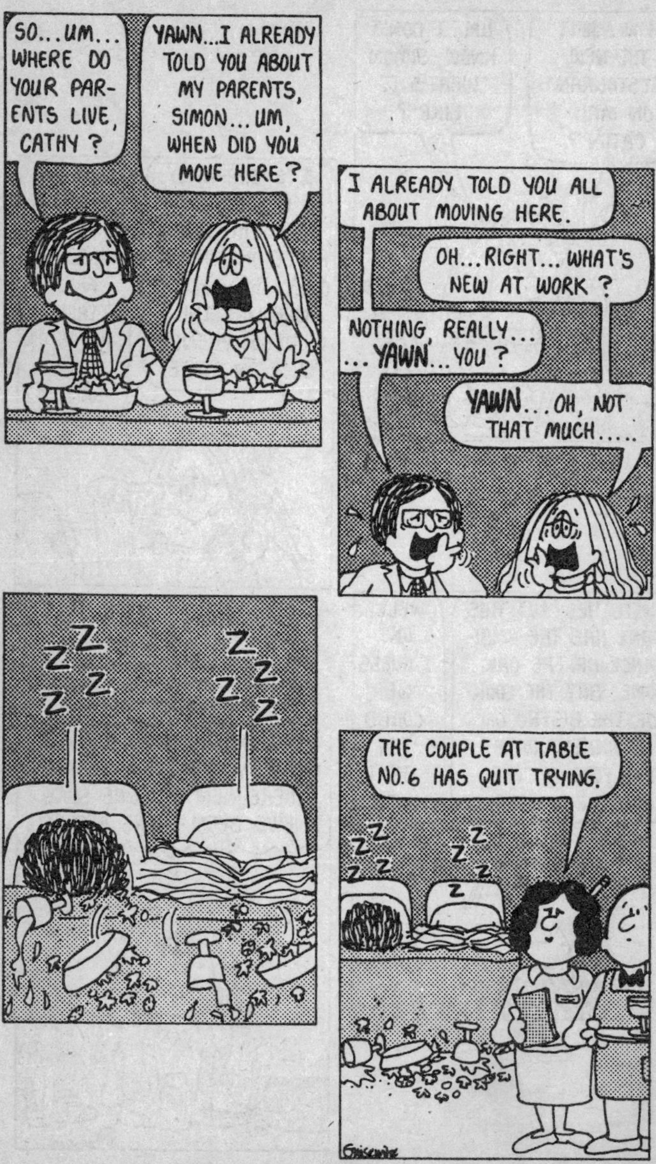
SO...UM... WHERE DO YOUR PARENTS LIVE, CATHY ?
YAWN...I ALREADY TOLD YOU ABOUT MY PARENTS, SIMON...UM, WHEN DID YOU MOVE HERE ?
I ALREADY TOLD YOU ALL ABOUT MOVING HERE.
OH...RIGHT... WHAT'S NEW AT WORK ?
NOTHING, REALLY... ...YAWN...YOU ?
YAWN...OH, NOT THAT MUCH.....
Z Z Z Z
Z Z Z Z
THE COUPLE AT TABLE NO.6 HAS QUIT TRYING.
Guisewite

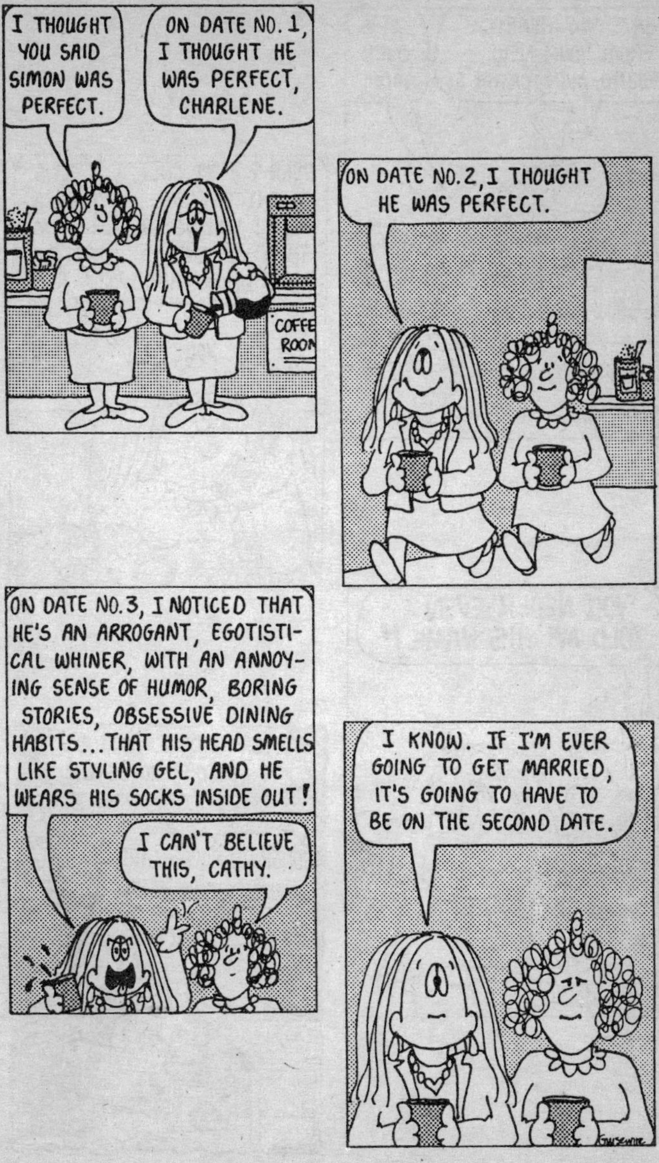
I THOUGHT YOU SAID SIMON WAS PERFECT.
ON DATE NO. 1, I THOUGHT HE WAS PERFECT, CHARLENE.
COFFE ROOM
ON DATE NO. 2, I THOUGHT HE WAS PERFECT.
ON DATE NO. 3, I NOTICED THAT HE'S AN ARROGANT, EGOTISTICAL WHINER, WITH AN ANNOYING SENSE OF HUMOR, BORING STORIES, OBSESSIVE DINING HABITS... THAT HIS HEAD SMELLS LIKE STYLING GEL, AND HE WEARS HIS SOCKS INSIDE OUT!
I CAN'T BELIEVE THIS, CATHY.
I KNOW. IF I'M EVER GOING TO GET MARRIED, IT'S GOING TO HAVE TO BE ON THE SECOND DATE.

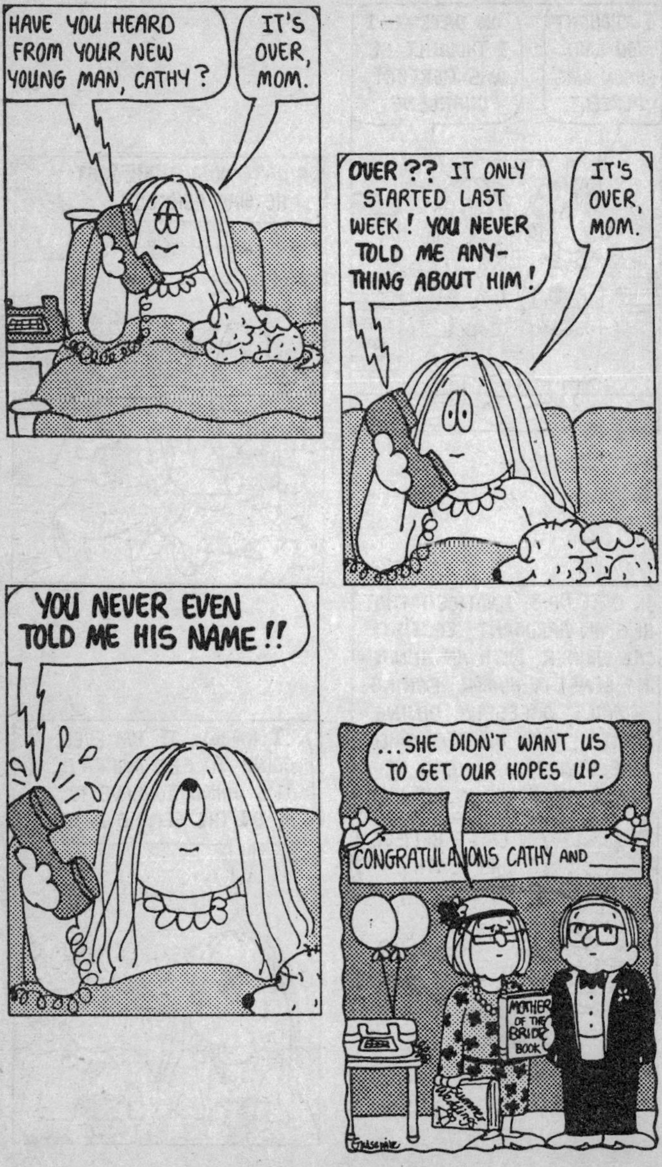
HAVE YOU HEARD FROM YOUR NEW YOUNG MAN, CATHY?
IT'S OVER, MOM.
OVER?? IT ONLY STARTED LAST WEEK! YOU NEVER TOLD ME ANYTHING ABOUT HIM!
IT'S OVER, MOM.
YOU NEVER EVEN TOLD ME HIS NAME!!
...SHE DIDN'T WANT US TO GET OUR HOPES UP.
CONGRATULATIONS CATHY AND ____
MOTHER OF THE BRIDE BOOK

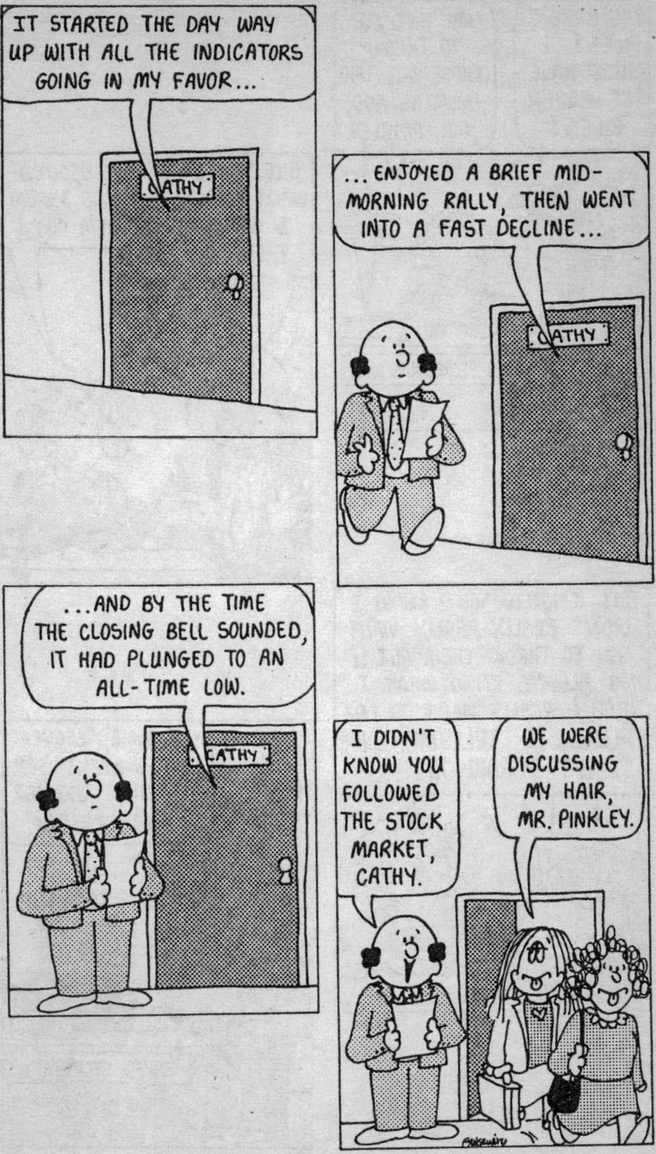
IT STARTED THE DAY WAY UP WITH ALL THE INDICATORS GOING IN MY FAVOR...
CATHY
...ENJOYED A BRIEF MID-MORNING RALLY, THEN WENT INTO A FAST DECLINE...
CATHY
...AND BY THE TIME THE CLOSING BELL SOUNDED, IT HAD PLUNGED TO AN ALL-TIME LOW.
CATHY
I DIDN'T KNOW YOU FOLLOWED THE STOCK MARKET, CATHY.
WE WERE DISCUSSING MY HAIR, MR. PINKLEY.

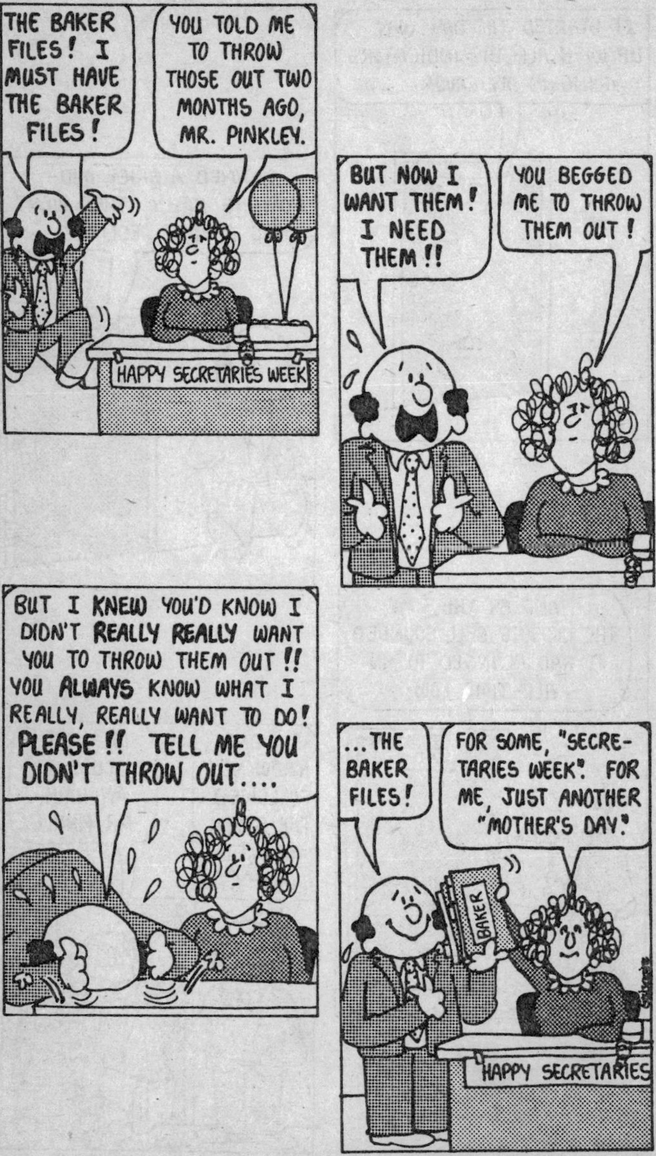
THE BAKER FILES! I MUST HAVE THE BAKER FILES!
YOU TOLD ME TO THROW THOSE OUT TWO MONTHS AGO, MR. PINKLEY.
HAPPY SECRETARIES WEEK
BUT NOW I WANT THEM! I NEED THEM!!
YOU BEGGED ME TO THROW THEM OUT!
BUT I KNEW YOU'D KNOW I DIDN'T REALLY REALLY WANT YOU TO THROW THEM OUT!! YOU ALWAYS KNOW WHAT I REALLY, REALLY WANT TO DO! PLEASE!! TELL ME YOU DIDN'T THROW OUT....
...THE BAKER FILES!
FOR SOME, "SECRETARIES WEEK". FOR ME, JUST ANOTHER "MOTHER'S DAY."
BAKER
HAPPY SECRETARIES

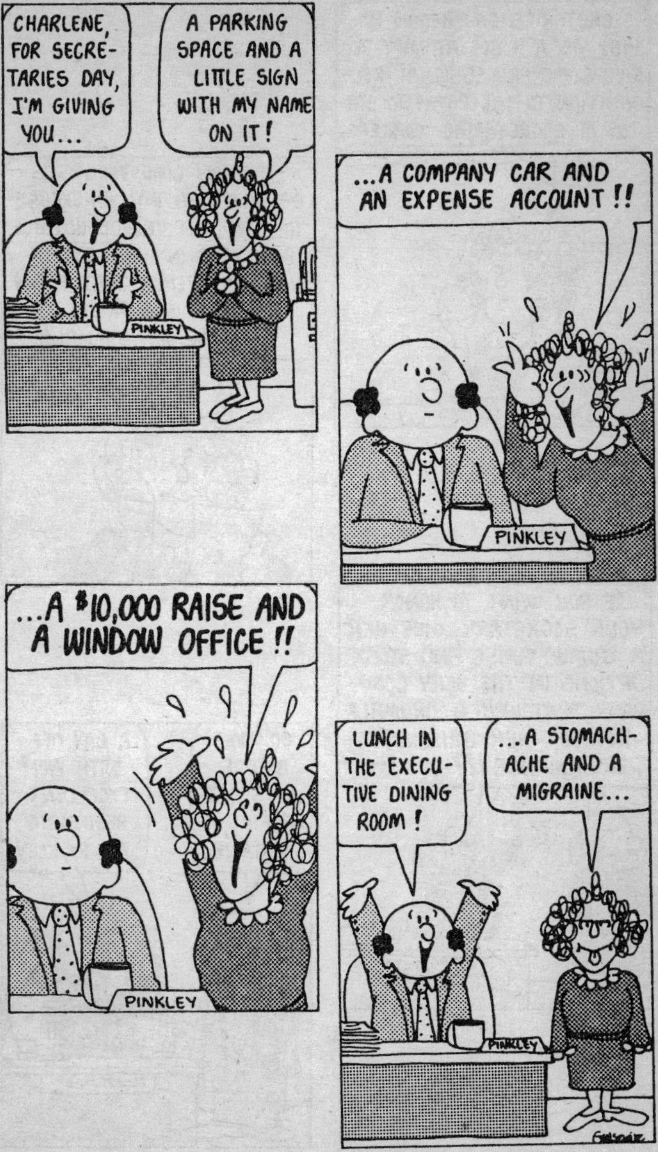
CHARLENE, FOR SECRETARIES DAY, I'M GIVING YOU...
A PARKING SPACE AND A LITTLE SIGN WITH MY NAME ON IT!
PINKLEY
...A COMPANY CAR AND AN EXPENSE ACCOUNT!!
PINKLEY
...A $10,000 RAISE AND A WINDOW OFFICE!!
PINKLEY
LUNCH IN THE EXECUTIVE DINING ROOM!
...A STOMACHACHE AND A MIGRAINE...
PINKLEY

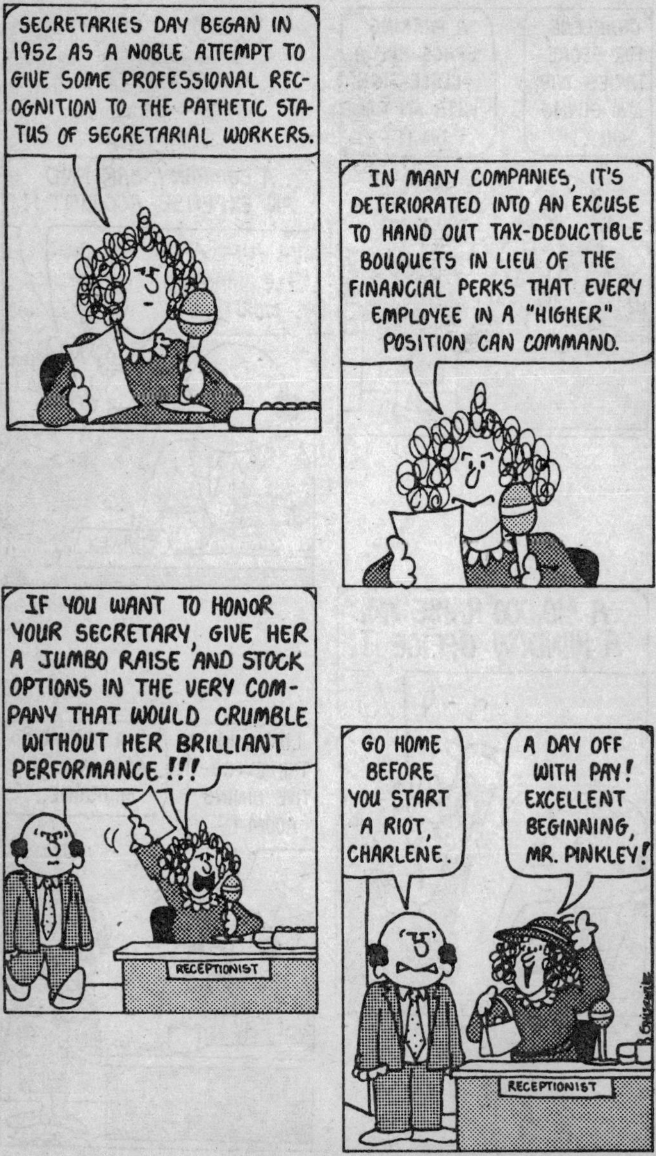
SECRETARIES DAY BEGAN IN 1952 AS A NOBLE ATTEMPT TO GIVE SOME PROFESSIONAL RECOGNITION TO THE PATHETIC STATUS OF SECRETARIAL WORKERS.
IN MANY COMPANIES, IT'S DETERIORATED INTO AN EXCUSE TO HAND OUT TAX-DEDUCTIBLE BOUQUETS IN LIEU OF THE FINANCIAL PERKS THAT EVERY EMPLOYEE IN A "HIGHER" POSITION CAN COMMAND.
IF YOU WANT TO HONOR YOUR SECRETARY, GIVE HER A JUMBO RAISE AND STOCK OPTIONS IN THE VERY COMPANY THAT WOULD CRUMBLE WITHOUT HER BRILLIANT PERFORMANCE!!!
RECEPTIONIST
GO HOME BEFORE YOU START A RIOT, CHARLENE.
A DAY OFF WITH PAY! EXCELLENT BEGINNING, MR. PINKLEY!
RECEPTIONIST

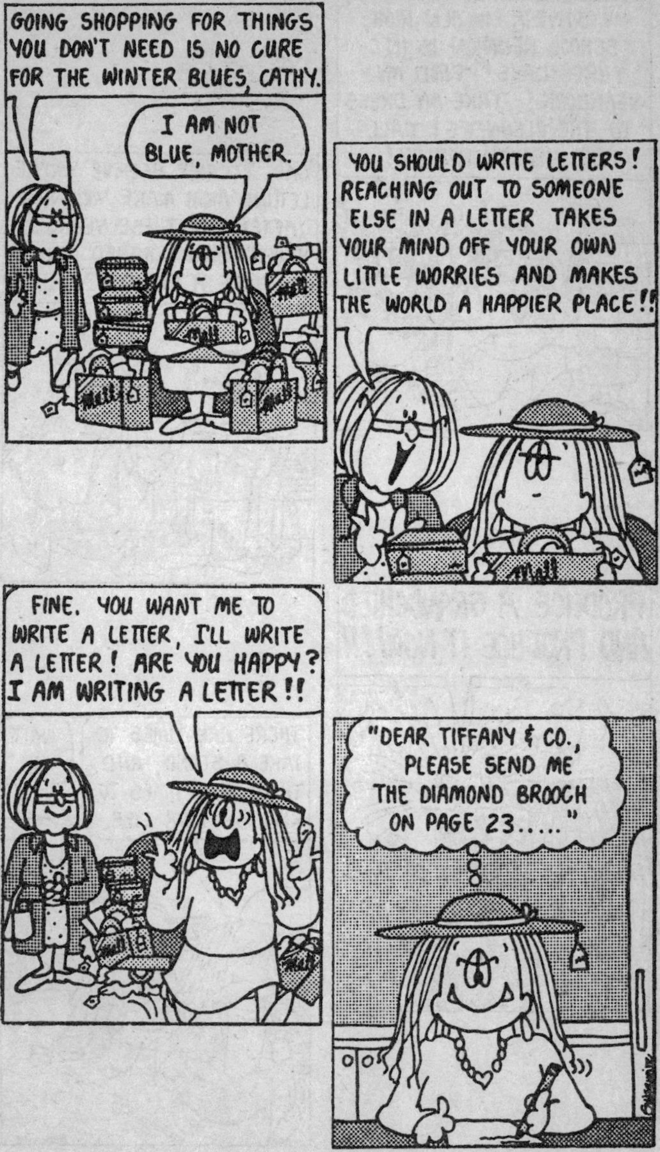
GOING SHOPPING FOR THINGS YOU DON'T NEED IS NO CURE FOR THE WINTER BLUES, CATHY.
I AM NOT BLUE, MOTHER.
YOU SHOULD WRITE LETTERS! REACHING OUT TO SOMEONE ELSE IN A LETTER TAKES YOUR MIND OFF YOUR OWN LITTLE WORRIES AND MAKES THE WORLD A HAPPIER PLACE!!
FINE. YOU WANT ME TO WRITE A LETTER, I'LL WRITE A LETTER! ARE YOU HAPPY? I AM WRITING A LETTER!!
"DEAR TIFFANY & CO., PLEASE SEND ME THE DIAMOND BROOCH ON PAGE 23....."

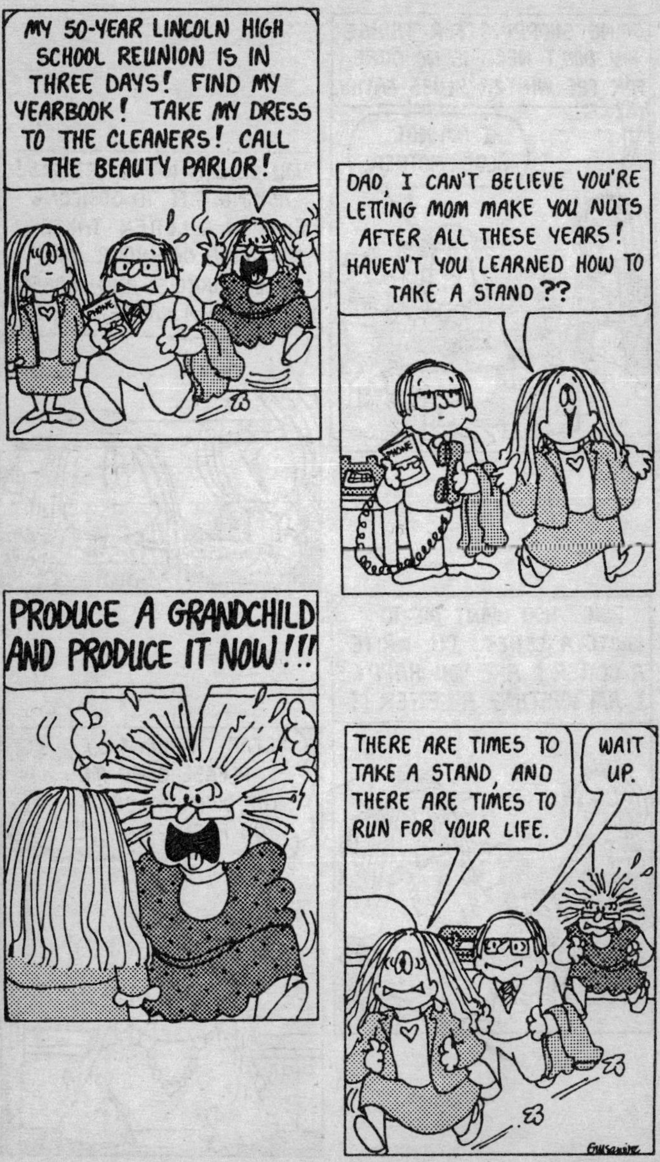
MY 50-YEAR LINCOLN HIGH SCHOOL REUNION IS IN THREE DAYS! FIND MY YEARBOOK! TAKE MY DRESS TO THE CLEANERS! CALL THE BEAUTY PARLOR!
PHONE
DAD, I CAN'T BELIEVE YOU'RE LETTING MOM MAKE YOU NUTS AFTER ALL THESE YEARS! HAVEN'T YOU LEARNED HOW TO TAKE A STAND??
PHONE
PRODUCE A GRANDCHILD AND PRODUCE IT NOW!!!
THERE ARE TIMES TO TAKE A STAND, AND THERE ARE TIMES TO RUN FOR YOUR LIFE.
WAIT UP.

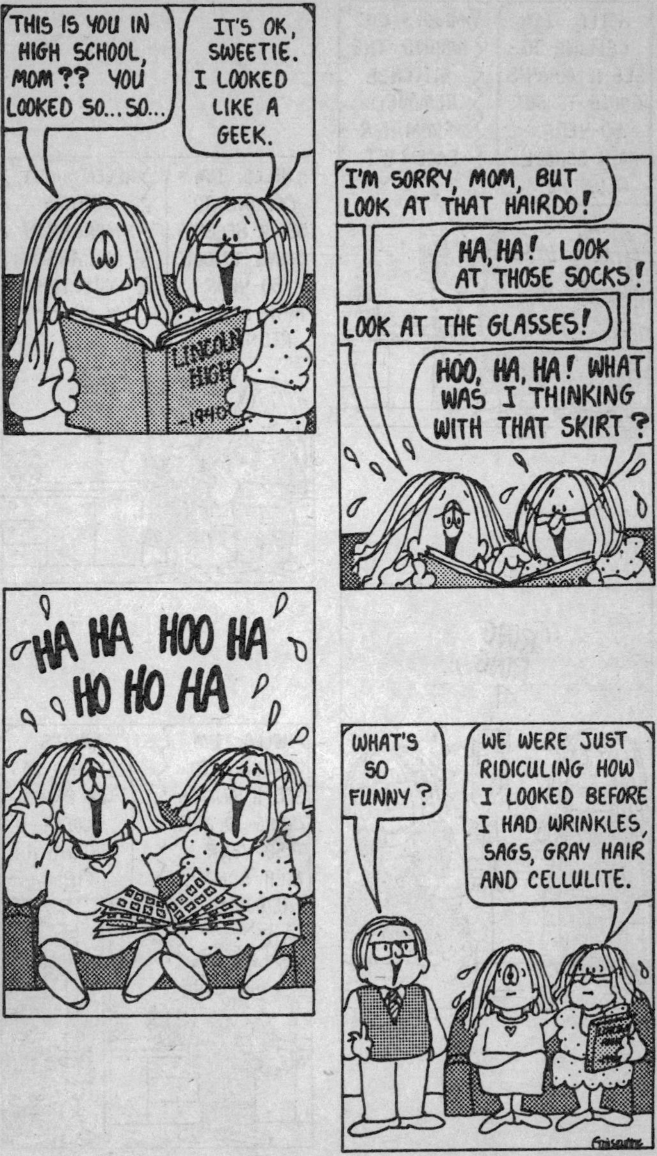
THIS IS YOU IN HIGH SCHOOL, MOM?? YOU LOOKED SO... SO...
IT'S OK, SWEETIE. I LOOKED LIKE A GEEK.
LINCOLN HIGH 1940
I'M SORRY, MOM, BUT LOOK AT THAT HAIRDO!
HA, HA! LOOK AT THOSE SOCKS!
LOOK AT THE GLASSES!
HOO, HA, HA! WHAT WAS I THINKING WITH THAT SKIRT?
HA HA HOO HA
HO HO HA
WHAT'S SO FUNNY?
WE WERE JUST RIDICULING HOW I LOOKED BEFORE I HAD WRINKLES, SAGS, GRAY HAIR AND CELLULITE.

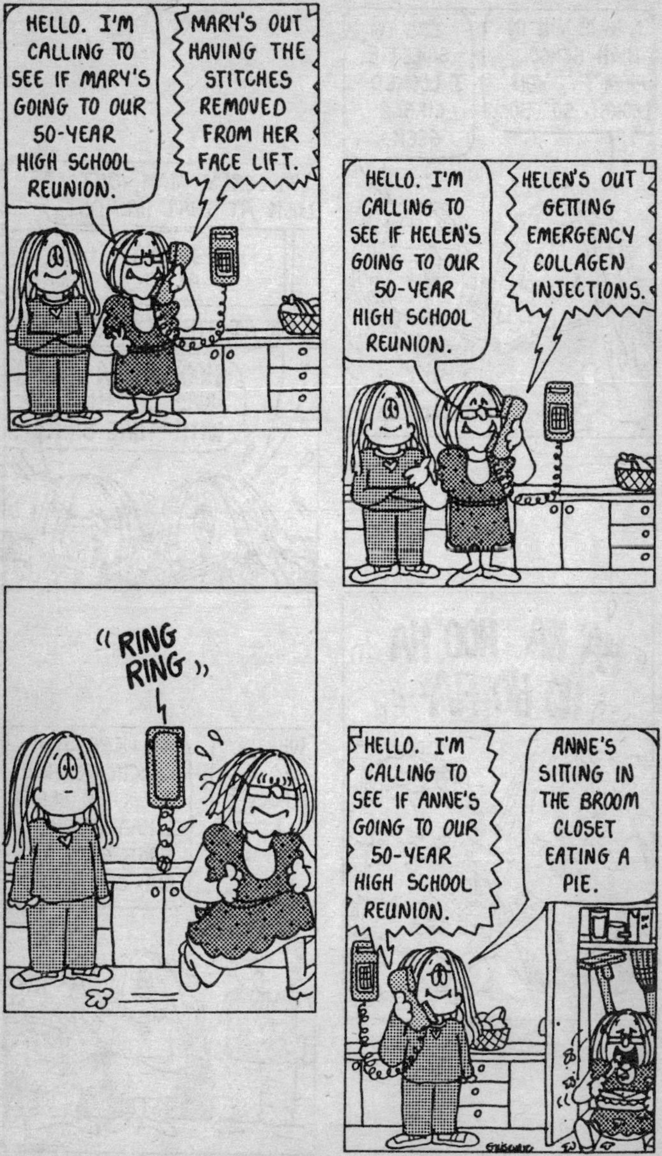
HELLO. I'M CALLING TO SEE IF MARY'S GOING TO OUR 50-YEAR HIGH SCHOOL REUNION.
MARY'S OUT HAVING THE STITCHES REMOVED FROM HER FACE LIFT.
HELLO. I'M CALLING TO SEE IF HELEN'S GOING TO OUR 50-YEAR HIGH SCHOOL REUNION.
HELEN'S OUT GETTING EMERGENCY COLLAGEN INJECTIONS.
"RING RING"
HELLO. I'M CALLING TO SEE IF ANNE'S GOING TO OUR 50-YEAR HIGH SCHOOL REUNION.
ANNE'S SITTING IN THE BROOM CLOSET EATING A PIE.

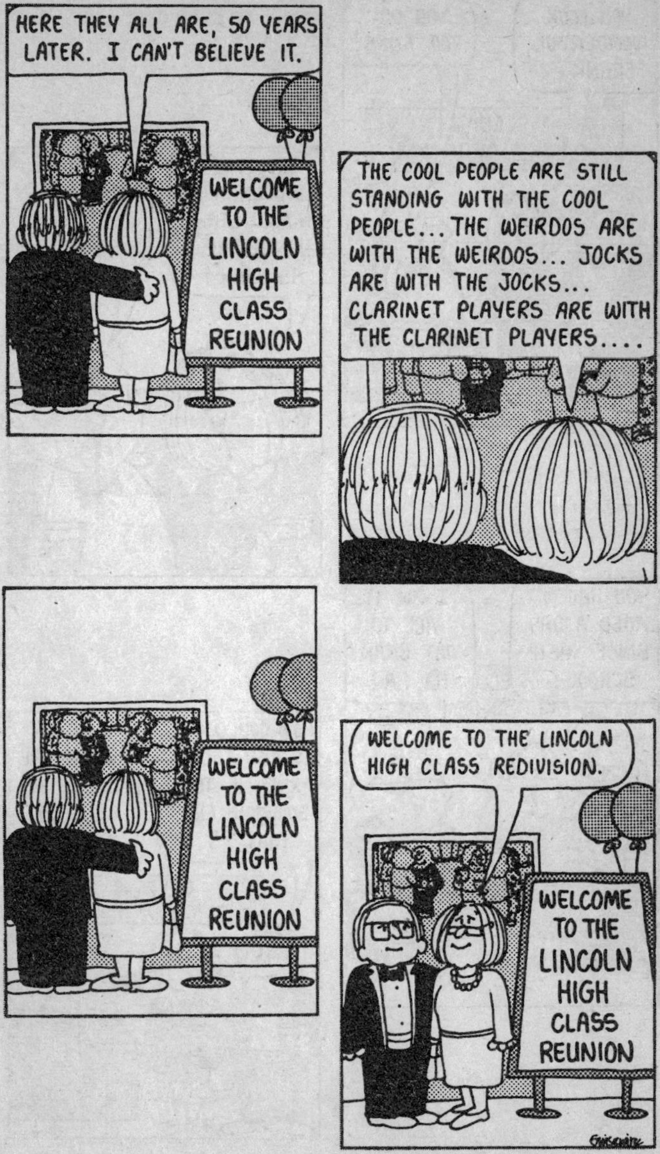
HERE THEY ALL ARE, 50 YEARS LATER. I CAN'T BELIEVE IT.
WELCOME TO THE LINCOLN HIGH CLASS REUNION
THE COOL PEOPLE ARE STILL STANDING WITH THE COOL PEOPLE... THE WEIRDOS ARE WITH THE WEIRDOS... JOCKS ARE WITH THE JOCKS... CLARINET PLAYERS ARE WITH THE CLARINET PLAYERS....
WELCOME TO THE LINCOLN HIGH CLASS REUNION
WELCOME TO THE LINCOLN HIGH CLASS REDIVISION.
WELCOME TO THE LINCOLN HIGH CLASS REUNION
GUISEWITE

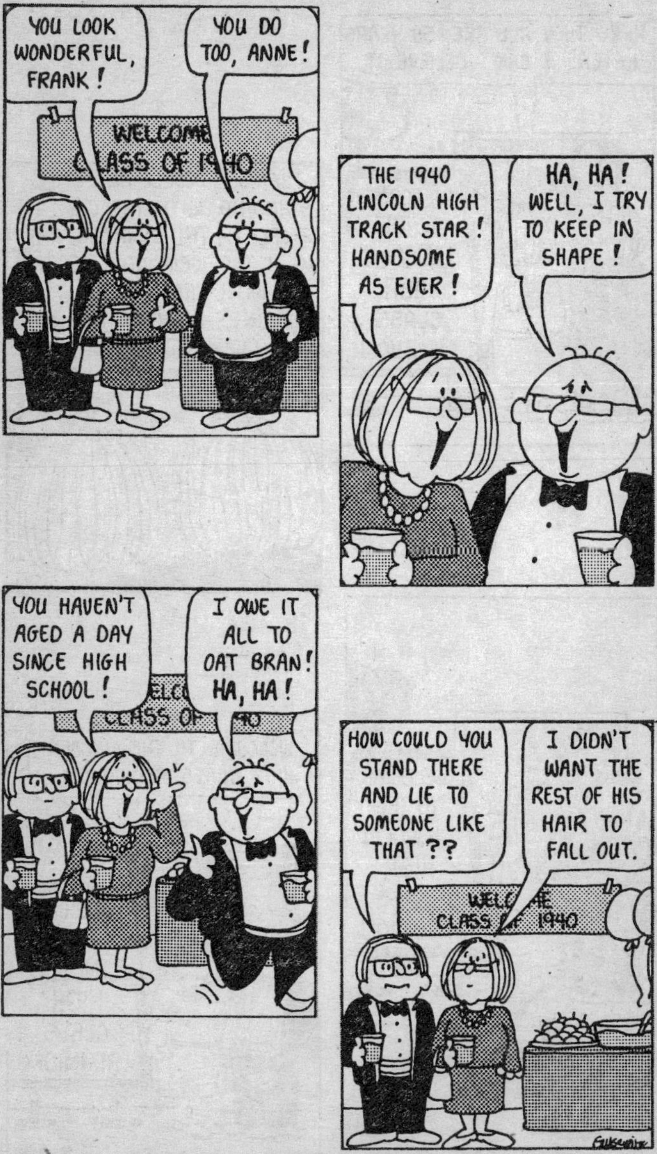
YOU LOOK WONDERFUL, FRANK!
YOU DO TOO, ANNE!
WELCOME CLASS OF 1940
THE 1940 LINCOLN HIGH TRACK STAR! HANDSOME AS EVER!
HA, HA! WELL, I TRY TO KEEP IN SHAPE!
YOU HAVEN'T AGED A DAY SINCE HIGH SCHOOL!
I OWE IT ALL TO OAT BRAN! HA, HA!
HOW COULD YOU STAND THERE AND LIE TO SOMEONE LIKE THAT??
I DIDN'T WANT THE REST OF HIS HAIR TO FALL OUT.

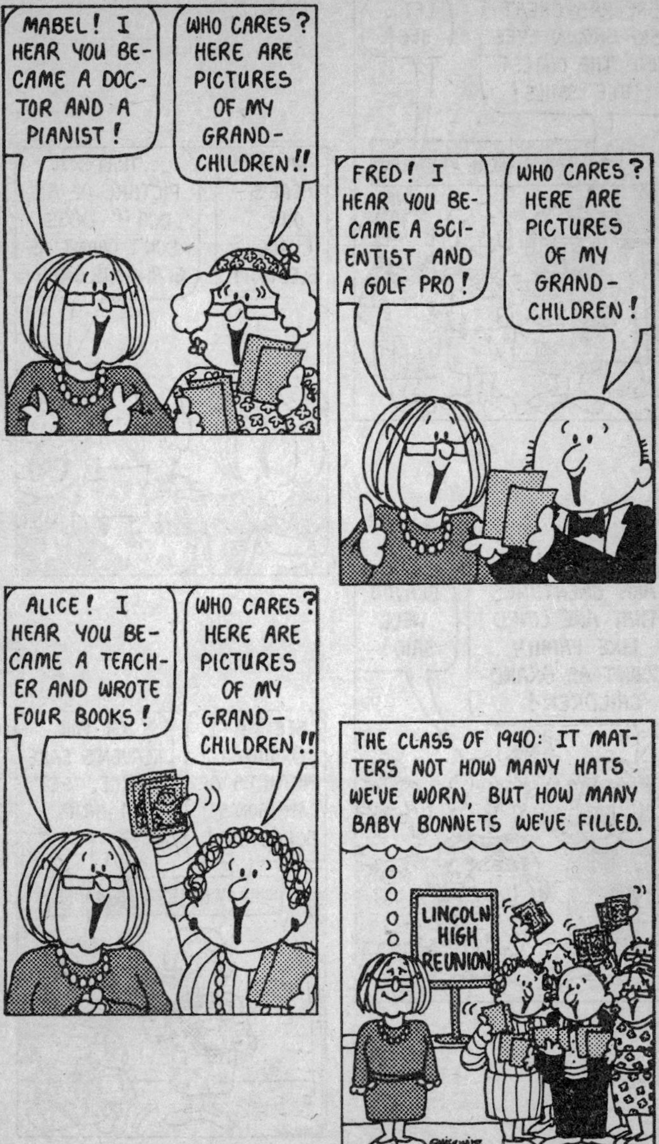

MABEL! I HEAR YOU BECAME A DOCTOR AND A PIANIST!
WHO CARES? HERE ARE PICTURES OF MY GRANDCHILDREN!!
FRED! I HEAR YOU BECAME A SCIENTIST AND A GOLF PRO!
WHO CARES? HERE ARE PICTURES OF MY GRANDCHILDREN!
ALICE! I HEAR YOU BECAME A TEACHER AND WROTE FOUR BOOKS!
WHO CARES? HERE ARE PICTURES OF MY GRANDCHILDREN!!
THE CLASS OF 1940: IT MATTERS NOT HOW MANY HATS WE'VE WORN, BUT HOW MANY BABY BONNETS WE'VE FILLED.
LINCOLN HIGH REUNION

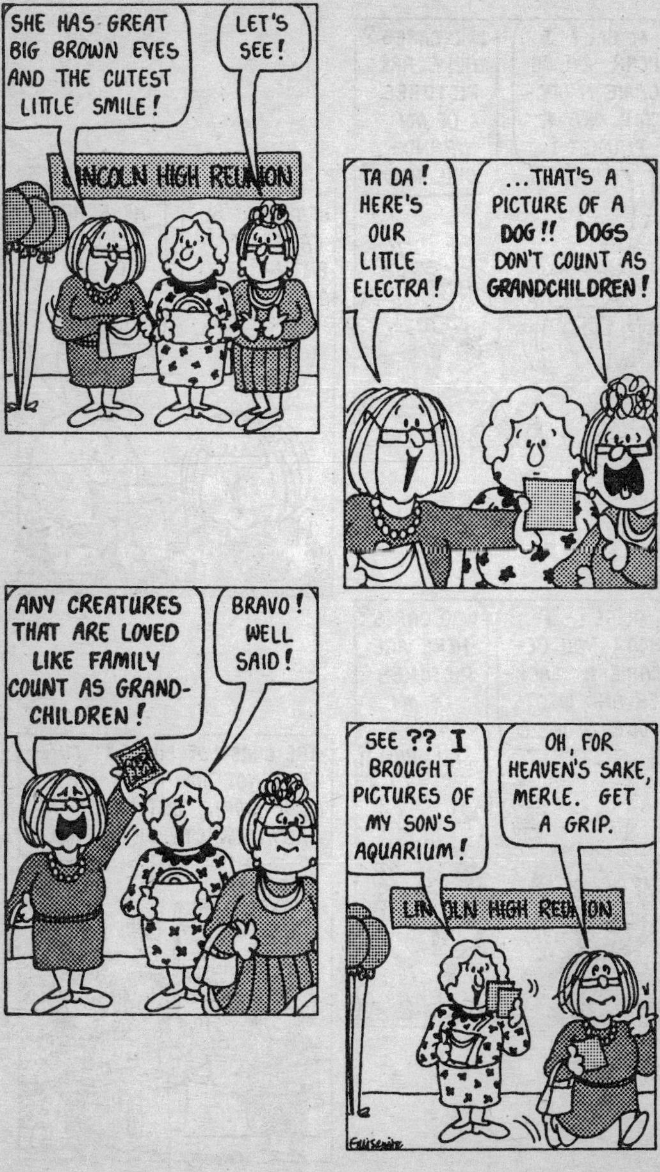
SHE HAS GREAT BIG BROWN EYES AND THE CUTEST LITTLE SMILE!
LET'S SEE!
TA DA! HERE'S OUR LITTLE ELECTRA!
...THAT'S A PICTURE OF A DOG!! DOGS DON'T COUNT AS GRANDCHILDREN!
ANY CREATURES THAT ARE LOVED LIKE FAMILY COUNT AS GRAND-CHILDREN!
BRAVO! WELL SAID!
SEE?? I BROUGHT PICTURES OF MY SON'S AQUARIUM!
OH, FOR HEAVEN'S SAKE, MERLE. GET A GRIP.
Guisewite

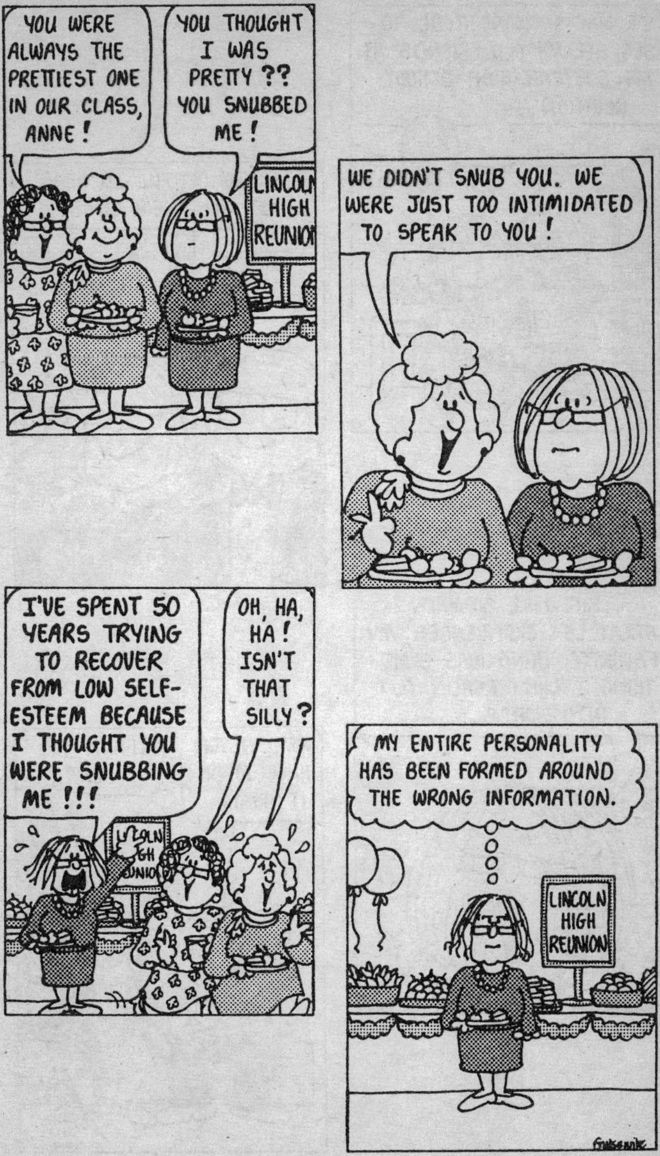
YOU WERE ALWAYS THE PRETTIEST ONE IN OUR CLASS, ANNE!
YOU THOUGHT I WAS PRETTY?? YOU SNUBBED ME!
WE DIDN'T SNUB YOU. WE WERE JUST TOO INTIMIDATED TO SPEAK TO YOU!
I'VE SPENT 50 YEARS TRYING TO RECOVER FROM LOW SELF-ESTEEM BECAUSE I THOUGHT YOU WERE SNUBBING ME!!!
OH, HA, HA! ISN'T THAT SILLY?
MY ENTIRE PERSONALITY HAS BEEN FORMED AROUND THE WRONG INFORMATION.
LINCOLN HIGH REUNION

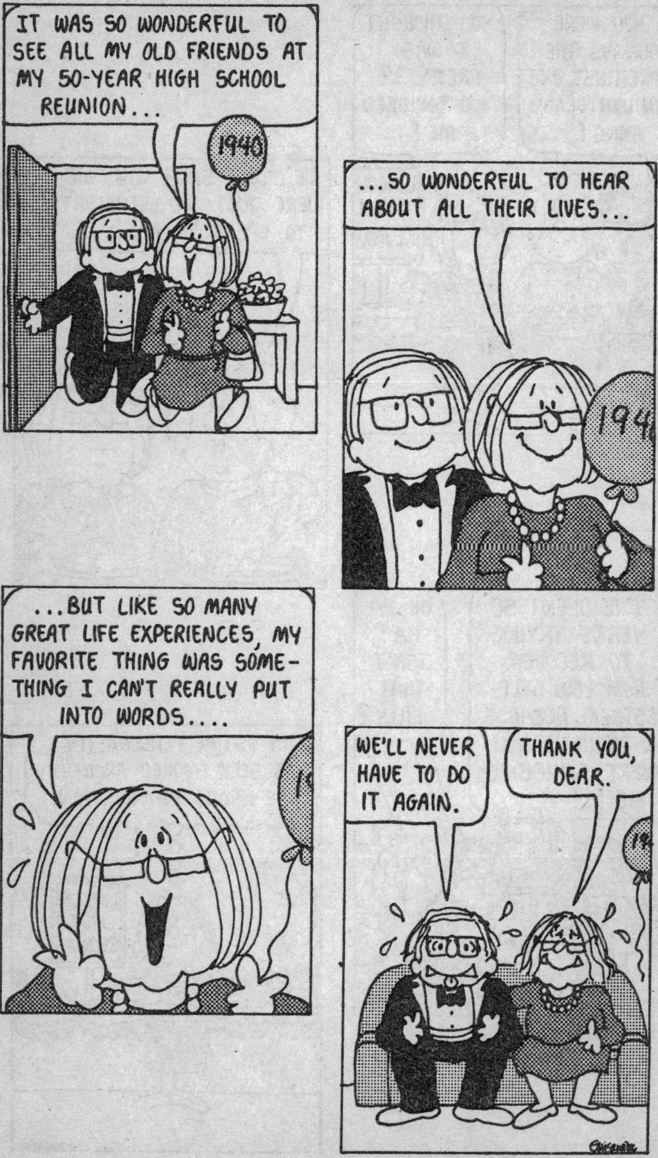
IT WAS SO WONDERFUL TO SEE ALL MY OLD FRIENDS AT MY 50-YEAR HIGH SCHOOL REUNION...
1940
...SO WONDERFUL TO HEAR ABOUT ALL THEIR LIVES...
...BUT LIKE SO MANY GREAT LIFE EXPERIENCES, MY FAVORITE THING WAS SOME-THING I CAN'T REALLY PUT INTO WORDS....
WE'LL NEVER HAVE TO DO IT AGAIN.
THANK YOU, DEAR.

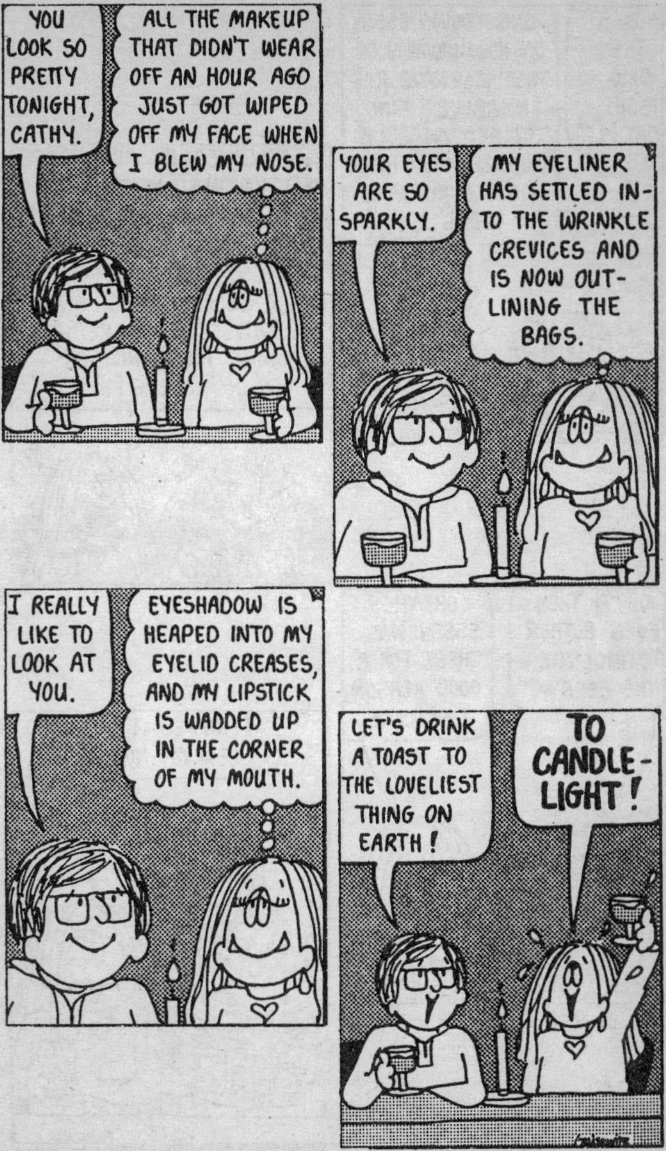
YOU LOOK SO PRETTY TONIGHT, CATHY.
ALL THE MAKEUP THAT DIDN'T WEAR OFF AN HOUR AGO JUST GOT WIPED OFF MY FACE WHEN I BLEW MY NOSE.
YOUR EYES ARE SO SPARKLY.
MY EYELINER HAS SETTLED INTO THE WRINKLE CREVICES AND IS NOW OUTLINING THE BAGS.
I REALLY LIKE TO LOOK AT YOU.
EYESHADOW IS HEAPED INTO MY EYELID CREASES, AND MY LIPSTICK IS WADDED UP IN THE CORNER OF MY MOUTH.
LET'S DRINK A TOAST TO THE LOVELIEST THING ON EARTH!
TO CANDLELIGHT!

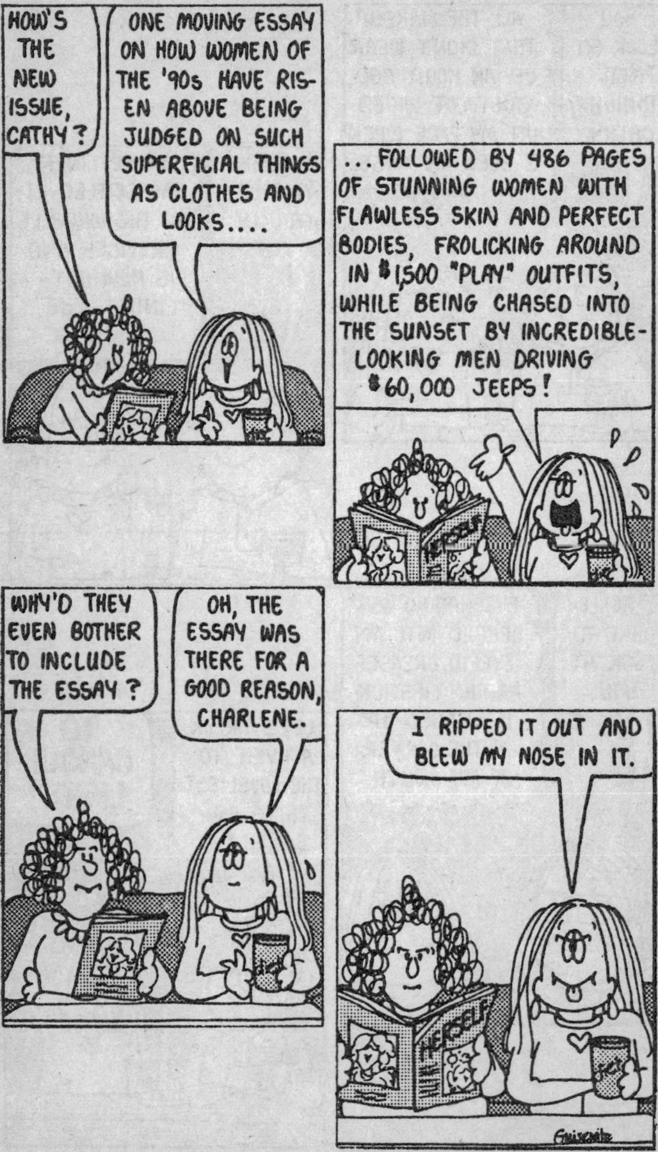
HOW'S THE NEW ISSUE, CATHY?
ONE MOVING ESSAY ON HOW WOMEN OF THE '90s HAVE RISEN ABOVE BEING JUDGED ON SUCH SUPERFICIAL THINGS AS CLOTHES AND LOOKS....
...FOLLOWED BY 486 PAGES OF STUNNING WOMEN WITH FLAWLESS SKIN AND PERFECT BODIES, FROLICKING AROUND IN $1,500 "PLAY" OUTFITS, WHILE BEING CHASED INTO THE SUNSET BY INCREDIBLE-LOOKING MEN DRIVING $60,000 JEEPS!
WHY'D THEY EVEN BOTHER TO INCLUDE THE ESSAY?
OH, THE ESSAY WAS THERE FOR A GOOD REASON, CHARLENE.
I RIPPED IT OUT AND BLEW MY NOSE IN IT.

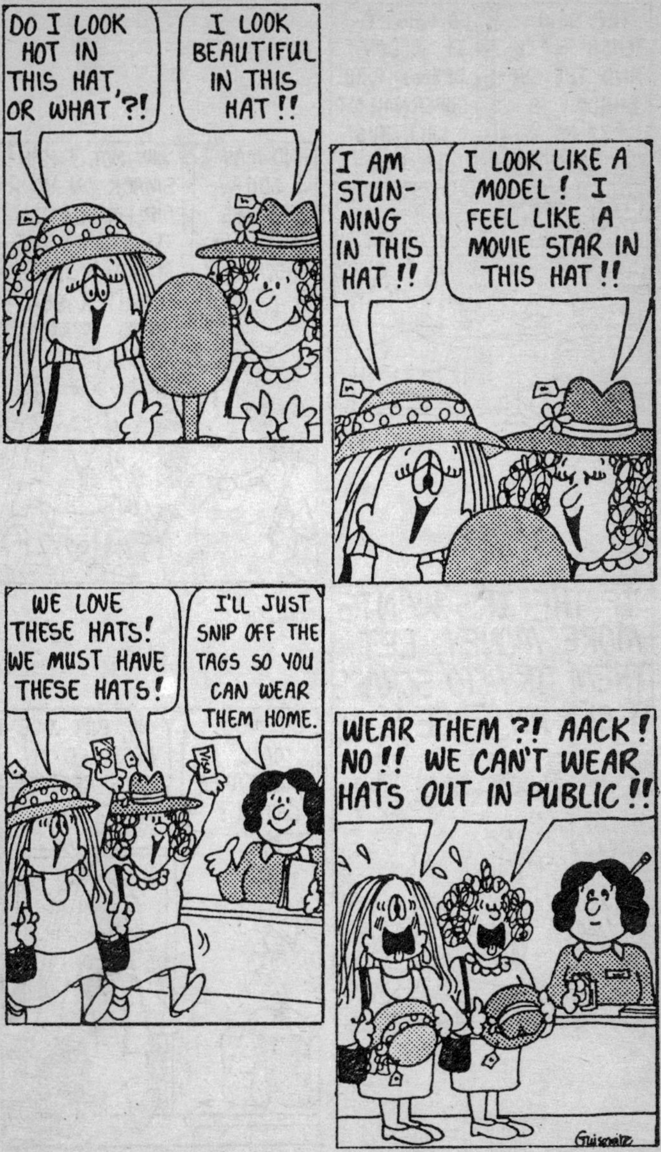
DO I LOOK HOT IN THIS HAT, OR WHAT?!
I LOOK BEAUTIFUL IN THIS HAT!!
I AM STUNNING IN THIS HAT!!
I LOOK LIKE A MODEL! I FEEL LIKE A MOVIE STAR IN THIS HAT!!
WE LOVE THESE HATS! WE MUST HAVE THESE HATS!
I'LL JUST SNIP OFF THE TAGS SO YOU CAN WEAR THEM HOME.
WEAR THEM?! AACK! NO!! WE CAN'T WEAR HATS OUT IN PUBLIC!!
Guisewite

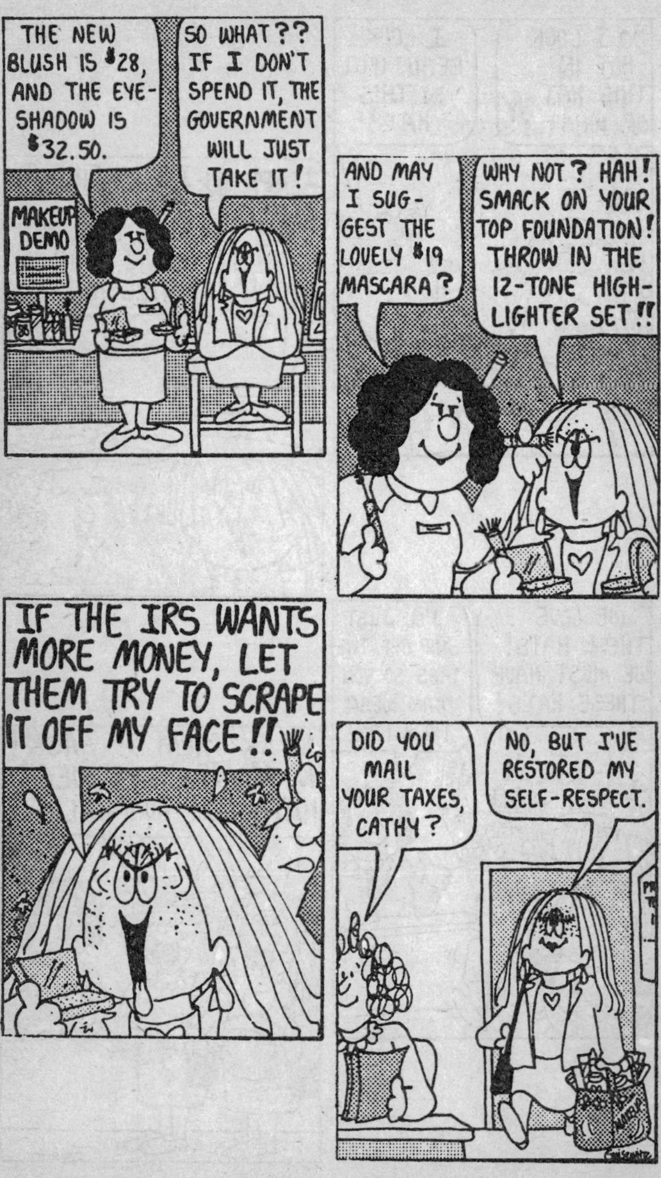
THE NEW BLUSH IS $28, AND THE EYE-SHADOW IS $32.50.
SO WHAT?? IF I DON'T SPEND IT, THE GOVERNMENT WILL JUST TAKE IT!
MAKEUP DEMO
AND MAY I SUGGEST THE LOVELY $19 MASCARA?
WHY NOT? HAH! SMACK ON YOUR TOP FOUNDATION! THROW IN THE 12-TONE HIGHLIGHTER SET!!
IF THE IRS WANTS MORE MONEY, LET THEM TRY TO SCRAPE IT OFF MY FACE!!
DID YOU MAIL YOUR TAXES, CATHY?
NO, BUT I'VE RESTORED MY SELF-RESPECT.

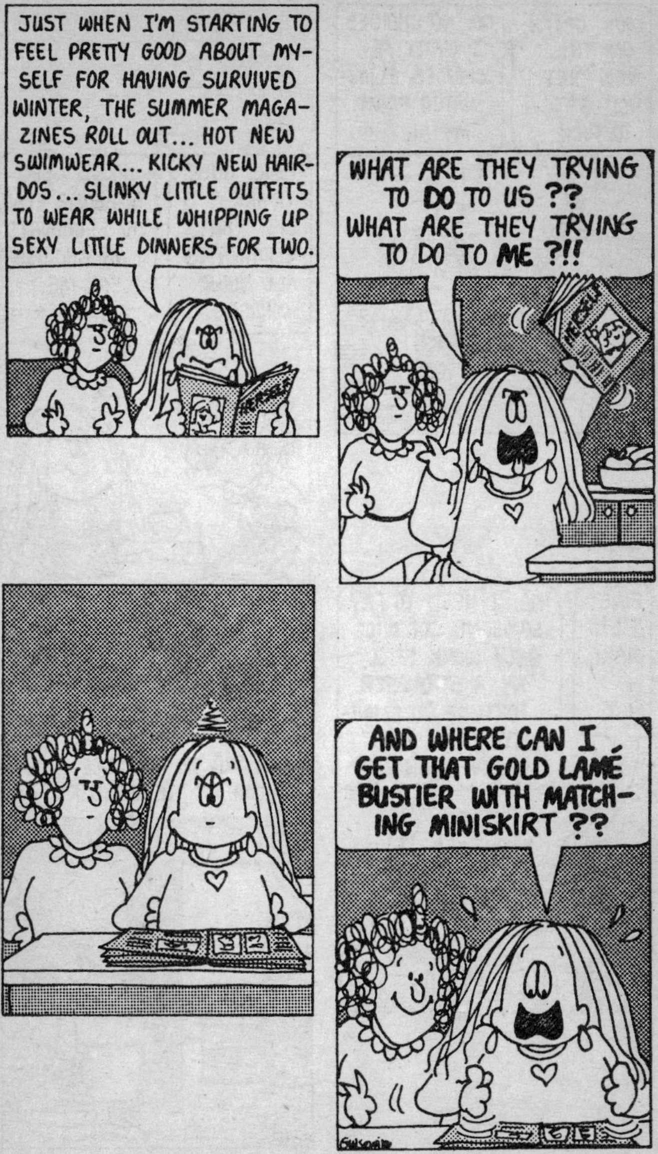
JUST WHEN I'M STARTING TO FEEL PRETTY GOOD ABOUT MY-SELF FOR HAVING SURVIVED WINTER, THE SUMMER MAGA-ZINES ROLL OUT... HOT NEW SWIMWEAR... KICKY NEW HAIR-DOS... SLINKY LITTLE OUTFITS TO WEAR WHILE WHIPPING UP SEXY LITTLE DINNERS FOR TWO.
WHAT ARE THEY TRYING TO DO TO US ?? WHAT ARE THEY TRYING TO DO TO ME ?!!
AND WHERE CAN I GET THAT GOLD LAMÉ BUSTIER WITH MATCH-ING MINISKIRT ??

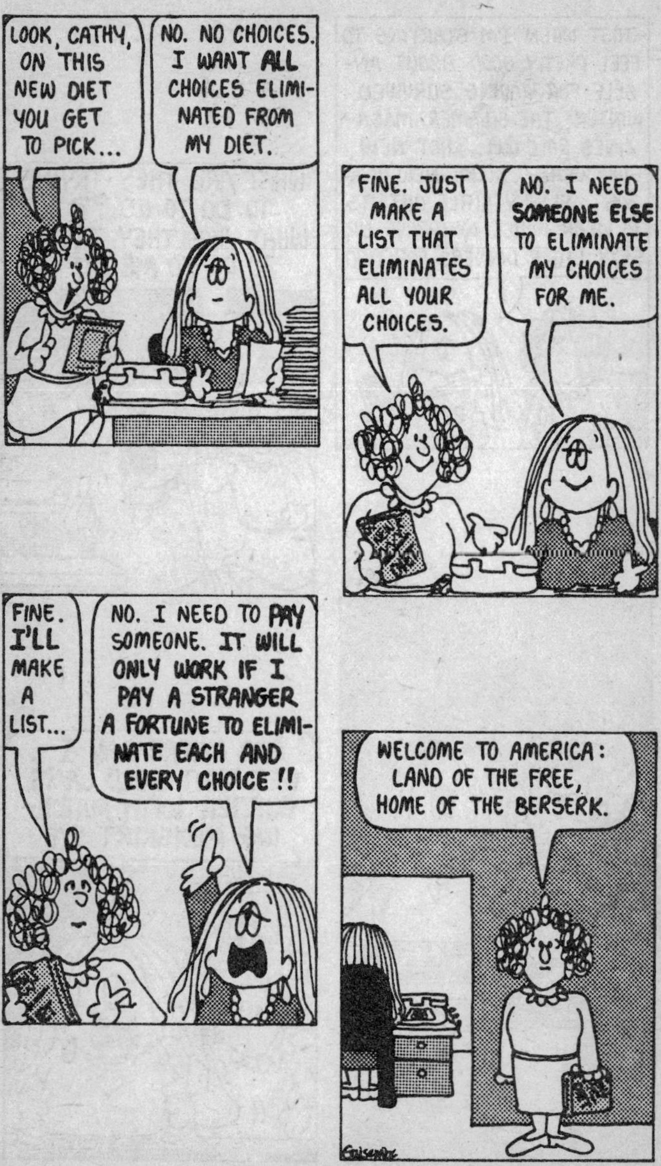
LOOK, CATHY, ON THIS NEW DIET YOU GET TO PICK...
NO. NO CHOICES. I WANT ALL CHOICES ELIMINATED FROM MY DIET.
FINE. JUST MAKE A LIST THAT ELIMINATES ALL YOUR CHOICES.
NO. I NEED SOMEONE ELSE TO ELIMINATE MY CHOICES FOR ME.
FINE. I'LL MAKE A LIST...
NO. I NEED TO PAY SOMEONE. IT WILL ONLY WORK IF I PAY A STRANGER A FORTUNE TO ELIMINATE EACH AND EVERY CHOICE!!
WELCOME TO AMERICA: LAND OF THE FREE, HOME OF THE BERSERK.